MEDITATIONS ON A HERITAGE

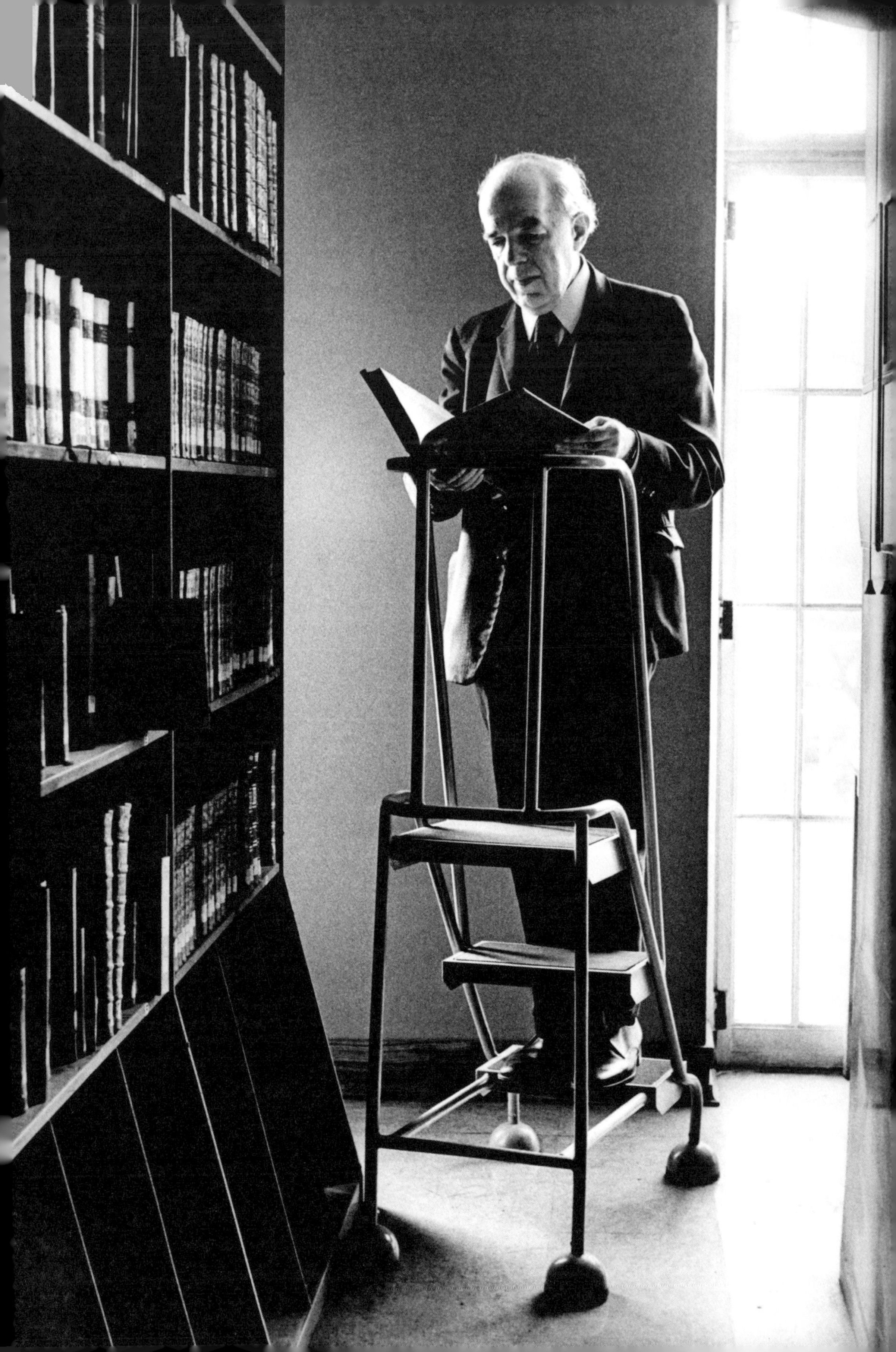

MEDITATIONS ON A HERITAGE

PAPERS ON THE WORK AND LEGACY OF

SIR ERNST GOMBRICH

Edited by Paul Taylor

CONTRIBUTIONS BY

Peter Burke | Roberto Casati | Paul Crossley
Charles Hope | Martin Kemp | Veronika Kopecky | John Kulvicki
Elizabeth McGrath | Harry Mount | Jeroen Stumpel | Paul Taylor

Paul Holberton publishing
in association with the Warburg Institute, London

A catalogue record for this book is available from the British Library

ISBN 978 1 907372 54 4

Produced by Paul Holberton publishing,
89 Borough High Street, London SE1 1NL
www.paul-holberton.net

Jacket design and book template by Philip Lewis;
execution by Laura Parker

Printed by E-Graphic, Verona

JACKET with acknowledgement to the design of E.H. Gombrich's early publications with Phaidon
FRONTISPIECE Photograph of Sir Ernst Gombrich in the library of the Warburg Institute,
London © Pino Guidolotti

CONTENTS

Preface

PAUL TAYLOR

ONLY SEVEN YEARS AFTER HIS DEATH, the staff of the Warburg Institute decided to celebrate the centenary of the birth of Sir Ernst Gombrich. I was asked by his successor as Director of the Institute, Charles Hope, to organize a commemorative colloquium for 2009.

The first letter of invitation I sent was to Gombrich's most celebrated pupil, Michael Baxandall. He declined, as I knew he would: he was in failing health, and died later that year. But he gave me some good advice: he told me that, if he were organizing a conference on his former supervisor, he would invite speakers who he would like to hear, whether or not they were experts on Gombrich's work, and would 'just let them get on with it'.

Baxandall's suggestion defined the character of the colloquium. The speakers were not specialists on Gombrich: they were historians, philosophers and scientists who over the years had read and thought about aspects of his work, had engaged with it in the course of their own research, and were entertaining lecturers; enthusiastic amateurs in the world of Gombrich studies, rather than scholars with the learning to assign him a fixed place in the historiography of art.

Another piece of advice which set the nature of the event was from Gombrich himself. He always felt – as Charles Hope notes on p. 6 below – that to contest the opinions of a scholar is to take his thought seriously, and his dictum 'We are not a mutual admiration society!' is often repeated in the institute he directed. I therefore made a point, when inviting speakers, of encouraging them to engage with his thought, to criticize and rethink his ideas rather than simply to analyse them as objects of academic study, as opinions consigned to history. Some of what follows, therefore, is combative rather than reverential, but that is only because the issues Gombrich dealt with are still alive and relevant today.

As Peter Burke notes in his paper in this volume, Gombrich was a polymath, who was able to give top-flight academic papers to art historians, historians, philosophers, psychologists and neurologists. This book does not reflect the full range of his work, and it also does not reflect the full range of speakers at the centenary colloquium: the archaeologist Robert Bagley, the psychologist Patrick

Cavanagh, and the visual psychophysicists Christopher Tyler and Jan Koenderink all gave engaging and brilliant papers, but, owing to other commitments, were unfortunately unable to take part in this volume. In what follows, then, eight art historians, two philosophers and a historian give their views; the last word on Gombrich's extraordinarily rich body of work is not likely to be said for some years, or possibly centuries, to come.

A proceedings volume like this would normally appear in the 'Warburg Institute Colloquia' series, published by the Institute. We felt, however, that the wide interest in Gombrich's work called for a professional publisher, and we thank Paul Holberton and Laura Parker for their work in crafting this beautifully designed book. I would also like to thank my colleagues Charles Hope, Elizabeth McGrath, Rembrandt Duits, Anita Pollard and Peter Mack for their assistance and advice over the years of organization and editing that have led to this volume.

Introduction

CHARLES HOPE

IN THE PUBLISHED TEXT of the speech that Ernst Gombrich delivered when he received the Hegel Prize he wrote: 'It cannot be too often repeated that the best tribute one can pay a scholar is to take him seriously and constantly to reappraise his lines of argument'. While this could be regarded as an elegant excuse for talking in critical terms about what he considered as Hegel's negative impact on the history of art, it was also something that Gombrich thought to be beyond dispute. Indeed, he made the same point about Riegl in his preface to *The Sense of Order*; and it could be taken as a justification for the conference at which the papers collected in this volume were delivered.

Implicit in Gombrich's remarks about Hegel and Riegl, of course, is the claim that their ideas about history, or, in the case of Riegl, more specifically about the history of art, were coherent and influential. But it is less easy to discern a comparably coherent group of ideas about such topics in Gombrich's large and very diverse body of published work. He had an unusual status among the art historians of his time, in that his exceptionally wide readership included not just his professional colleagues but also, and in greater numbers, members of the general public. In this respect the success of the *The Story of Art*, first published in 1950, was obviously crucial. Its appeal was based not just on the lucidity of the style and the fact that it was more than a mere chronological survey, but that it included an original and interesting argument. But many of those who read it were evidently also willing to read other things by him, even on much more specialised topics. They did so because in almost everything that he wrote he managed to construct an argument with wide implications, generally expressed in a clear and readable way. On the rare occasions when his meaning was difficult to follow, one could usually be confident that he was not entirely convinced by what he was saying.

The ideas in *The Story of Art*, as Gombrich himself made clear on many occasions, were related to some of those that he subsequently explored in *Art and Illusion*. But in his later years, he sometimes seemed to imply that that there was a more general agenda in his work. Thus in the introduction to his longest book, *The Sense of Order* (1979), he referred to the complementary character of it and the earlier *Art and Illusion*

(1960), 'one concerned with representation, the other with pure design'. He went on to say: 'I hope that the book on *Symbolic Images* (1972) and other matters I have written on narrative and illustration can now be seen as fragments of an even more ambitious project: to study some of the fundamental functions of the visual arts in their psychological implications'.

Just what he meant by 'other matters I have written on narrative and illustration' is not immediately clear, given that almost everything that he had published on narrative and illustration, as distinct from representation, had been included in *Symbolic Images*, but in 1987 he made much the same point about his general intentions, in a talk in which he explained why he had decided after his work on *Art and Illusion* to turn his attention to decoration. As he put it: 'My ambition – and it was rather a lofty ambition – was to be a kind of commentator on the history of art. I wanted to write a commentary on what actually happened in the development of art. I sometimes see it as representation in the centre with symbolism on the one hand and decoration on the other. One can reflect about all these things and say something in more general terms. It was my ambition to do precisely this.'[1]

But when did this 'ambitious project' take form? And how important was it in Gombrich's total output? At first sight the implication seems to be that he had long had a specific intellectual agenda that he gradually fulfilled. But this does not seem to have been exactly the case. So, for example, the idea of publishing a volume of his collected writings on iconography did not come from him, but from Michael Baxandall, as a sensible way of dividing up his publications on Renaissance art, which could not be accommodated in a single volume.[2] It is true that *Symbolic Images* contained much new material, some of which could, without undue strain, be said to involve the study of some 'of the fundamental functions of the visual arts in their psychological implications', but this does not apply to everything in the book.

However, even if some of Gombrich's statements could imply that his work had a greater degree of coherence than was actually the case, there were consistent themes and approaches that were present in much of what he wrote throughout his career. This applies most obviously to psychology and its application to the history of art. The topic was characteristic of Viennese art history well before Gombrich's time, and he attended lectures on psychology during his student years and later acknowledged his debt to Karl Bühler. He was encouraged to maintain his interest in the subject by Ernst Kris's invitation to collaborate on a book on caricature. However, the task that he was then hired to carry out at the Warburg Institute, that it to say to work on the founder's *Nachlass*, and especially the *Bilderatlas*, involved him in investigating problems of a very different kind.

Gombrich did not choose his next project either. He was asked by the Director of the Courtauld Institute to collaborate with Otto Kurz on an introduction to iconography for Courtauld students. The book was put aside during the war and never completed, but much of the text still survives in typescript at the Warburg Institute. When writing their book, Kurz and Gombrich were certainly aware of Panofsky's *Studies in Iconology*, published in 1939 and accessioned in the Warburg Library in that year. But their approach was very different, in two ways. First, they were not much interested in problem pictures, which were the main focus of Panofsky's text, but instead concentrated on the standard genres and subjects of figurative art. Second, Gombrich, at least implicitly, did not accept the validity of the distinction made by Panofsky, in his introduction, between pre-iconographic description (the identification of what is actually shown in a picture), iconography (the identification of the subject) and iconography in a deeper sense (later called by Panofsky iconology, and concerned, it would seem, with the associations and implications of the subject). For Gombrich the distinction between the first two categories was artificial, because in many cases the identification of what the artist had depicted could not be separated from the recognition of the subject.[3]

Gombrich's starting point here, as in his earlier work on caricature, was evidently the psychology of perception; and this would seem to be one way in which his thinking on narrative and illustration was related to their psychological implications. But whereas in the study of caricature Gombrich was interested in the ways in which someone acquainted with the person represented would recognise who was shown, despite the distortions introduced by the artist, in their studies of iconography both Gombrich and Panofsky were mainly writing about the ways in which their contemporaries, and especially contemporary art historians, might recognise subjects represented long before, even if they also sometimes considered what these themes meant to people in the past. Neither writer, however, had much to say about whether and, if so, how the original viewers might themselves have identified the subjects. We get closer to this issue in Gombrich's observation that a narrative painting necessarily does not resemble a photograph,[4] because the artist is forced to use various non-naturalistic devices for telling the story; and this implies that an understanding of such devices on the part of the viewer is not necessarily strongly historically based.

From the surviving fragments of the book, it is evident that Gombrich's approach was much more wide-ranging than that of Kurz, and would have included, for example, some discussion of symbols, child art and primitive art. Although the text was never completed, Gombrich continued to think about the problems he had tried to address in it, even while engaged on his study of Warburg's ideas. The bulk of the text on Warburg dates from 1946 or 1947 but, due to circumstances beyond his control, it did not appear until 1972, with the addition of some biographical material.[5] At the same period Gombrich explored, if only in a limited way, the psychological implications of symbolic figures, notably personifications, in his essay on 'Icones symbolicae', published in 1947, and also produced an outline for a book to be entitled *The Realm and Range of the Image*, which he unsuccessfully proposed to publishers in 1947 and

1952.[6] This was to be divided into three parts: Image and Reality, Image and Meaning and Image and Belief. The second and third parts, of course, were closely related to the abandoned book on iconography, including an examination of the persistence of magical ideas associated with images, while the first part anticipated many of the themes that would appear in *Art and Illusion.*

The Realm and Range of the Image was the first book planned by Gombrich from the outset on his own initiative, and, apart from *The Preference for the Primitive* (2002), the only one.[7] The project was unrealistically vast, and this may partly explain why he failed to find a publisher. It demonstrates both the range and originality of his interests as well as his intellectual ambition, but also what was to become a characteristic of his work, a failure to appreciate the difficulty of sustaining a clear argument over the length of an entire book. In this case, it is clear from his later writings on similar topics that he wanted his work to be accessible to general readers and at the same time tried to make his arguments rigorous and comprehensive. But these two aims were often in conflict. The problem is not evident in his book on Warburg or in *The Story of Art*, probably because in both cases he was more or less obliged to adopt a chronological structure.

Gombrich had accepted, evidently rather reluctantly, a commission for *The Story of Art* during the war. At the end of 1945 he returned to the Institute as a senior research fellow, in order to continue his work on Warburg, and the then director, Fritz Saxl, was understandably anxious that this task should have priority over his general book. But after Saxl's death in 1947 Gombrich became a permanent member of staff and was able to complete the text, which was finished in 1949. The focus of the book is on the different tasks that artists were required or expected to carry out at different times and places, and on the means that they adopted or invented for doing this; and the simplicity of the argument owed much to the fact that it was intended, in the first instance, for teenagers, although its appeal was certainly not limited to them. It was largely limited to representational art and was vastly more interesting than earlier general histories of the subject. In particular, it was distinctive in treating successive artistic styles primarily as responses by individual artists to new demands and new circumstances, rather than as expressing the character of a particular society, or, as Wölfflin had argued, as changing in accordance with certain general principles.

The Story of Art established Gombrich's reputation, but his interests lay elsewhere, as is evident from his attempts to find a publisher for *The Realm and Range of the Image.* He would later say that *Art and Illusion* (1960) 'can be seen as a commentary' on *The Story of Art*, but that was essentially just a way of saying that it was about representational art, and, in part, addressed the question of why such art has a history.[8] As Richard Woodfield has recently pointed out, it is difficult to extract a coherent argument from the book as a whole, which originated in a series of lectures.[9] Part of the problem was that Gombrich was trying to address two types of audience at the same time: those familiar with the psychology of perception and therefore aware of the complexities of the problems he was discussing, and a much broader public without this kind of specialist knowledge. But the fame of the book is justified and its impact easy enough to understand. For many readers its most striking feature must be the way in which Gombrich took as his theme pictorial representation in the broadest sense, neither excluding nor confining himself to the canon of Western art. This in itself set *Art and Illusion* apart from all other books about the history of art, whether intended for a general or a scholarly audience. Equally striking were the way in which he argued that artists did not, at any period, simply paint what they saw, and his explanation of the difficulty they had had in achieving the apparent mastery of representation finally acquired in the nineteenth century. The book was remarkable because it illuminated the history of Western art by drawing on insights from psychology, in an original, broadly accessible and authoritative way.

Gombrich explained in the preface to *The Sense of Order* (1979) that he had already been interested in ornament and decoration in his childhood, but there is no indication that he thought of studying the topic in any depth until some time after the appearance of *Art and Illusion*, the index of which does not include a reference to decoration. According to his own account, the idea developed gradually as he received various invitations to deliver lectures. Thus while it does not seem to be the case that in this book, the longest that he wrote, Gombrich was completing a longstanding project about art and psychology, it is certainly true that the relationship between art and psychology was a central interest for most of his life. It was the red line running through his scholarly activity.

As in *Art and Illusion*, in *The Sense of Order* the transition from a lecture format to a book is not entirely successful, because Gombrich seems to have been trying to do several different things simultaneously: to provide a historical survey of attitudes towards decoration, to offer a psychological explanation for the popularity of forms of visual decoration across different cultures, and to discuss a number of disparate problems relating to the use and development of ornament, whether in architecture or clothing or even heraldry. As a result, the reader is often left puzzled as to where he or she is being led, and why. It is a text in need of a strong-minded editor, but despite this it is still more wide-ranging, original and interesting that almost any other art-historical book in English of its period.

Gombrich's last book, *The Preference for the Primitive*, again grew out of various lectures, mostly given decades before its publication. To a much greater degree even than *The Sense of Order*, it is a historical narrative based on original research, but here too there is also a discussion of psychological issues, which fits rather uneasily with the rest and in which Gombrich developed and in places modified ideas already examined in *Art and Illusion*. *The Preference for the Primitive* has so far had rather limited impact, partly because it addresses an aspect of the history of taste on which there was

     Charles Hope

already a substantial scholarly literature, but, like his previous book, it demonstrates the remarkable range of Gombrich's knowledge of works of art of all types and from all periods, and his deep familiarity with the writings of past European historians and critics.

The common belief that he had a particular expertise in or affinity with the art of the Italian Renaissance is certainly mistaken. He published extensively on that period, and his production included several highly influential articles, but this was not so much because he retained a special interest in the topic as because it was central to his teaching activity at the Warburg Institute. It was almost inevitable that in choosing to write about patronage or iconography, taste or art criticism, he should often have taken examples from the Renaissance; and his many studies of Leonardo are surely not just the result of a particular admiration for this artist but also depend on the fact that Leonardo's recorded comments on paintings and his legacy of drawings are extraordinarily abundant, even compared with painters of later periods.

Gombrich was evidently most comfortable in writing articles, reviews or single lectures, and the greater part of his published work belongs in these categories. However, he largely or entirely avoided two of the main types of art-historical writing: connoisseurship, and the publication of new historical information. Instead, he devoted much effort to criticising, sometimes explicitly but usually implicitly, some widespread approaches to the history of art. Chief among these, of course, was the idea, which he categorised as Hegelian, that art reflects the spirit of the age. All his writings on changes in style and fashion can be seen as related to this issue. Equally important were his criticisms of the kind of elaborate iconographic speculation common in the middle decades of the last century.

Much of what he wrote on such topics has, inevitably, lost some of its force, since art history has moved on, and many of the battles that he fought no longer seem very relevant, because they have been won. But it is easy to forget that, when he was writing, the ideas that he opposed still exerted a powerful hold on many art historians. The efforts on the part of mainly German-speaking art historians to impose some kind of overarching scheme on the subject, to find some kind of inevitability in the changes that had taken place, were still regarded with perhaps excessive respect. At the same time, connoisseurship possessed an enormous and not always justified prestige, while much of the writing about individual works consisted of critical appreciation of a kind that would not have surprised Walter Pater. Unlike many art historians, Gombrich did not claim that his own responses to works of art of the past had any special authority. Instead, he recognised that it was a legitimate historical challenge to understand how their original audience would have responded to such works, and his many contributions to the study of this problem, which occupied him increasingly in the latter part of his career, are likely to be of lasting importance.

Art historians often treat their predecessors whose names are attached to a

particular approach or theory with a perhaps excessive reverence, Morelli, Wölfflin
and Warburg being obvious examples. It is unlikely that Gombrich will achieve this
kind of status, or would have wished to do so. The importance of his work on the
history of taste has yet to be fully recognised, but his most influential contribution
was and is likely to remain in the application of developments in psychology to the
visual arts, and he made it because he took the trouble to familiarise himself with
another discipline in addition to the visual arts. There was nothing distinctive about
his method (as distinct from his style), and he certainly regarded his conclusions as
necessarily provisional. Even if and when they are superseded, however, much of his
work will surely continue to be read, because of its extraordinary range and intrinsic
interest, and for the clarity of the exposition.

    Charles Hope

1 'An autobiographical sketch', reprinted in *The Essential Gombrich*, ed. Richard Woodfield, London, 1996, p. 34; also quoted in Richard Woodfield, 'Ernst Gombrich: Iconology and the "linguistics of the image"', *Journal of Art Historiography*, 5, December 2011, http://arthistoriography.files.wordpress.com/2011/12/woodfield.pdf, p. 11.

2 E.H. Gombrich, *Norm and Form: Studies in the Art of the Renaissance*, London, 1966, p. vii.

3 See Gombrich's draft introduction for the projected book on iconography, p. 1: 'The very act of perception of forms and valeurs [sic] is governed and regulated by the steering force of recognising and naming of "subjects."' (quoted in C. Hope, 'How Gombrich will be remembered', *Wiener Jahrbuch für Kunstgeschichte*, LIX, 2010, p. 268).

4 Draft introduction (n. 3 above), p. 4; Hope, 'Gombrich' (n. 3 above), p. 268.

5 When Gombrich had completed his study of Warburg's ideas, the intention was that it should be published with a biography of Warburg by Gertrud Bing. This was never written, and after her death in 1964 Gombrich decided to revise his text for publication: see E.H. Gombrich, *Aby Warburg: An Intellectual Biography*, London, 1970, pp. 3-5.

6 On this project see Hope, 'Gombrich' (n. 3 above), p. 268, and Woodfield, 'Iconology' (n. 1 above), pp. 9-11.

7 *A Little History of the World* and *The Story of Art* were both proposed by publishers; *Art and Illusion* and *The Sense of Order* were based respectively on Gombrich's Mellon Lectures and Wrightsman Lectures.

8 E.H. Gombrich, *A Lifelong Interest: Conversations on Art and Science with Didier Eribon*, London, 1993, p. 97.

9 Woodfield, 'Iconology' (n. 1 above), p. 10.

  Gombrich's Search for Cultural History

Gombrich's Search for Cultural History

PETER BURKE

ERNST GOMBRICH WAS A POLYMATH, perhaps one of the last of this endangered species. To write about him we need to cut his work up into fragments. In this paper I shall be discussing Gombrich's views on cultural history, expressed most famously - though not, of course, exclusively - in his lecture 'In Search of Cultural History'.[1] In what follows I shall try to insert this lecture into Gombrich's career and also into the career of cultural history, situating him within some of the intellectual movements of his time.

I

The lecture in question was the Philip Maurice Deneke Lecture given at Oxford (more exactly at Lady Margaret Hall) in 1967 and published two years later, in other words over forty years ago. The lecture was part of a prestigious series, in which Gombrich's predecessors included the classicist Sir Gilbert Murray, the physicist, astronomer and mathematician Sir James Jeans and the physiologist, neurologist and pathologist Sir Charles Sherrington.

Of the hundreds of lectures that Gombrich gave in public, the vast majority were concerned with art. Why then did he speak about cultural history on this occasion? A possible answer to the question is that his intellectual biography of Aby Warburg, which was nearing completion, encouraged or provoked him to choose this theme, in order to explain to the world why the Director of the Warburg Institute was not a Warburgian, at least as far as *Kulturwissenschaft* was concerned.[2]

In its expanded and printed version, 'In Search of Cultural History' is extremely well-known, so it will be summarized here only very briefly – at the price, needless to say, of simplifying its central argument. Gombrich argues that 'we are today in search of cultural history' because '*Kulturgeschichte* has been built, knowingly and unknowingly, on Hegelian foundations which have crumbled',[3] notably the ideas of *Zeitgeist* and *Volksgeist*.[4] He goes on to describe later cultural historians, especially Burckhardt, Lamprecht and Huizinga, as having attempted 'to salvage the Hegelian assumption without accepting Hegelian metaphysics'.[5] 'It is this belief in the existence of an independent supra-individual collective spirit', Gombrich declares, 'which seems … to have blocked the emergence of a true cultural history'. What is to be done?

'Cultural history will make progress', he says, if it 'fixes its attention firmly on the individual human being'.[6]

Any listener or reader who was familiar with Gombrich's earlier work would have seen this central argument coming. In 1953, for instance, in a review of Arnold Hauser's *Social History of Art*, Gombrich had criticized the author for attempting to write 'the social history of the western world' as reflected in art, and also because he had 'caught himself in the intellectual mousetrap of "dialectical materialism"'.[7]

The central argument of 'In Search of Cultural History' would be repeated in later years, in the lecture on 'Art History and the Social Sciences' (1973),[8] for instance, with its critique of Marxism, and in remarks at a symposium in 1988, where he dismissed 'the mythological tendencies of romantic historiography' such as *Zeitgeist* and *Volksgeist*.[9] However, Gombrich's preoccupation with this theme appears to have been particularly intense in the late 1960s. In a short piece on Aby Warburg that was first published in 1966, Gombrich described three books by Carl Justi as 'masterpieces of cultural history'; the books were all monographs on individuals – Winckelmann, Michelangelo and Velázquez.[10]

Again, in a famous essay published in 1967, 'From the Revival of Letters to the Reform of the Arts', Gombrich used if anything even stronger language than before. He declared that 'Cultural history is passing through a crisis, the crisis engendered by the slow demise of Hegelian "historicism"' and attacked 'the pseudo-explanation of a "spirit"' and 'the metaphysics of history'. In order to escape the crisis, Gombrich once again advised his readers to look at 'living people in concrete situations'.[11]

We might describe the almost obsessive concern with the idea of the *Zeitgeist* as a *Leitmotiv* in Gombrich's work, alongside his recurrent critique of cultural relativism and of course more positive motifs such as the importance of the schema. We might also describe 'In Search of Cultural History' as a manifesto for what Gombrich's friend and mentor Karl Popper famously described as 'methodological individualism'.

In history, economics, sociology, and other social studies, there is a long-standing conflict between two groups, individualists and holists, each side defining its position against the other over the generations, from the early nineteenth century onwards. On one side, the individualists claim that 'the "behaviour" and the "actions" of collectives, such as states or social groups, must be reduced to the behaviour and to the actions of human individuals'.[12] On the other side, the holists or as Popper called them, the 'methodological collectivists', believe that something important is lost by this reductionism and so they emphasize the importance of systems of different kinds.

Gombrich adopted a relatively extreme position in favour of the methodological individualists, memorably expressed in 1950 in the first and most famous sentences of his most famous book. 'There really is no such thing as art. There are only artists'.[13] A quarter of a century later, in the lecture on art history and the social sciences, Gombrich re-iterated his emphasis on 'the situation in which the artist found himself, the options he had, and the decisions he made within the tradition in which he was bound to work', leaving systems aside.[14]

The problem is that for methodological individualists, or 'atomic' individualists as I would prefer to call them, it is difficult if not impossible to write cultural history, at least in the sense of a general history of culture as distinct from the so-called 'special' histories of art, philosophy, music, literature and so on. Atomic individualism is compatible with an internalist approach to the history of the arts and sciences, one that emphasizes problems and solutions, as Gombrich did, but it is rather less compatible or less easily compatible with an externalist approach, one that stresses social or cultural contexts.

In this context it is surely significant that cultural variations in perception is a theme that receives relatively little emphasis in Gombrich's most brilliant book, *Art and Illusion*, which contains a small handful of references to native Australian and American peoples;[15] even though the anthropologist W. H. R. Rivers had suggested over half a century earlier that there are cultural differences in the susceptibility to optical illusions, and the point has been re-iterated by some psychologists since then.[16]

To sum up so far: Gombrich was extremely interested in individuals on one side and on the other in what he called 'the common ground of universally human response'. He was considerably less comfortable with what lies in between, cultural variation and cultural change. It is all too easy to imagine what he must have thought about his Warburg colleague Michael Baxandall's concept of 'the period eye'.[17] Gombrich associated the study of cultural wholes with what he called 'totalitarian habits of mind'[18] and had a deep distrust of the 'historical collectivism' that he associated with Hegel and Marx. In his wide multi-disciplinary reading, he preferred zoology and experimental psychology to sociology and anthropology, suspecting cultural anthropologists in particular of 'Hegelianism and holism'.[19]

II

Let us now take a few steps back in order to see a bigger picture. Ernst Gombrich was part of a major cultural movement of the 1930s, a movement in the literal sense of the term, the great diaspora of Central European intellectuals, mainly German-speaking and Jewish, taking refuge from the dictatorships of Hitler and Mussolini in Britain and in the USA as well as in other places from Turkey (in the case of Erich Auerbach, for instance) to New Zealand (in the case of Popper).

The cultural encounter between German scholars and Anglo-American traditions and institutions, recently described by Nicholas Mann as a new *translatio studii*, had important consequences for the development of a number of academic disciplines, from art history to sociology, as well as for the individual émigrés, whether they adapted themselves or indeed refused to adapt themselves to unfamiliar environments.[20]

At first sight, Gombrich's methodological individualism looks like an adaptation to English culture on the part of an immigrant. In this sense it resembles the transformation of Nikolaus Pevsner from a foreign refugee into a national institution thanks to his architectural guides to English counties, or indeed the transformation of

the Kulturwissenschaftliche Bibliothek Warburg into the Warburg Library and later
the Warburg Institute, gradually losing its former German accent.

Gombrich certainly became attached to some features of English or British culture,
though not to all (he never really understood his colleagues' interest in cricket and
other sports).[21] He admired the philosophy and the prose of David Hume,[22] and
made regular use of Ockham's razor to cut away fuzzy thinking, as in his claim that
'The history of art as a history of formal solutions can apply Ockham's razor and do
away with the spirit of the age'.[23] There is also an affinity, to put it mildly, between
Gombrich's methodological individualism and the tradition of British empiricism,
the cult of facts and brass tacks, not to mention British individualism in the everyday
sense of the term. It was after all a British Prime Minister who affirmed that 'there is
no such thing as society'. Directing some of his most vigorous critiques against the
holism of German-speaking scholars, from Hauser to Panofsky, Gombrich might well
seem to have become more English than the English.

Of course, this is not the whole story. Methodological individualism is associated
not only with Englishmen such as John Stuart Mill, but also with thinkers from the
Continent, especially, intriguingly enough, from Gombrich's native Austria. It was an
Austrian, Popper, who criticized Karl Marx together with the Hungarian émigré Karl
Mannheim as 'methodological collectivists'. Prominent methodological individualists
also include a quartet of Austrian economists: Carl Menger, Josef Schumpeter (who
later recanted), Ludwig von Mises and Friedrich von Hayek (who became Mrs
Thatcher's guru).[24] Perhaps we should speak of individualism as an Austrian cultural
tradition or better still as an Anglo-Austrian one, given the earlier connections
between Austrian and British scholars. Theodor Gomperz translated John Stuart
Mill, for instance, while the Vienna school of economics was inspired by the British
classical economists.[25]

It is important not to oversimplify the position of these economists, who believed
in the power of the invisible hand of the market as well as in individual freedom.
In Gombrich's case too, we should not overlook cross-currents in his work, minor
themes as well as dominant ones. We should be aware of ambiguity, ambivalence and
the tension between different ideas. Although Gombrich thought cultural history too
vague, for instance, he also found art history too narrow and insisted that it 'cannot be
isolated' from economic, social or religious history. As Willibald Sauerländer has put
it, he was 'reluctant to see himself as a conventional art historian'.[26]

Again, Gombrich never denied the value of what might be called a microsocial
history of art of the kind practised by Aby Warburg.[27] He praised that aspect of
Hauser's book in 1953 and twenty years later he was still supporting the history of
'social conditions, workshop organizations, or the motivations of patronage'.[28]

On occasion, Gombrich sounds more like a holist than an individualist. As a
young man he had learned from Max Dvořák, so he later confessed, that art is 'a
marvellous key to the past',[29] though he seems to have repudiated Dvořák by the
time that he was reviewing Arnold Hauser. He was not an opponent of Hegel in all
respects, as his lecture on 'The Father of Art History' makes particularly clear.[30] As

David Summers has suggested, he engaged in a dialogue with Hegel, 'a dialogue integral with the successive definition of his own positions'.[31] Although he rarely cited continental philosophers, he learned and used a few of their ideas, for example the 'horizon of expectations' discussed by Husserl, his pupil Heidegger and Heidegger's pupil Gadamer, though Gombrich confessed that 'I owe this phrase to K. H. Popper'.[32]

From time to time, Gombrich wrote and spoke about cultures, about 'Chinese culture', for instance. 'There is no culture or subculture', he argued, 'where you could not watch' an emergence of standards. Although he criticized the idea of cultural morphology, dear to Huizinga among others, Gombrich was prepared to admit that 'there are sometimes patterns' of culture, adding cautiously that 'they needn't necessarily be all-pervasive'.[33] He noted problems that the art historian shares with 'those who teach the history of music, or literature, or perhaps the dance'.[34]

Again, Gombrich remarks on occasion that 'there is such a thing as a mental climate',[35] defined as 'the mentality or outlook dominant in a class, generation or nation'.[36] The scholar who passionately rejected the metaphor of the 'spirit of the age' seems to have found nothing objectionable in that of 'climate of opinion'. Most important of all, Gombrich sometimes describes art in collective terms as an institution or as a language, or more conventionally as a set of styles and genres, without developing those ideas very far. In a late interview he had good words to say about Pierre Bourdieu, despite Bourdieu's emphasis on systems.[37] Sometimes I think that there must have been two Gombrichs, like Dr Jekyll and Mr Hyde (the one I prefer is Hyde).

III

I promised to say something about the intersection between Gombrich's career and the career of cultural history. It is well known that both the term *Kulturgeschichte* and the practice of cultural history, as distinct from the history of particular arts and sciences, go back to the late eighteenth century. In other words, they go back a generation before Hegel, undermining the suggestion that the practice is built on 'Hegelian foundations'. Flourishing in Germany and in areas of German cultural hegemony such as Switzerland, Denmark and the Netherlands in the nineteenth and early twentieth centuries, cultural history was taken less seriously in Britain until quite recently. At the time of Gombrich's arrival here in 1936, I rather doubt whether more than a handful of English scholars would have described themselves as cultural historians. Christopher Dawson, almost certainly. Arnold Toynbee, possibly, although he preferred the term 'civilization' to 'culture'. It is difficult to think of a third name.

Today, of course, the situation has changed quite dramatically, like the style of cultural history itself. Indeed, it is not easy to say these days who is not a cultural historian and what is not cultural history. What would Gombrich have thought, or what did he think of the so-called 'new cultural history'? When I began writing this paper, I thought that this question was unanswerable. However, a brief investigation online – I still cannot bring myself to call this 'research' – turned up a radio interview from 1973, printed in *The Listener*, in which Gombrich was asked to respond to questions about new trends in cultural history.[38] At that point the phrase 'new cultural history' had not yet been coined.[39] I should have remembered this interview, since I happen to have been the interviewer.

Anyway, asked what he thought about the history of mentalities, or the social history of culture, Gombrich expressed what might be called a kind of open scepticism. That is, he did not dismiss these approaches out of hand, but he did not warm to them either, preferring to place the emphasis on difficulties.

On the study of mentalities, for instance, 'I never quite know how this should be done'. Again, admitting that 'it is indeed most important to clarify what section of the population was really involved' in certain cultural activities, Gombrich expressed discomfort with the idea of the social history of culture. He agreed that 'the most important task for the future of the history of art is to clarify' the problem of function, but went on to say that the task was not easy. My impression was and remains that if it had been possible to ask Aby Warburg the same questions fifty years earlier, he would have been more positive in his responses. Warburg, interested as he was in anthropology, in memory, and in cultural studies, was closer to the New Cultural History than his successor.

To conclude by returning to the search for 'a true cultural history'. Did Gombrich ever find what he was looking for? He certainly found parts of cultural history, but if the famous lecture is to be understood as a programme for the future development of the subject, there are some surprising absences or blind spots. There is no place, for instance for the history of cultural conflicts and cultural encounters (though elsewhere Gombrich praised Otto Kurz for his 'exploration of culture contacts').[40] There was little place for the reception of cultural artefacts until the late work on The Preference for the Primitive, despite the interest Gombrich expressed elsewhere for 'the beholder's share'.

Gombrich was of course a brilliant practitioner of cultural history at the micro-level, beginning with his interpretation of Mannerism in the 1930s as a response to the court milieu in Mantua and elsewhere rather than to a general spiritual crisis. In this respect his essay on the early Medici as patrons of art[41] rivals Warburg's famous essay on Sassetti's will.[42] On the other hand, he shied away from cultural history at the macro-level, associating it with Hegel. He threw out the baby, *Zusammenhang*, with the bathwater of the *Zeitgeist*. In this respect and possibly in others, the celebration of Gombrich's many achievements needs to be combined with attempts to go beyond them.[43]

   Gombrich's Search for Cultural History

1 E.H. Gombrich, *In Search of Cultural History*, the Philip Maurice Deneke Lecture, Oxford, 1969, reprinted in Gombrich, *Ideals and Idols: Essays on Values in History and in Art*, Oxford, 1979, pp. 24-59. All subsequent references are to *Ideals and Idols*.

2 E.H. Gombrich, *Aby Warburg: an Intellectual Biography*, London, 1970.

3 Gombrich, *In Search* (n. 1 above), p. 28.

4 Ibid., pp. 36, 47.

5 Ibid., p. 43.

6 Ibid., p. 50.

7 E.H. Gombrich, review of A. Hauser, *The Social History of Art*, New York, 1951, in *The Art Bulletin*, 35, 1953, pp. 79-84; reprinted as 'The Social History of Art' in Gombrich, *Meditations on a Hobby Horse and Other Essays on the Theory of Art*, London, 1963, pp. 86-94 (88). References are to *Meditations on a Hobby Horse*.

8 E.H. Gombrich, *Art History and the Social Sciences*, the Romanes Lecture, Oxford, 1973; reprinted in Gombrich, *Ideals and Idols* (n. 1 above), pp. 131-66. References are to *Ideals and Idols*.

9 E.H. Gombrich, 'Approaches to the History of Art: Three Points for Discussion', introductory remarks to the Erasmus Symposium in Holland in 1988; published in Gombrich, *Topics of Our Time: Twentieth-Century Issues in Learning and in Art*, London, 1991, pp. 63-73 (p. 64), and reprinted in *The Essential Gombrich*, ed. R. Woodfield, London, 1996, pp. 355-68 (p. 357). This piece may have been aimed at Tim Clark in particular, in reply to the *Times Literary Supplement* article of 1974 discussed below by Harry Mount (p.23).

10 E.H. Gombrich, 'The Ambivalence of the Classical Tradition: the Cultural Psychology of Aby Warburg (1866-1929)', an address given at Hamburg University on 13 June 1966 on the centenary of Aby Warburg's birth; published in Gombrich, *Tributes: Interpreters of our Cultural Tradition*, Oxford, 1984, pp. 116-37 (p. 120).

11 E.H. Gombrich, 'From the Revival of Letters to the Reform of the Arts: Niccolò Niccoli and Filippo Brunelleschi', in *Essays Presented to Rudolf Wittkower on his Sixty-Fifth Birthday*, ed. D. Fraser, H. Hibbard and M.J. Lewine, 2 vols., London 1967, I, pp. 71-82 (p. 71); reprinted in Gombrich, *The Heritage of Apelles: Studies in the Art of the Renaissance III*, London, 1976, pp. 93-110 (p. 93).

12 K. Popper, *The Open Society and its Enemies*, London, 1945, p. 349.

13 E.H. Gombrich, *The Story of Art*, London, 1950, p. 5.

14 Gombrich, *Social Sciences* (n. 8 above), p. 148.

15 E.H. Gombrich, *Art and Illusion: A Study in the Psychology of Pictorial Representation*, London, 1960, pp. 90-91, 119, 228.

16 W.H.R. Rivers, 'The Colour Vision of the Eskimo', *Proceedings of the Cambridge Philosophical Society*, 11, 1901, pp. 143-49; cf. M.H. Segall, D.T. Campbell and M.J. Herskovits, *The Influence of Culture on Visual Perception*, Indianapolis, 1966, pp. 62-65.

17 M. Baxandall, *Painting and Experience in Fifteenth-Century Italy*, Oxford, 1972, pp. 29-108. In an interview with Allan Langdale in 1994, Baxandall referred to Gombrich's 'suspicious reaction' to this concept: A. Langdale, 'Aspects of the Critical Reception and Intellectual History of Baxandall's Concept of the Period Eye', in *About Michael Baxandall*, ed. A. Rifkin, Oxford, 1999, pp. 17-35 (pp. 21, 33, 346).

18 Gombrich, *Art and Illusion* (n. 15 above), p. 17.

19 P. Burke, interview with E.H. Gombrich, *The Listener*, 90, 1973, pp. 881-83; available online at *The Gombrich Archive*, ed. Richard Woodfield, http://www.gombrich.co.uk.

20 N. Mann, '*Translatio Studii*: Warburgian *Kunstwissenschaft* in London, 1933-45', in *The Migration of Ideas*, ed. R. Scazzieri and R. Simili, Sagamore Beach, MA, 2008, pp. 151-60; P. Burke, '*Translatio Studii*: the contribution of exiles to the establishment of sociology and art history in Britain, 1933-1960', *Arbor*, 185, 2009, pp. 903-08.

21 E.H. Gombrich, 'The Tradition of General Knowledge', oration delivered at the London School of Economics in 1961, published in *Ideals and Idols* (n. 1 above), pp. 9-23 (p. 12).

22 E.H. Gombrich, 'Preface' to *Hobby Horse* (n. 7 above), pp. IX-XII (p. XI). I thank Richard Woodfield for providing me with this and the preceding reference.

23 E.H. Gombrich, 'Norm and Form: the Stylistic Categories of Art History and their Origins in Renaissance Ideals', in Gombrich,

Norm and Form: Studies in the Art of the Renaissance I, London, 1966, pp. 81-98 (p. 95).

24 F. von Hayek, 'Economic Thought: the Austrian School', in *International Encyclopaedia of the Social Sciences*, ed. D.L. Sills, 18 vols., New York, 1968, vol. 4, pp. 458-62.

25 These examples come from C. Fleck, 'Emigration of Social Scientists' Schools from Austria', in *Forced Migration and Scientific Change*, ed. M.G. Ash and A. Söllner, Cambridge and Washington, D.C., 1996, pp. 198-223 (p. 220).

26 W. Sauerländer in *E.H. Gombrich: A Commemoration*, London, 2002, pp. 16-20 (p. 17).

27 E.g. A. Warburg, *Bildniskunst und florentinisches Bürgertum*, Leipzig, 1902, tr. D. Britt as 'The Art of Portraiture and the Florentine Bourgeoisie', in A. Warburg, *The Renewal of Pagan Antiquity*, Los Angeles, 1999, pp. 184-221; idem, 'Francesco Sassettis letztwillige Verfügung', in *Kunstwissenschaftliche Beiträge August Schmarsow gewidmet*, Leipzig, 1907, pp. 129-52; translated as 'Francesco Sassetti's Last Injunctions to His Sons', in *Renewal*, pp. 223-62.

28 Gombrich, *Social Sciences* (n. 8 above), p. 134.

29 E.H. Gombrich, 'An Autobiographical Sketch', transcribed from the tape recording of an informal talk given at Rutgers University, 1987; published in Gombrich, *Topics of our Time* (n. 9 above), pp. 11-24 (p. 14); reprinted in *Essential Gombrich* (n. 9 above), pp. 21-36 (p. 24).

30 E.H. Gombrich, '"The Father of Art History": A Reading of the *Lectures on Aesthetics* of G.W.F. Hegel (1770-1831)', lecture given as acceptance of the Hegel Prize in Stuttgart in 1977; published in Gombrich, *Tributes* (n. 10 above), pp. 51-69.

31 D. Summers, 'E.H. Gombrich and the Tradition of Hegel', in *Companion to Art Theory*, ed. P. Smith and C. Wilde, Oxford, 2002, pp. 139-49 (p. 139).

32 Gombrich, *Art and Illusion* (n. 15 above), p. 340 (note to p. 53).

33 Burke, *Listener* (n. 19 above), p. 881.

34 E.H. Gombrich, 'The Necessity of Tradition: an Interpretation of the Poetics of I.A. Richards (1893-1979)', the Darwin Lecture given at Cambridge University in 1979; published in *Tributes* (n. 10 above), pp. 185-210.

35 Gombrich, 'The Social History of Art' (n. 7 above), p. 91.

36 Gombrich, *Art and Illusion* (n. 15 above), p. 17.

37 E.H. Gombrich and D. Eribon, *A Lifelong Interest: Conversations on Art and Science with Didier Eribon*, London, 1993, pp. 166 and 172-73.

38 Burke, *Listener* (n. 19 above).

39 The name goes back to *The New Cultural History*, ed. L. Hunt, Berkeley, 1989.

40 E.H. Gombrich, 'The Exploration of Culture Contacts: the Services to Scholarship of Otto Kurz (1908-1975)'; memoir from the *Proceedings of the British Academy*, 65, 1979, pp. 719-35; reprinted in Gombrich, *Tributes* (n. 10 above), pp. 235-50.

41 E.H. Gombrich, 'The Early Medici as Patrons of Art', in *Italian Renaissance Studies: A Tribute to the late Cecilia M. Ady*, ed. E.F. Jacob, New York, 1960, pp. 279-311; reprinted in Gombrich, *Norm and Form* (n. 23 above), pp. 35-57.

42 A. Warburg, 'Sassetti' (n. 26 above).

43 C. Pavur, 'Restoring Cultural History: beyond Gombrich', *Clio*, 20, 1991, pp. 157-67.

     Gombrich's Search for Cultural History

Gombrich and the Fathers of Art History

HARRY MOUNT

THAT GOMBRICH WAS ONE OF THE MOST IMPORTANT art historians of the twentieth century would seem to go without saying.[1] As such, one might expect him to feature prominently in the numerous surveys, guides and introductions to the history and methods of art history produced during the past two decades. Precisely the opposite, however, is the case. In many of these works Gombrich is a peripheral figure; in some he is hardly mentioned at all.[2] The authors of one survey, Michael Hatt and Charlotte Klonk, even go so far as to apologise for leaving Gombrich out, but they do not explain why they chose to do so.[3] While recent anthologies of art historical writings do usually find room for a little Gombrich, their choices of which bleeding chunk to include are both curious and revealing: Eric Fernie chose the attack on Hegel's theory of history from 'In Search of Cultural History', Steve Edwards chose the attack on Heinrich Wölfflin's formalism from 'Norm and Form', while Donald Preziosi chose the essay on 'Style' which attacks both Hegel and Wölfflin.[4] The editors of these anthologies evidently felt that Gombrich was better represented by one of his attacks on what he did not believe in than by any statement or example of what he did believe in. Or, to put it another way, they seem to have found it difficult to say where exactly Gombrich fits into the grand scheme of things. Such difficulties would appear to confirm the paradox expressed by Willibald Sauerländer, who, when speaking at Gombrich's posthumous commemoration, concluded that his friend's 'position in the field of "official" art history was at once dominant and peripheral'.[5]

Those who, since the 1970s, have challenged 'official' art history, calling for major changes in art historical practice and aligning themselves with what has come to be known as the new art history, have not found Gombrich any easier to pigeon-hole. These radicals have often identified Gombrich as the figurehead of an art historical *ancien régime* which rejected political and sociological theory, believed profoundly in a canon of great works and had a lamentable tendency to omit women artists from introductory surveys.[6] But having cast Gombrich as stage villain the authors in question at times seemed reluctant to drop him through the trapdoor of oblivion. Among the contributors to the 1986 volume entitled *The New Art History*, for example, some were simply dismissive of Gombrich, but others were moved to admit that his work might, sphinx-like, hold some hitherto undisclosed significance. The introduction to this book featured both a claim that radical scholars abroad valued Gombrich's work alongside that of Jacques Derrida and a suggestion that Gombrich might one day be revealed as the F.R. Leavis of art history.[7] That Gombrich might be likened to both Leavis and Derrida in such quick succession suggests just how little consensus there was about his place in the history of ideas.

Still more revealing is the celebrated essay published by T. J. Clark in the *Times Literary Supplement* in 1974.[8] In this piece Clark not only called for a new social history of art, but also harked back to the golden age of Alois Riegl, Max Dvořák and Heinrich Wölfflin, and lamented that art historians had lost the capacity to ask the big questions which had driven those heroic figures. Instead, Clark complained, we have come down to an art history not of ideas but of methods, an art history in which, for example, reactionaries had the temerity to belittle Hegel for his lack of attention to the particular. The reactionaries in question are not named, but, as the Hegel example suggests, Gombrich stomps round Clark's article like the elephant in the room, continually alluded to but never mentioned. That Clark does not mention Gombrich is especially curious given that his critique of modern art history seemed to owe much to the famous attacks on the reactionary empiricism of British intellectual life voiced by Perry Anderson during the 1960s, attacks which explicitly listed Gombrich among the so-called White or right-wing of the intellectual diaspora from totalitarian Europe who ended up in Britain, while the Red or left-wing went to France or the USA.[9] Why did Clark feel unable to repeat the thorough-going attack on Gombrich mounted by Anderson, when it seemed so logical to do so? Was it just good manners, or was it because there was something about Gombrich's approach which made it too difficult simply to write him off?

One might object at this point that there is one set of big ideas with which Gombrich has been readily associated – those derived from his work on the relationship between art and psychology, and particularly his theories of perception, representation and decoration. It was also these ideas that inspired the most substantive critique of Gombrich to emerge from the new art history, that voiced by Norman Bryson.[10] It is, however, significant that none of the surveys or anthologies mentioned above does more than allude briefly to this aspect of Gombrich's work. It was as if those engaged in plotting the route map of art history saw Gombrich's work on art and psychology as an unusually impressive branch line, one which, while admirable in itself, failed to link up with any subsequent developments in the field and, perhaps, led outside of it altogether, into the realms of aesthetics and perceptual psychology. And there is, perhaps, some justification for this view.[11] Gombrich's work in these areas remains something of a thing apart; that it is still to this day discussed predominantly in terms of the rights and wrongs of Gombrich's own arguments is

   Gombrich and the Fathers of Art History

indicative of how reluctant other art historians have been to carry forward his work in this area.

Aside from the specific difficulties of incorporating his work on art and psychology, there are, I believe, two main reasons why it has been so hard to find a clearly defined space for Gombrich in recent accounts of the history and methodology of art history. The first stems from the nature of his work and the way he presented it. The second stems from the distinctive ways in which art historians, or at least certain art historians, have chosen to shape the stories they tell themselves about the development of their field, stories in whose construction Gombrich himself has played a major and, I will argue, ultimately self-annihilating role.

The most obvious answer to the question of why it has been so hard to accommodate Gombrich stems from the protean quality of his work, the sheer extent of the ground he covered, the extraordinary range of the issues he discussed. This partly explains why no abstract noun attaches itself to his name with the readiness of iconology to Erwin Panofsky, formalism to Heinrich Wölfflin, or feminism to Linda Nochlin. But that this is the case is also a consequence of the way in which Gombrich presented his work. Unlike Panofsky, who covered almost as wide a range, or Clark, he did not start his books with expansive statements about his own historical method. When Didier Eribon pointed this out to him and asked why there was no such thing as a Gombrichian method, Gombrich replied, 'I don't want one. I just want common sense!'[12] The riposte may have been faux-naïf, but it underlines one of the most characteristic features of Gombrich's thought, his consistent resistance to being associated with any clearly defined movement or big idea. Even *Art and Illusion*, which did, one might think, advance just such a big idea, was described by Gombrich himself as a specific investigation into a tightly defined set of problems, not an all-embracing theory of art history.[13] And there were, of course, many instances, both published and unpublished, in which those who attempted to pin down the core ideas of that book were told by its author, often in a distinctly prickly fashion, that they had misunderstood him.[14] That this famously clear and lucid communicator could, on his own estimation, have been so repeatedly misunderstood is a paradox perhaps best explained by his own aversion to being too closely associated with any readily reducible grand theory.

But there was more to Gombrich's relentlessly unaccommodating responses to all attempts to pigeon-hole him than a desire to remain free from the restrictions of any deterministic strait-jacket. For Gombrich was, notoriously, every bit as mistrustful of the grand theories of others as he was of the grand theories others associated with him. The enduring leitmotifs of Gombrich's writings are their attacks on Hegel's historicism and *Geistesgeschichte*, and on the offspring of those ideas in the cultural history of Jacob Burckhardt, the periodisation of Heinrich Wölfflin and the iconology

     Harry Mount

of Erwin Panofsky.[15] The anthology-compilers have not been so very wrong in choosing Gombrich's critiques of this tradition as representative of his writing, while Clark would have been at least partially justified had he named Gombrich among the enemies of the big-ideas art history which he wanted to revive.

But are we then compelled to define Gombrich only in negative terms, to see his primary importance as lying in his dismantling of the theories of others? While Gombrich's attacks on the grand theories of his predecessors and his fears that they could lead to racist generalisations and totalitarian myth-making are well-known,[16] much less attention has been devoted to the model of historical practice which Gombrich wanted to set in their place. That this has been so is, again, attributable in part to Gombrich's coyness about his own methods, his tendency to substitute such seemingly transparent but actually obfuscating terms as 'common sense' for the statements of method that one might have expected. But we do not have to look very hard to find the approach which Gombrich does recommend, in essay after essay. This lies in an attendance not to generalisations but to the specifics of individual cases, individual cases assessed through a forensic analysis of factual evidence derived from primary sources.[17] When Gombrich wished to deflate the big theories of his predecessors his standard method of dispatch was to deploy the killer counter-example, the specific case which was incompatible with the broad generalisations of his adversary.[18] And when he wanted to make a case himself his characteristic method was to cite a chain of examples, a chain which had a disturbing tendency to culminate not in the general conclusion one might have expected, but in a joke, a self-deprecating dying fall or just one further final example.[19]

So was this actually a method, or was it an anti-method, constructed in reaction against the grand theorizing which Gombrich so distrusted? Or, to put it another way, did Gombrich's method stem from a theory of practice, or was it, as some critics of art history have suggested, a striking embodiment of the discipline's naïve desire to have practice without theory?[20] I would argue that Gombrich was far too sophisticated to fall into this fallacy and was very well aware of what he was up to, for all his reluctance to talk about it too openly. His occasional throw-away admissions to being a nominalist, a wry reference to the medieval philosophers who believed in concrete and individual cases and not in universals, were made only half in jest.[21] These apparently light-hearted admissions chime with Gombrich's approval of the 'methodological individualism' advocated by his friend Karl Popper, with its focus on particular cases rather than collectives or universals.[22] Echoes of another of Popper's ideas have been discerned by Ján Bakoš, who has pointed out the resemblances between Gombrich's use of anomalous examples to deflate the claims of grand theories and Popper's principle of falsification, in which scientific hypotheses are tested against specific examples.[23]

A further theory advanced by Popper featured in one of Gombrich's most extended examinations of his own method, the essay entitled 'The Logic of Vanity Fair'. This essay, though written earlier, achieved its first prominent publication in 1974.[24] This was the same year as Clark's *Times Literary Supplement* article, and the two pieces bear some surprising similarities. Like Clark, Gombrich began by proclaiming the death of the big-ideas, historicist art history which had originated with Hegel.[25] Although Gombrich was much less regretful about its disappearance than Clark, he agreed with him in seeing something deeply inadequate in the art history that had replaced it, referring to the current approach as a mere 'desire for facts, a hope to get on with the business of cataloguing items without much interference from theorizers.' Gombrich advised art historians to turn instead to Popper's call for 'a more detailed analysis of the logic of situations'.[26] As far as its application to art history was concerned, Gombrich took the logic of situations to mean a close attention to the ways in which individuals and institutions respond to specific social situations, responses which have perforce to be addressed as separate cases because the logic of each individual circumstance is different. In this, too, there were resemblances to Clark, for Gombrich's interpretation of the logic of situations implied, in its attention to context, a specifically social history of art, albeit one purged of Hegelian historicism and seemingly lacking in the neo-Marxian attention to class ideologies enjoined by Clark. But unlike Clark's new social history of art, Gombrich's logic of situations never took hold; few art historians now even know the phrase, let alone regard it as one of the key methods of the discipline. That this has come to pass has been not only because Gombrich made his case less polemically than Clark, and not only because he did not, unlike Clark, publish at the same time two major books which explicitly showed his favoured approach in action.[27] Nor was it because the logic of situations was such a controversial or repugnant concept. Just the opposite, indeed, was the case; I would argue that the logic of situations had so little impact precisely because it was, essentially, what many art historians, at least in Britain, were doing already. While the focus on social circumstances might have been somewhat less widespread in the 1960s and 1970s than it is today, a careful attention to the logic of individual cases, assessed through facts derived from primary sources, was already the normative procedure. And, at least in Anglophone art history, it has remained so.

What I am arguing here is that Gombrich's approach has been so hard to identify as being an approach at all because that approach is, in its essence, already so deeply ingrained within the discipline of art history; so deeply ingrained, indeed, as to be almost beneath notice. When noticed at all this approach is at times labelled as empiricism.[28] In advocating falsification and the logic of situations Gombrich was, in effect, doing no more nor less than offering theoretical descriptions of empirical practices that were already central to the discipline. Art historians have been looking at specific cases (logic of situations) and deriving their estimations of whether their

     Harry Mount

hypotheses about them were right or wrong from the facts of those cases (falsification) for a very long time, and, for all the new angles of attack thrown up over the last three decades they have, by and large, continued to do so. I should hasten to add that I am referring here predominantly to Anglophone and, in particular, British art history. The predominantly empirical tenor of British art history in the post-war decades might, indeed, render plausible Perry Anderson's claim that Gombrich and his fellow immigrants made an important contribution to British intellectual life by offering theoretical justifications for empirical procedures which were in fact already endemic, if largely untheorised, in the national culture.[29]

The extent to which this was the case has been obscured by Gombrich's own determination to distance himself from empiricism. Following Popper, Gombrich repeatedly attacked purely inductive empiricism – that which starts with the facts and attempts to build generalisations – as pointless, even impossible. Facts had, he claimed, to be approached through ideas and hypotheses before they could become meaningful. He associated a purely inductive empiricism with a positivistic searching for facts for their own sake, an erroneous or dull practice into which, he claimed, the art history dominant in Britain was inclined to lapse.[30] Gombrich's belief in traits of human nature which are universal, and must thus by definition exist prior to individual experience, also distances him epistemologically from a purely inductive empiricism.[31] But while there may have been clear water philosophically between Gombrich and empiricism, or at least empiricism thus construed, his attempts to distance his own art historical method from those he accused of empiricism are undermined by the sheer effectiveness of his attack on purely inductive approaches, which he showed to be not only weak but, in practice, non-existent. For if, as he argued, a purely inductive approach would lead to nothing but a random jumble of facts, it follows that any historian who produces anything more ordered, even something as seemingly untheorised as a chronology or catalogue entry, must have started with a question or hypothesis of some sort. Or, to put it another way, if Gombrich's refutation of purely inductive empiricism is correct, then all empiricism must make some use of the process of hypotheses-tested-against-facts which Gombrich himself advocated. Gombrich had, in other words, destroyed his inductive-empirical straw man so effectively that it no longer served as a model of practice to set against his own, leading to the conclusion that there was no *essential* difference between the 'empirico-deductivist' procedure advocated by Gombrich, starting with a hypothesis and then proceeding to test it against the facts, and that employed by the empiricist art historians he encountered in Britain.[32] The only differences would be ones of degree, in how self-conscious authors were about the nature of the theory they were using, and in the level of complexity and ambition of that theory itself. That Gombrich's approach so closely resembled that dominant in his adopted country may not only explain, as Anderson argued, how well he settled here, but also, conversely, how keen he was to establish that there really was a difference between British empiricism and his own method.

This paper is not for one moment trying to appropriate Gombrich for British empirical art history. He was right to claim that he was often asking more ambitious questions of the evidence than his British counterparts, and in ways that were more self-conscious about the underlying theories involved. And empiricism was, of course, far from being an exclusively British phenomenon. As Jaś Elsner has argued, empiricism was an important aspect of the practice of the Vienna School from which Gombrich emerged,[33] and he himself claimed that he derived his determination to assess each case as an individual entity and to test every theory against primary evidence from his teacher, Julius von Schlosser.[34] If our task were that of writing Gombrich's intellectual biography and trying to work out whence his empiricism stemmed, then Vienna would be a good place to start. But if our task is to understand Gombrich's importance within the on-going discipline of art history then we must also consider the wider significance of his espousal of empiricism.

For what Gombrich did that was of such importance was to transfer the debate between grand historical theory and empirical testing which was being conducted in 1920s Vienna into a British and, more broadly, Anglophone context, a context in which it meant something very different. He did so, as we have seen, through his use of empiricism to attack the historicist *Geistesgeschichte* practised by Hegel and his followers. Gombrich's regular devouring of the liver of the Hegelian Prometheus was not, however, in itself of great significance for Anglophone art history, because that art history had never had much time for the grand historical theories of Hegel and his followers anyway. Gombrich's contribution was, rather, to demonstrate just how inimical grand historical theories and empirical testing were, just how difficult it was to get them to lie down peacefully together. In doing so he laid bare, in a way beyond the understanding or interest of most of his new compatriots, just why it was that Britain, in which empirical patterns of thought had been dominant since the seventeenth century, proved so consistently resistant to the blandishments of grand theory. So deeply did these empirical presumptions run among British art historians that even Clark in his *Times Literary Supplement* article admitted that 'we need facts – about patronage, about art dealing, about the status of the artist, the structure of artistic production – but we need to know what questions to ask of the material'.[35] In its insistence on a theoretically aware empiricism it was a sentence that might have been written by Gombrich himself. And Gombrich might in his turn have respected the way in which Clark, for all his theoretical ambitions, gave each of his historical studies a tight geographical and temporal focus, a focus which allowed for a process of verification through research in primary sources.[36] For all that modern social historians of art like to trace what they do back to Clark, their practice, with its close looking at specific cases, its assessment of the relationships between individuals and institutions and the social contexts they inhabit, and its use of primary sources to test the validity of interpretations, often bears as close a resemblance to that advocated in 'The Logic of Vanity Fair' as it does to the model set out by Clark in his article in the *Times Literary Supplemen*. This is especially the case now that the Marxian reference points of Clark's thought have become less fashionable.

What I am arguing here is that Gombrich's importance for the history of art history stems above all from his status as, in effect, the greatest and most articulate apologist for an empirical approach to the history of art. Because empirical art history, especially in its British variant, is usually just *done*, rather than spoken about, it took someone from a different tradition, one in which grand theory was far more important, to offer an articulate defence of the value of what was being done here anyway, and to proffer useful advice on how it might be done better and in a more theoretically informed way. If we want to find a clearly defined place for Gombrich in the surveys of the history of art history then his role as champion of empiricism should, I believe, be it.

To give him this role would be doubly valuable, as it would also compel us to give more recognition to empiricism, an approach which, while of great importance in the history of art history, has to date largely been ignored in accounts of that history. That this has been the case owes much to the ways in which accounts of that history have been written. In recent years, in particular, descriptions of the origins and development of art history have become so standardised that they have begun to harden into myth. After a brief nod back to Giorgio Vasari and other precursors, most recent accounts present Johann Winckelmann and Hegel as the true fathers of modern art history. Art history's Tree of Jesse then moves on through a sequence of great names – Burckhardt, Wölfflin, Panofsky, Clark – each one standing for a different method which is held to have developed or supplanted those which precede it.[37] The model echoes that traditionally used in histories of philosophy, in which each great thinker follows and supplants the one who went before. In philosophy this method has some justification, in the sense that philosophy can plausibly be seen as having developed through a series of paradigm shifts initiated by the conceptual leaps made by great individual thinkers. For all its supposed Hegelian origins, however, art history is fundamentally a historical, and not a philosophical, discipline. It is, as a consequence, simplistic to reduce its development to a series of conceptual stepping stones, each one marking the impact of a great thinker or a new method. The water that flows around those stepping stones, the water formed by the vast, slow-moving process of knowledge accretion which goes on all the time in archives, libraries, museums and now in conservation labs, is also of immense importance in the development of the discipline. Often the individual advances made by this work are so incremental that they make little noticeable impact, and yet their cumulative importance is great. Panofsky's 1934 article on Van Eyck's *Arnolfini* portrait is one of the landmarks of iconography; but without the archival researches of J.A. Crowe, G.B. Cavalcaselle and W.H.J. Weale it could not have been written.[38]

In recent books on the history and methodology of art history this empirical work has largely been ignored, disregarded as meaningless noise wafting around the clarion calls of the great art historians. For Clark it was something worse, it represented the decline of the discipline from the golden age of the great Germans. But Clark was wrong, in the sense that this sort of art history had always been going on, not only during the so-called golden age, but also back through the nineteenth century, back through the eighteenth, even into the sixteenth, from Vasari's occasional bouts of fact-checking to the voluminous notes of George Vertue or the catalogues of Pierre-Jean Mariette.[39] When art history first supplanted classical art theory in Britain as the dominant discourse through which art was discussed, a development which can be dated to the second quarter of the nineteenth century, the figures who effected this shift were not academic art historians but a motley collection of dealers, curators, critics, practising painters and writers of popular books. And while the likes of Maria Callcott, Charles Eastlake, Anna Jameson, Thomas Phillips and John Smith certainly kept an eye on intellectual developments in Germany,[40] the German writers on art they were most interested in were not Hegel nor the other 'critical historians of art' who followed his lead but archival historians, connoisseurs and museum directors like Franz Kugler, Carl Friedrich von Rumohr, Gustav Waagen and Johann Passavant – fact-gatherers, categorizers and attributors rather than grand theorists.[41]

It is not difficult to see why this empirical strain has been so systematically under-rated in histories of art history. Many of those who carried it out in the past were connoisseurs, amateurs and antiquarians. To admit that so much of what we know about art's past derives from those concerned primarily with buying or selling art or with grubbing up facts for their own sake might seem to diminish a discipline which already suffers, at least in the English-speaking world, from a long-standing inferiority complex. Far better to assert the seriousness of art history by affirming that what defines it as a discipline is its commitment to grand theories and big questions, and to locate this essentialist version of art history firmly within the professional world of the universities. Far better still to trace the origins of the discipline back to an irreproachably big name, to cast Hegel as the Giotto of art history, with Winckelmann as his Cimabue. The insistence with which art historians now refer to Hegel as the father of art history not only echoes those apocryphal noble families who liked to trace their ancestry back to William the Conqueror, it also plays a similar role. For who could under-estimate a discipline with such a distinguished and powerful blood-line? It was for a return to this same blood-line that Clark called in his *Times Literary Supplement* article, a blood-line that should, he argued, be purged of the inferior collateral branches which art history had, in his view, sprouted.[42] And yet, as I have been arguing, there is more than a whiff of creation myth about this habitual tracing

     Harry Mount

of the origins of the entire discipline of art history back to one man. Even seeing
Hegel as the originator of the particular form of cultural history with which he is
most closely associated entails, as Peter Burke has shown, a radical simplification of
the historiography.[43] And Hegel's form of art history is, anyway, very far from being
the only sort of art history, then or now. Art history is not a monolithic discipline;
it has many fathers, and even a few mothers too. The now commonplace casting of
Hegel as the father of art history works to obviate any further enquiry into these
multivalent origins, and encourages the fiction that art history is one single discipline
with a common core of principles and methods. Art history may, as Gombrich himself
argued, not even be a discipline at all, but rather a loosely grouped cluster of practices
and techniques, many borrowed from other fields, which hover around that equally
loosely defined thing called art.[44] To gain a genuine understanding of its development
we will need a historical approach closer to that which Gombrich himself advocated,
one that is less committed to the promotion of a grand historicist narrative and more
attuned to the vagaries of individual cases.[45]

The paradox here, of course, is that it was Gombrich himself who was, perhaps
more than anyone else, responsible for the perpetuation of this mythologisation of art
history's history. It was he who seems to have coined the phrase 'father of art history'
for Hegel,[46] and he who repeatedly wrote about the great tradition which stemmed
from Hegel. Not only could he be disparaging about the empirical art history going
on around him in his adopted country, he was also inclined to marginalise the
connoisseurs who had, historically, played such an important role in producing that
history.[47] And yet the construction of art history's history promoted by Gombrich,
and obediently followed by so many of those now writing the history of the discipline,
has turned out to be peculiarly ill-equipped to do justice to the approach of which
Gombrich himself was the most eloquent advocate.

Now Gombrich would, I am sure, have hated the idea that he might be associated
with empirical art history, not only because of his doubts about the limitations of
empiricism but also because of his loathing for being associated with any method or
movement, his favoured branch of the School of Vienna solely excepted. It would,
moreover, be far too crude to see him only as an empiricist, and, since there are many
shades of empiricism, any honest assessment of Gombrich's work would have to be
very careful in pinning down precisely what sort of empiricist he was. But this same
honest assessment should, I believe, identify Gombrich's empirical scepticism as one
of his supreme contributions to the discipline. Such an understanding might not
only prompt those writing art history's history to give empiricism its due, but also
to accord Sir Ernst Gombrich the prominence within that history which he so richly
deserves.

     Gombrich and the Fathers of Art History

1 Numerous statements to this effect may
be found. For Eric Fernie, writing in 1995,
Gombrich was a 'pivotal figure in the world
of contemporary art history' (*Art History and
its Methods: A Critical Anthology*, ed. E. Fernie,
London, 1995, p. 223); for Steve Edwards
he was 'one of the twentieth century's most
influential art historians' (*Art and its Histories:
A Reader*, ed. S. Edwards, New Haven and
London, 1999, p. 72); while for Jaś Elsner he
was 'the most magisterial, indeed dominant,
art-historical voice of the third quarter of the
twentieth century' (J. Elsner, 'The Birth of
Late Antiquity: Riegl and Strzygowski in
1901', *Art History*, 25, 2002, pp. 358-79
(p. 359)).

2 Among books in which Gombrich hardly
features see e.g. L.S. Adams, *The Methodologies
of Art: An Introduction*, New York, 1996; V.H.
Minor, *Art History's History*, New York, 1994;
D. Preziosi, *Rethinking Art History*, New
Haven and London, 1989. Some books on the
methods of art history from this period do not
mention Gombrich at all, e.g. *The Subjects of
Art History*, ed. M.A. Cheetham, M.A. Holly,
K. Moxey, Cambridge, 1998.

3 M. Hatt and C. Klonk, *Art History: a Critical
Introduction to its Methods*, Manchester and
New York, 2006, p. 3.

4 Fernie, *Art History* (n. 1 above), pp. 223-36;
Edwards, *Art and its Histories* (n. 1 above),
pp. 72-78; *The Art of Art History: A Critical
Anthology*, ed. D. Preziosi, Oxford, 1998,
pp. 150-63. The Gombrich essays in question
are, respectively, *In Search of Cultural History*,
the Philip Maurice Deneke Lecture, Oxford,
1969, reprinted in Gombrich, *Ideals and Idols:
Essays on Values in History and in Art*, Oxford,
1979, pp. 24-59 (all subsequent references
are to *Ideals and Idols*); 'Norm and Form: the
Stylistic Categories of Art History and their
Origins in Renaissance Ideals', in Gombrich,
*Norm and Form: Studies in the Art of the
Renaissance I*, London, 1966, pp. 81-98; and
'Style', in *International Encyclopaedia of the Social
Sciences*, ed. D.L. Sills, 18 vols., New York,
1968, vol. 15, pp. 352-61.

5 *E.H. Gombrich: A Commemoration*, London,
2002, p. 18. The same paradox is explored
by James Elkins in 'Ten Reasons why E.H.
Gombrich is not connected to Art History',

Human Affairs, 19, 2009, pp. 304-10.

6 For a neat summation of this view of
Gombrich see J. Harris, *The New Art History:
A Critical Introduction*, Abingdon, 2001, p. 37.

7 'Introduction', in *The New Art History*, ed. A.L.
Rees and F. Borzello, London, 1986, p. 9.

8 T.J. Clark, 'The Conditions of Artistic
Creation', *Times Literary Supplement*, 24 May
1974, pp. 561-62, reprinted in Fernie, *Art
History* (n. 1 above), pp. 248-53. All subsequent
references are to the latter publication.

9 See especially P. Anderson, 'Components
of the National Culture', *New Left Review*,
1st series, no. 50, July/August 1968, pp. 3-57
(especially pp. 12-20, 38-41).

10 See especially N. Bryson, *Vision and Painting*,
New Haven and London, 1983.

11 See also Elkins, 'Ten Reasons' (n. 5 above),
pp. 306-07.

12 E.H. Gombrich and D. Eribon, *A Lifelong
Interest: Conversations on Art and Science with
Didier Eribon*, London, 1993, p. 139.

13 E.g. in E.H. Gombrich, 'The Logic of Vanity
Fair: Alternatives to Historicism in the Study
of Fashions, Style and Taste', in *The Philosophy
of Karl Popper*, ed. P.A. Schilpp, La Salle,
Illinois, 1974, pp. 925-57; reprinted in *Ideals
and Idols* (n. 4 above), pp. 60-92 (p. 61). All
subsequent references are to *Ideals and Idols*.

14 See, for example, David Carrier's account of
Gombrich's response to his interpretation of
Art and Illusion, in D. Carrier, *Principles of Art
History Writing*, University Park, Pennsylvania,
1991, pp. 238-39. Cf. *A Lifelong Interest* (n. 12
above), pp. 101-03.

15 There are many examples, but on all these
authors see E.H. Gombrich, '"The Father
of Art History": A Reading of the *Lectures
on Aesthetics* of G.W. F. Hegel (1770-1831)',
lecture given as acceptance of the Hegel Prize
in Stuttgart in 1977, published in Gombrich,
Tributes: Interpreters of our Cultural Tradition,
Oxford, 1984, pp. 51-69, esp. pp. 62-63.
On Hegel and Burckhardt see especially
Gombrich, *In Search* (n. 4 above); on Wölfflin
see especially Gombrich, 'Norm and Form'
(n. 4 above); on Panofsky see the largely
implicit criticisms voiced in E.H. Gombrich,
'Aims and Limits of Iconology', in Gombrich,
*Symbolic Images: Studies in the Art of the
Renaissance II*, Oxford, 1972, pp. 1-22, and the

    Harry Mount

more explicit comments in Gombrich and Eribon, *A Lifelong Interest* (n. 12 above), pp. 135-37, 153-55.

16 See e.g. Gombrich, *In Search* (n. 4 above), p. 50. Both Vardan Azatyan and Andrew Hemingway have, for example, recently sought to contextualize these attacks within the wider rhetoric of individualistic freedom promoted by the West during the Cold War. See V. Azatyan, 'Cold-War Twins: Mikhail Alpatov's *A Universal History of Arts* and Ernst Gombrich's *The Story of Art*', *Human Affairs*, 19, 2009, pp. 289-96 (especially p. 292); A. Hemingway, 'E.H. Gombrich in 1968: Methodological Individualism and the Contradictions of Conservatism', *Human Affairs*, 19, 2009, pp. 297-303.

17 See e.g. Gombrich, *In Search* (n. 4 above), pp. 50-55; Gombrich, review of A. Hauser, *The Social History of Art*, New York, 1951, in *The Art Bulletin*, 35, 1953, pp. 79-84, reprinted as 'The Social History of Art' in Gombrich, *Meditations on a Hobby Horse and Other Essays on the Theory of Art*, London, 1963, pp. 86-94.

18 Among numerous examples see especially Gombrich, 'The Social History of Art' (n. 17 above). See also Gombrich, *In Search* (n. 4 above), p. 48.

19 A typical example is Gombrich, 'Vanity Fair' (n. 13 above).

20 See e.g. J. Elkins, 'Art History without Theory', *Critical Inquiry*, 14, 1988, pp. 354-78.

21 E.g. E.H. Gombrich, 'The Cartoonist's Armoury', first given as a lecture at Duke University in 1962, published in *Hobby Horse* (n. 17 above), pp. 127-42 (p. 128); *A Lifelong Interest* (n. 12 above), p. 71.

22 Gombrich, 'Vanity Fair' (n. 13 above), p. 61. Cf. K.R. Popper, *The Poverty of Historicism*, London, 1957, p. 149. On Gombrich and methodological individualism see Hemingway, 'Gombrich in 1968' (n. 18 above), p. 300.

23 J. Bakoš, 'The Vienna School's Hundred and Sixty-eighth Graduate: the Vienna School's Ideas Revised by E.H. Gombrich', in *Gombrich on Art and Psychology*, ed. R. Woodfield, Manchester, 1996, pp. 234-57 (pp. 237, 248). Cf. K.R. Popper, *The Logic of Scientific Discovery*, New York, 1959. For Gombrich's approval of this principle see Gombrich, 'Father of Art History' (n. 15 above),

pp. 62-63, and 'Focus on the Arts and Humanities', first delivered as a lecture to the American Academy of Arts and Sciences in 1981, published in Gombrich, *Tributes* (n. 15 above), pp. 11-27 (17).

24 Gombrich, 'Vanity Fair' (n. 13 above) was written in 1965.

25 Gombrich, 'Vanity Fair' (n. 13 above), p. 60; see also Gombrich, *In Search* (n. 4 above), pp. 52-53.

26 Gombrich, 'Vanity Fair' (n. 13 above), pp. 60-62. See also Hemingway, 'Gombrich in 1968' (n. 18 above), p. 300.

27 Clark's books were *Image of the People: Gustave Courbet and the 1848 Revolution*, London, 1973, and *The Absolute Bourgeois*, London, 1973.

28 For example by James Elkins, who offers one of the few analyses of the prevalence of empiricism in art historical practice in Elkins, 'Art History' (n. 22 above).

29 Anderson, 'Components of the National Culture' (n. 9 above), p. 233.

30 See e.g. Gombrich, *In Search* (n. 4 above), pp. 41-42; Gombrich, 'Vanity Fair' (n. 13 above), pp. 60-61; Gombrich and Eribon, *A Lifelong Interest* (n. 12 above), p. 161. On the Popperian origins of Gombrich's attack on inductive empiricism see Hemingway, 'Gombrich in 1968' (n. 18 above), pp. 299-300.

31 See e.g. E.H. Gombrich, *Art and Illusion: a Study in the Psychology of Pictorial Representation*, London, 1960, pp. 86-89. For a discussion of this aspect of Gombrich's thought and of its parallels in that of Popper see Hemingway, 'Gombrich in 1968' (n. 18 above), p. 301.

32 'Empirico-deductivist' is a term tellingly applied by Andrew Hemingway to Popper's favoured method and, by inference, to that advocated by Gombrich. See Hemingway, 'Gombrich in 1968' (n. 18 above), p. 300.

33 Elsner, 'Birth of Late Antiquity' (n. 1 above), pp. 358-79. See also Peter Burke's claim in his essay, above, p. 15, on the interest in 'methodological individualism' evident among both English and Austrian thinkers.

34 See e.g. E.H. Gombrich, 'Art and Scholarship', first delivered as a lecture at University College London in 1957, published in *Hobby Horse* (n. 17 above), pp. 106-19 (p. 112); *A Lifelong Interest* (n. 12 above), p. 71.

     Gombrich and the Fathers of Art History

35 Clark, 'Conditions of Artistic Creation' (n. 8 above), p. 251.

36 I am not the first to notice points of resemblance between the ideas of Gombrich and those of Clark. See also Paul Overy, 'The New Art History and Art Criticism', in *New Art History* (n. 7 above), pp. 133-45.

37 Fernie's *Art History* (n. 1 above) and Hatt and Klonk's *Critical Introduction* (n. 3 above) are typical examples.

38 Erwin Panofsky, 'Jan van Eyck's *Arnolfini* Portrait', *Burlington Magazine*, LXIV, 1934, pp. 117-27; J.A. Crowe and G.B. Cavalcaselle, *The Early Flemish Painters*, London, 1857, pp. 65-66; W.H.J. Weale, *Hubert and John van Eyck*, London, 1908, p. 73. For the contributions of Crowe, Cavalcaselle and Weale see Lorne Campbell, *National Gallery Catalogues: The Fifteenth Century Netherlandish Schools*, London, 1998, p. 193.

39 On Vasari's researches see P.L. Rubin, *Giorgio Vasari: Art and History*, New Haven and London, 1995, pp. 168-77, 215-27. See also George Vertue, 'The Vertue Note Books', *The Walpole Society* 18, 1929-30; 20, 1931-32; 22, 1933-34; 24, 1935-36; 26, 1937-38; 29, 1940-42; 30, 1948-50; *Abecedario de P.J. Mariette et autres notes inédites de cet amateur sur les arts et les artistes*, ed. P. de Chennevières and A. de Montaiglon, 6 vols., Paris, 1851-60.

40 See Mrs [Maria] Callcott, *Essays Towards the History of Painting*, London, 1836; Charles Eastlake, *Materials for a History of Oil Painting*, London, 1847; Anna Jameson, *Memoirs of the Early Italian Painters*, London, 1845; Thomas Phillips, *Lectures on the History and Principles of Painting*, London, 1833; John Smith, *A Catalogue Raisonné of the Works of the Most Eminent Dutch, Flemish, and French Painters*, 9 vols., London, 1829-42.

41 On the Hegelian tradition in nineteenth-century Germanophone art history see Michael Podro, *The Critical Historians of Art*, New Haven and London, 1982. On the importance of Kugler, Rumohr, Waagen and Passavant in Britain see e.g. Francis Haskell, *Rediscoveries in Art*, Oxford, 1976, pp. 152-54; William Vaughan, *German Romanticism and English Art*, New Haven and London, 1979, pp. 86-89. Kugler was, of course, a theorist of history as well as an archival historian, but

significantly Charles Eastlake, in his notes to the English translation of Kugler's *Handbuch*, attacked one of Kugler's more Hegelian and historicist pronouncements in favour of an attention to the specific determinants of the individual case. See F. Kugler, *A Handbook of the History of Painting*, Part One, London, 1842, pp. 45-46 and n., and, for a discussion of the interaction, Vaughan, *German Romanticism and English Art*, pp. 88-89.

42 Clark, 'Conditions of Artistic Creation' (n. 8 above), pp. 249-50.

43 P. Burke, *Varieties of Cultural History*, Ithaca, 1997, p. 21.

44 On Gombrich's scepticism about the existence of disciplines in the humanities see Gombrich, *In Search* (n. 4 above), p. 57; E.H. Gombrich, 'Research in the Humanities: Ideals and Idols', first published in *Daedalus*, Spring 1973, reprinted in *Ideals and Idols* (n. 4 above), pp. 112-22 (p. 119). On Gombrich's scepticism about art as a unified concept see the famous opening words of the introduction to *The Story of Art*, London, 1950: 'There really is no such thing as Art. There are only artists.' See also Gombrich and Eribon, *A Lifelong Interest* (n. 12 above), pp. 71-74.

45 One, perhaps, closer to that adopted by Francis Haskell in *History and its Images*, New Haven and London, 1993. In the light of the argument I make below it is, however, significant that Gombrich, in the course of a generally positive review of this book, felt that Haskell had presented his findings in too atomized a fashion and that he had specifically underestimated the importance of Hegel and the tradition to which he belonged. Gombrich's review originally appeared in the *New York Review of Books*, 21 October 1993, pp. 60-62, and was reprinted with revisions in E.H. Gombrich, *The Uses of Images: Studies in the Social Function of Art and Visual Communication*, London, 1999, pp. 262-72 (pp. 263-64).

46 In Gombrich, 'Father of Art History' (n. 15 above), see both the title and p. 51. The quotation marks within which he places the phrase in the title suggest an attempt to distance himself from the soubriquet, but within the article itself Gombrich argues that Hegel should indeed be regarded as the father

     Harry Mount

of art history, just as he had cast him as the
founder of cultural history in *In Search* (n. 4
above), pp. 28-47.

47 For Gombrich's scepticism about the practices
of connoisseurs see, for example, his 'The
Rhetoric of Attribution – a Cautionary Tale',
first published as 'Rhétorique de l'attribution:
reductio ad absurdum', *Revue de l'art*, no. 42,
1978, pp. 23-25, republished in translation
in E.H. Gombrich, *Reflections on the History
of Art: Views and Reviews*, ed. R. Woodfield,
Oxford, 1987, pp. 91-96.

Gombrich and 'Warburgian' Iconography*

ELIZABETH MCGRATH

Gombrich's interest in iconography

'ICONOGRAPHY TREATS OF THE SUBJECT MATTERS OF WORKS OF ART; its method is that of interpretation'. These are the words with which Ernst Gombrich, some time around 1940, planned to open a projected handbook of iconography. The handbook never materialised.[1] But his words of introduction sum up what it was – at that time, and thereafter – that Gombrich found especially interesting about the study of iconography: its relevance to issues surrounding the interpretation of images. He always had in mind the question as to what makes a given reading of an image a valid one. Starting from the notion that, in content as in style, not everything is possible at every period,[2] he sought to define and delimit the iconographic choices available to individual artists in particular situations at particular times. He aimed thereby to understand not only why certain themes were illustrated in certain ways, but how, as historians, we can plausibly construct guidelines for the comprehension of the content and meaning of a work of art. In his essays on iconography, then, as so often elsewhere in his writings, he was concerned with the processes of making and of deciphering images. Gombrich's engagement with iconographic interpretation illustrates how, within the context of research and teaching at the Warburg Institute – the context in which he operated for most of his working life – he found material that would feed into his other investigations into representation.

I underline the working context since, although he habitually protested against the widespread association of the Warburg Institute with iconography,[3] Gombrich accepted that the study of the subject-matter of art, particularly of Renaissance art in its relationship to humanism, was and should be a characteristically 'Warburgian' pursuit. Late in his life he described his book *Symbolic Images* as 'the most Warburgian of my books'.[4] This work is devoted to Renaissance iconography. Published in 1972, it consists of a collection of essays, for the most part already printed in some form (usually in the *Journal of the Warburg and Courtauld Institutes*), prefaced by some general observations and principles that are at once down-to-earth and subtle. The volume contains incisive short pieces on specific topics, such as 'Tobias and the Angel', first published in 1948, which explains how Renaissance pictures usually identified by this title are intended not as illustrations of an Old Testament story but as images of St (Archangel) Raphael with the attribute (Tobias) by which he can be recognised.[5] There are also lengthy and more difficult studies, revisions of articles dating from around the same period, which involve erudite commentary and Neoplatonic interpretation.[6] The opening essay, entitled 'Introduction: Aims and Limits of Iconology', is, however, altogether new, and far-reaching in its approach – an introduction not so much to the book as to iconographic method. It represents a distillation of ideas about meaning and interpretation that had been developed over the years by Gombrich, particularly while teaching a series of classes on iconography for the postgraduate course on the Renaissance at the Warburg. At the same time, by giving his introductory essay the title he did, Gombrich signalled two things. First, his intention to challenge, or at least provide an alternative to, Erwin Panofsky's famous theoretical essays of 1939 and 1955.[7] Second, in his reference to 'limits' of iconology, a wish to campaign against the sort of over-interpretation and search for hidden meanings that was common at the time, and had been encouraged by some of Panofsky's work.[8]

Iconology and iconography

The term 'iconology' had been employed by Aby Warburg to characterise something of his approach to the study of images. Warburg never attempted a definition, and he seems to have used the word in slightly different ways in the course of his life,[9] but he certainly meant by it something distinct from iconography.[10] He particularly applied it to his lecture of 1912 about the frescoes in Palazzo Schifanoia in Ferrara, which he called an 'iconological analysis'.[11] There he presented a notable *iconographic* discovery: the identification of the strange decan figures in the Sala dei Mesi. But this discovery was, to Warburg, only a stepping stone towards an interpretation that sought to show how ancient astral imagery had been misunderstood and disguised in medieval Europe, and had appeared in debased form, through the distorting lens of orientalising and Arabic sources, before recovering appropriate shape and meaning in the High Renaissance. Images were for Warburg the ideal vehicle for charting change in ideas and cultural values over time, especially in relation to the heritage of classical antiquity.[12] By following a specific iconographic theme through different stylistic and expressive manifestations he sought insights into the evolution of the human mind, confronted, as he saw it, with conflicting forces of superstition and enlightenment.[13]

It was Erwin Panofsky who gave the word 'iconology' its currency among the art historians of the last century, especially through the two essays in which he set out to define the pursuit and distinguish it from iconography.[14] Though never on the staff either of the Bibliothek Warburg in Hamburg or of the Warburg Institute in London, Panofsky was a close friend and sometime collaborator of Warburg's

successor as Director, Fritz Saxl, and a great admirer of Warburg. There is no
doubt that Panofsky's impulse to interpret images in terms of the world view of
a period was influenced by Warburg's ideas, even if Panofsky, by contrast, seems
to have thought of reconstructing this *Weltanschauung* primarily through texts
and then bringing the results to bear on a particular object of study. He certainly
used terminology reminiscent of Warburg, talking of iconology as a means of
understanding, through iconographic analysis, how the 'essential tendencies of the
human mind' were expressed at a given period; 'the medieval mind' too is something
he appeals to on occasion.[15] This sort of phrase, with its aura of the 'spirit of the age',
was for Gombrich, at the time he was writing the introduction to *Symbolic Images*
(around 1970), a provocation; his anti-Hegelian reflexes were by this period strongly
developed.[16] He, for his part, advised iconologists to start from the limiting factors of
artistic genres, conventions and practical requirements, and then consider individual
choices within these. 'All iconological research', Gombrich pronounces, 'depends
on our prior conviction of what we look for, in other words, on our feeling for what
is or is not possible within a given period or milieu'.[17] Like Panofsky himself, he is
not altogether clear or consistent in what he means by the term *iconology*, though
he sets out to demystify the word. In the Preface to the book he talks of it as 'the
systematic study of Renaissance symbolism'.[18] But in the introduction he comments:
'By and large we mean by iconology, since the pioneer studies of Panofsky, the
reconstruction of a programme rather than the identification of a particular text [i.e.
behind an individual work]'.[19] By programme he means not only the instructions that
might have been given for the content of a specific painting, but the overall scheme
guiding the choice and combination of themes for a given setting – a case in point
being Raphael's frescoes in the Stanza della Segnatura, discussed by him in terms of
traditional cycles that combine personifications of different branches of knowledge
with historical figures who are representative of each discipline.[20] I am not sure that
this was indeed how the term 'iconology' was generally used at the time – to describe
the 'reconstruction of a programme' – but at any rate it allowed Gombrich to present
his message that we should look first to artistic genre and context, to proceed from
the known in iconography to the unknown; and that, without strong indications
otherwise, we should favour the obvious, primary meaning of a work, rather than
looking for hidden signification. Here he was consciously taking a stand not only
against Panofsky but against Edgar Wind's *Pagan Mysteries in the Renaissance* (1958),
and in particular the remarks made there about how looking at 'the commonplace
in history' was no way to approach great works of art.[21] For Gombrich, Raphael's
genius lay in the wonderfully inventive and suggestive way he treated his essentially
conventional subject matter; and it was this artistry that had encouraged scholars to
think that the 'programme' behind it must have been remarkably sophisticated.[22]

    Elizabeth McGrath

How Gombrich came to the Warburg Institute

Both Panofsky and Wind had known Aby Warburg and saw themselves in a direct line leading from him. Gombrich, by contrast, never met Warburg, nor came under the spell of his magnetic personality. Indeed, though this may seem surprising to the many people who now associate the Warburg Institute with Gombrich, it was more by accident than by design that Gombrich came to be there. A student of Julius von Schlosser in Vienna, he finished his dissertation in 1933 on Giulio Romano as the architect of the Palazzo del Te, and found himself unable to obtain employment. Through his friend and fellow student, Otto Kurz, he managed to get some work in a private capacity as an assistant to Ernst Kris, who was collecting material on caricature. It was through Kris that Gombrich became interested in the topic of caricature, which came to be such an important theme in his work, even though the book that Kris and Gombrich were writing in the 1930s was never published in the way they intended.[23] Kris, who had connections with the Warburg Library in Hamburg, had already organised some work there for Kurz in 1932. He now asked Saxl to find a job for Gombrich too, in the new Institute in London. This job turned out to be the difficult, indeed ultimately hopeless, task of preparing Warburg's notes and drafts for publication, and in particular of using these fragments to provide textual accompaniment to the project which had occupied the last years of Warburg's life: the so called Mnemosyne Atlas, a compendium of images intended to illuminate themes of change and continuity in the afterlife of antiquity.[24] Saxl's colleague Gertrud Bing, who had been Warburg's closest collaborator in his last years, was to act as guide in making sense of the notes. Gombrich often talked of the shock he got when he saw the scattered and incoherent material he was supposed to bring into order.[25] Still worse, he found himself unsympathetic to many of Warburg's grander ideas, something that Saxl and Bing quickly picked up on and worried over.[26]

Gombrich's association with the Warburg Institute did not then begin from a particular appreciation of Aby Warburg or a sense of intellectual affinity with his scholarly approach. It was more a matter of practical necessity, economic and political. It was expedient for Gombrich to leave Austria; and the Warburg Institute, a Germanic institution transplanted to London, offered him the opportunity of employment, as an art historian with expertise in the Renaissance. Crucial, however, for Gombrich's decision to come to the Warburg Institute in London and, still more importantly, to stay at it, was the presence of Kurz – the fact that he was already there, working on various Institute projects and publications. The two friends and fellow students of Schlosser now shared lodgings, as well as ideas and problems. A rare photo of the pair at this period (fig. 1) shows them on a trip to an unidentified seaside town in the company of Ilse Gombrich and Trude Weiss,[27] well wrapped against an English summer on the promenade. Among the many ways their friendship affected Gombrich's work was in the pursuit of iconographical research.[28]

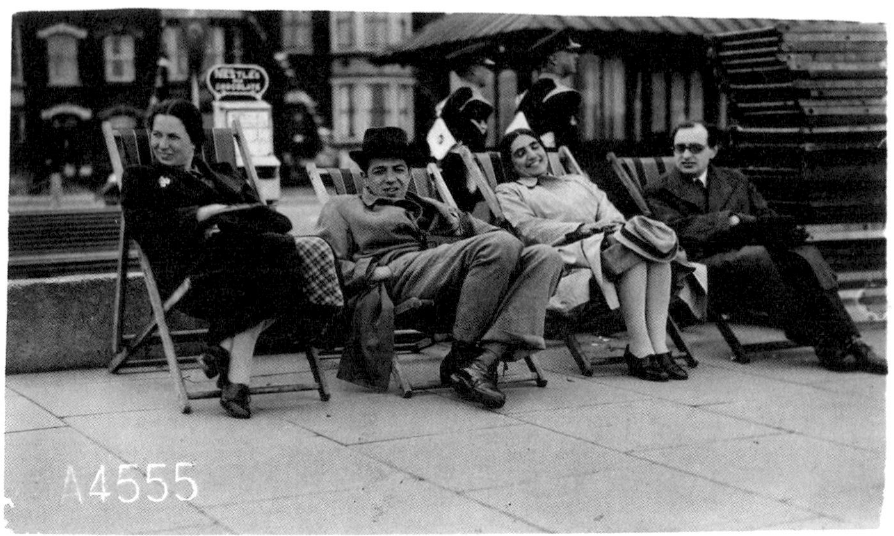

FIG. 1 Photograph of Ilse Gombrich, Ernst Gombrich, Trude Weiss and Otto Kurz
on the promenade in an English seaside town, 1937–38

An iconographic partnership

I was lucky enough to be able to witness the interaction of Gombrich and Kurz at
the Institute in the late 1960s and early 1970s and to observe how well their talents
and personalities complemented one another. Kurz was gentle and good humoured,
never showing resentment or annoyance, ready to listen to anyone. Gombrich, as he
himself would have been the first to admit, was easily irritated by ideas and behaviour
that he found disagreeable. In their scholarship Kurz almost always started from the
particular, some object or document, often from an out-of-the-way place, whereas
Gombrich was usually stimulated by some hypothesis or theory, or perhaps, rather,
by a sceptical reaction to a hypothesis or theory.[29] In the seminars which Gombrich
conducted at the Institute when he was Director, and which staff, fellows and students
were expected to attend, he never failed to appeal to Kurz for an opinion during
the question session which followed the talk – and then Kurz would come up with
what generally was not a judgement but rather some very relevant point of fact or
information. Sometimes indeed his intervention might demolish the very basis of the
speaker's argument, though in such circumstances he would avoid making the matter
explicit in public discussion. From his immense reserves of varied knowledge Kurz
regularly provided Gombrich himself with examples and documentation to underpin
or undermine a hypothesis. This was the case with Gombrich's interpretation of
Hieronymus Bosch's *Garden of Earthly Delights* (fig. 2) as the days before the Flood
of Noah.[30] In this study Gombrich drew attention to certain passages in Petrus

     Elizabeth McGrath

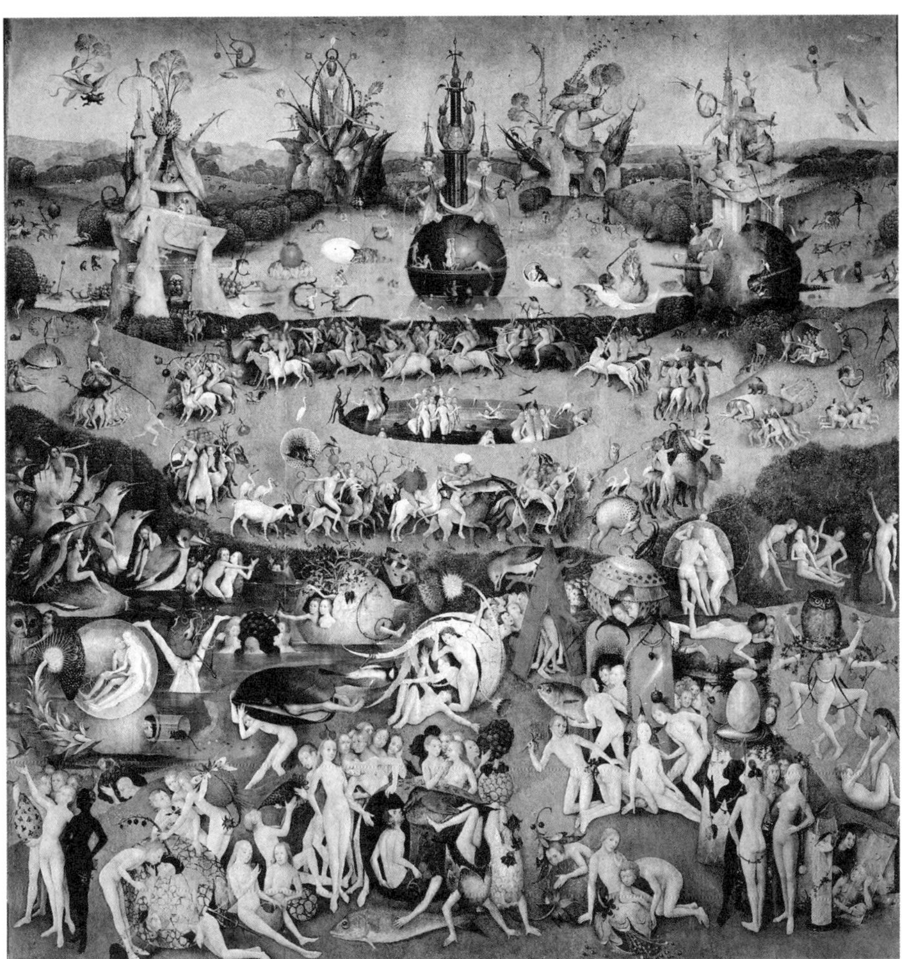

FIG. 2 Hieronymus Bosch, The 'Garden of Earthly Delights', central panel of a triptych, Madrid, Museo del Prado

Comestor and other medieval writers which talk of the time before Noah's Flood, when people were given over to lust and luxury: God supposedly sent the Flood to punish them. Gombrich related this story to ancient Greek and Roman accounts, known in medieval versions, of how, when the world was young, Nature produced 'experiments', strange creatures which combined different species. At this time too, in the youth of the world, excessive fertility meant that some animals and fruits grew extra large, out of control. Gombrich thanks Kurz in this article for a crucial reference in an old inventory to a painting of the subject of the days before the Flood, which he thought might have been a copy of Bosch's picture;[31] but Kurz certainly supplied more extensive help, general and particular. In fact Gombrich tells us as much. In one of

     Gombrich and 'Warburgian' Iconography

his obituaries of Kurz he remarks that it was his 'invariable rule' to submit any idea to Kurz, and that when he put forward his proposal that Henry III of Nassau had owned the picture, Kurz 'opened a drawer in his desk and produced a voluminous folder about this and other works of Bosch which confirmed my hypothesis'.[32] He adds that Kurz only published his own 'Four Tapestries after Hieronymus Bosch' in the same issue of the *Journal of the Warburg and Courtauld Institutes* to oblige his friend.

I emphasize their collaboration as it had a very specific bearing on Gombrich's engagement with iconography. Not long after Gombrich arrived at the Warburg, the Institute was packed away into storage, since its first home in London was no longer available.[33] Making the most of this enforced break from Warburg's papers, Gombrich taught at the Courtauld Institute, as also did Kurz, and it was the director of the Courtauld, T. S. R. Boase, who suggested that the two of them compile a series of handbooks for students of art history, with methodological case-studies and examples, and relevant bibliography.[34] Significantly, the first was to be on iconography. Drafts of a large portion of the projected book still exist.[35] Kurz's part is in a fairly finished state, with relevant photos even included; Gombrich's text is much further from completion. But it illustrates clearly how they tried to start, not by addressing exceptional or esoteric images, but by providing straightforward explanations of the range of themes at any period, as well as the functions and traditions of genres of art, and how they planned to go on to deal with individual works within these contexts.

An early text for the 'Foreword' to Kurz's first volume, on religious iconography, survives with the drafts of the Handbook. I suspect that it was written largely by Saxl. Not only does it refer to Kurz in the third person, it contains echoes of Warburg's thinking on iconology, talking of how the book 'deals with typical examples of religious iconography at different periods of European history, and attempts to illustrate the forms of expression used and the ideas underlying them', adding that the 'recurrence of particular forms in varying contexts is another essential part of any such study and one that often reveals curious links in the development of human thought'. This Foreword indicates too that initially Kurz alone was involved as author;[36] as yet there is no mention of who might undertake the second part.[37] But Gombrich must have quickly come on board to write the section on secular iconography, for which Kurz was to contribute only a short essay on portraiture. The joint book had evidently begun to be planned, as an Institute project, by the late summer of 1938. For, in a letter to Panofsky of 6 September, Saxl talks of the 'Kurz-Gombrichische Untersuchung' with which he is very busy.[38] This is certainly the iconographic handbook. Gombrich later commented that the war pushed it aside. He had been assigned to 'war work' in 1939 – with the BBC Monitoring Service (Listening Post) at Wood Norton, near Evesham, translating and interpreting foreign radio broadcasts, especially German ones;[39] and this job kept him and his family isolated in the English countryside and away from libraries. But he was evidently still working on the handbook, in any

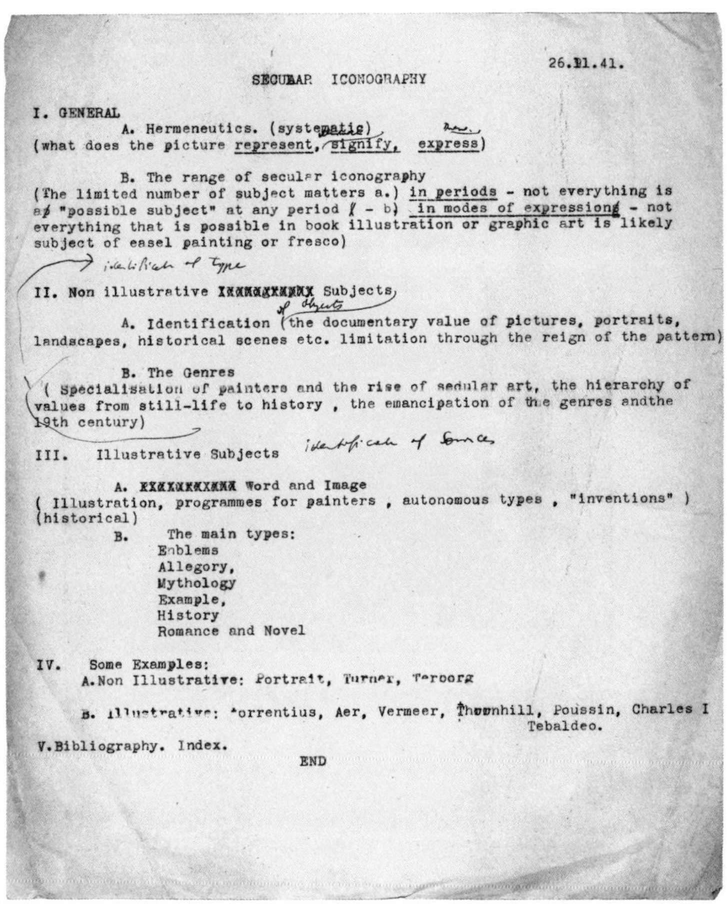

FIG. 3 Gombrich's outline of the section on secular iconography for the *Iconographic Handbook*, November 1941

spare time he got, at least during the early years of the war. A plan for Gombrich's part, first set down on 1 July 1941 and revised at the end of November (fig. 3), shows that it was to start with an introduction on interpretation, and the matter of why it is that we can manage to identify subjects at all. 'Not everything is a "possible subject" at any period', he says. And he adds that certain subjects that are possible in book illustration are not likely to be found in a fresco. There follows a division of subject-matter into 'non-illustrative' (e.g. portraits and still lifes) and 'illustrative' (e.g. histories, mythologies and allegories), which, in his handwritten corrections to the typescript Gombrich also associates respectively with the identification of objects

    Gombrich and 'Warburgian' Iconography

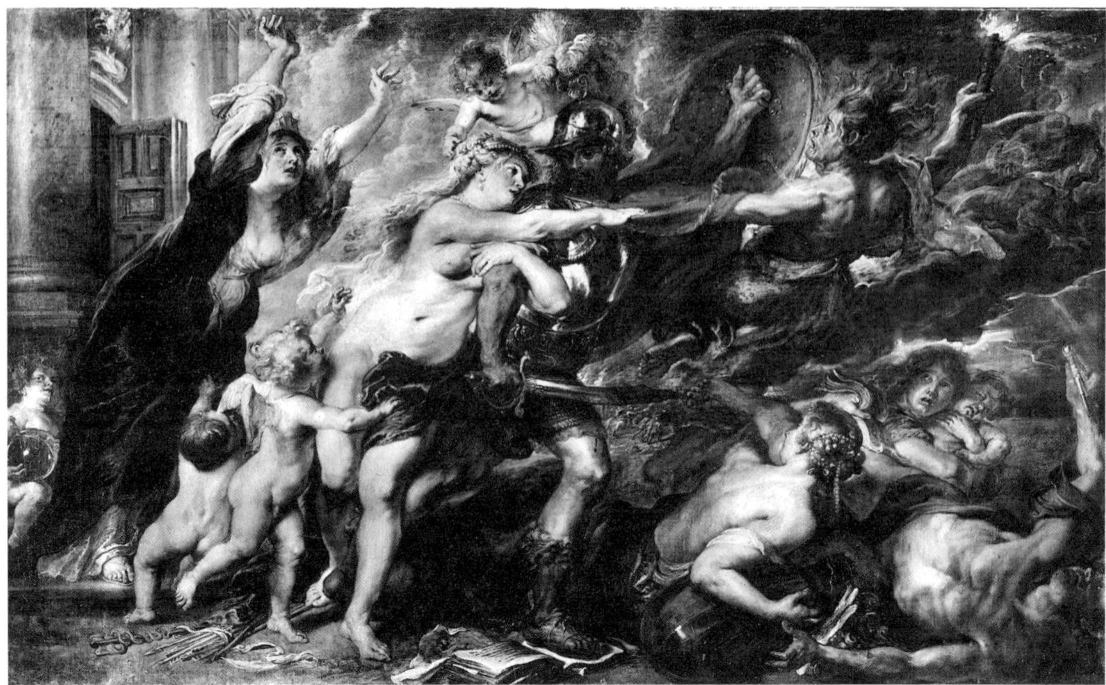

FIG. 4 Peter Paul Rubens, *Allegory of War*, Florence, Palazzo Pitti

and the identification of sources. More general essays, on the genres, for example, or programmes for painters, are included within one or the other category (though obviously there is a certain overlap). The plan for the book was that it should end with a series of telling case studies from the different categories, with some relevant text or document, ideally a statement by the artist concerned. Turner's *Liber Studiorum*, for example, was to feature for its evidence about the classification of landscape; Thornhill's Greenwich ceiling and various notes and studies the artist made in preparation were to be used for allegory; Torrentius' still life of 1614 (Rijksmuseum, Amsterdam) for emblems; and Poussin's *Orion* (Metropolitan Museum, New York), with the explanatory text of Natale Conti, for classical mythology.[40] Draft essays are extant for these, as well as a few other case studies that must have been added later: Titian's *Cupids* (Madrid, Museo del Prado) with its textual source in Philostratus, for example, and Rubens' *Horrors of War* (Florence, Palazzo Pitti; fig. 4) along with the artist's description of it, for mythology (in the latter case, transformed into allegory).

Despite remaining unpublished,[41] the handbook has had a lasting impact on the pursuit of iconography at the Warburg Institute. I already mentioned the iconography course that Gombrich taught to students at the Institute in the 1960s and 1970s. This course was conducted in collaboration with Kurz, and the abandoned book provided

    Elizabeth McGrath

a structure for the individual classes. Indeed it long continued to do so. Gombrich
handed me the drafts of the book when he retired in 1976 and Charles Hope and
I took over the teaching of this course. We may have dealt with different examples
from those used by Gombrich, and disputed a few of Gombrich's interpretations of
pictures, but we never felt the need to change the basic format of the classes since it
seemed to provide the best approach to the interpretation of Renaissance art: by first
establishing the categories and intended functions of imagery produced at the period
and then investigating the extent to which great works of art, including the famous
iconographic 'puzzles', could or could not be accommodated within them.

Symbolic images revisited

Gombrich of course exploited some of the material from the abandoned book in his
publications over the years – he was an inveterate recycler. As is evident even from
the summary of its projected contents written in November 1941 (fig. 3), Gombrich
developed the general themes of the handbook in the introduction to his *Symbolic
Images*, published in 1972. Having, I suspect, decided by the late 1960s that this
coming publication was likely to be the nearest thing to a book on iconography that
he would ever write, he worked into a couple of the essays ideas that had been tried
out in the handbook and tested in his later classes. This particularly applies to the
essay which gave the book its title, *Icones Symbolicae.* The original version of this essay
had been published in the *Journal of the Warburg and Courtauld Institutes* for 1948;
and it is one of the most learned pieces of 'Warburgian' scholarship Gombrich ever
produced.[42] It had begun as an investigation of Ficino and Neoplatonism and the
relationship of both to art. Gombrich's initial conclusions on this topic, outlined in
a lecture given at Oxford early in 1948,[43] rather downplayed the connection of art to
Neoplatonic philosophy, but a discovery he made when leafing through the volumes
of an eighteenth-century collection of Latin texts (Graevius' *Thesaurus Antiquitatum…
Italiae*) changed the perspective. This was a publication of 1626 (*Icones Symbolicae*) by
a Barnabite preacher and eventual bishop called Cristoforo Giarda which suggested
that personifications could be viewed as images of Platonic ideas.[44] Giarda's text
encouraged Gombrich in a theory that had intrigued him since he began studying
art history in Vienna: the status of those heavenly women (for, given the demands
of Latin and Italian gender, personified abstractions are almost always women)
who occupy so much space among the clouds on Baroque ceilings. In the revised
version of this essay, however, where his starting point was art rather than Platonic
abstraction, he realised that he should not try to make so much of Platonism; Giarda's
theory had very little to do with the larger story of the representation of allegorical
figures, which Gombrich now treated in a new and extensive introduction dealing
with the traditions of personification in European art. Here he produced, among

other interesting examples, a brilliant analysis of Rubens' *Horrors of War* (fig. 4), exploring the inventive interplay of symbolism and 'reality' in that picture, so unlike earlier, more straightforwardly allegorical treatments of the theme of war and peace. Rubens, he showed, 'knew how to turn the thought into a human drama', by evoking classical myth and poetry and making the goddess of love herself the figure of Peace who opposes the warlike Mars. Lucretius' invocation, in the first lines of *De rerum natura*, of the benevolent and nurturing Venus who can seduce and thus subdue the god of war is here inverted in an image that is at the same time inspired by a memory of Titian's famous group of the goddess clinging desperately to Adonis, her doomed young lover. Rubens' painting, and the long letter the artist wrote about it shortly after he had made it, had been intended as one of the case studies in the iconography book. I regret, however, that a sense of intellectual economy led Gombrich to persist in reworking the 1948 article rather than leaving it as it was and embarking on a completely fresh piece on the general subject of allegory, or expanding his material into a book. In trying to qualify the earlier text and bring it up to date he sacrificed its original coherence. The new material fits awkwardly with the old *Icones Symbolicae*: the device of contrasting an 'Aristotelian tradition' of allegory with the Platonic approach is rather artificial, and disguises the fact that this study now ranges widely over modes of symbolic thought and imagery. As a result the important and richly suggestive essay on allegory in the volume of 1972 has not had the impact it should have done.

The *Primavera* article

There is another Neoplatonic essay in the 1972 collection, on Botticelli's Mythologies, centred on the *Primavera* (fig. 5).[45] It was a version of an article that had appeared in the *Journal of the Warburg and Courtauld Institutes* of 1945 – actually published a couple of years after the end of the war.[46] In this case, despite the inclination to do so, Gombrich seems to have found it impossible to revise and update the original essay to any significant degree, resorting instead to providing an apologetic introduction. Here he admits that his interpretation has not fared well in the literature; indeed he more or less confesses that he himself is not really convinced any more. He had proposed that the painting's theme was a sort of allegorical representation of the Judgement of Paris, referring to (rather vague) analogies with a pageant of that subject which includes Venus, the Graces and the Horae in Apuleius' *Golden Ass*.[47] And he went on to argue that this garden of spring and Venus is not so much a pleasure grove as a place of instruction for a teenage boy from the Medici family, to encourage him to read Neoplatonic philosophy. Curiously, he cites as supporting evidence Botticelli's much more sober and very different version of what demonstrably *is* a moralising subject, showing a young Florentine being led to philosophical study (fig. 6). In this mural, detached from a decorative cycle in the Villa Lemmi near Florence which has been

     Elizabeth McGrath

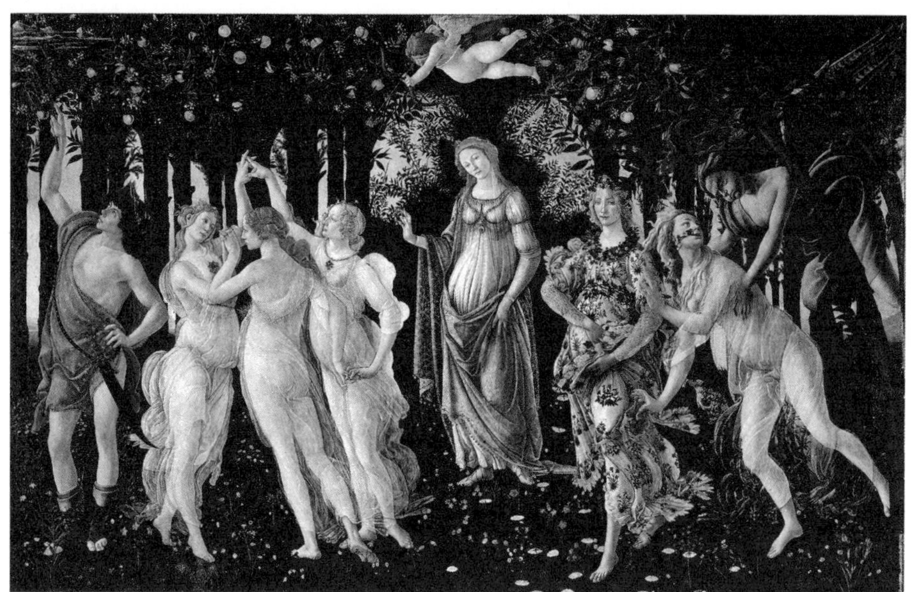

FIG. 5 Sandro Botticelli, '*Primavera*', Florence, Uffizi

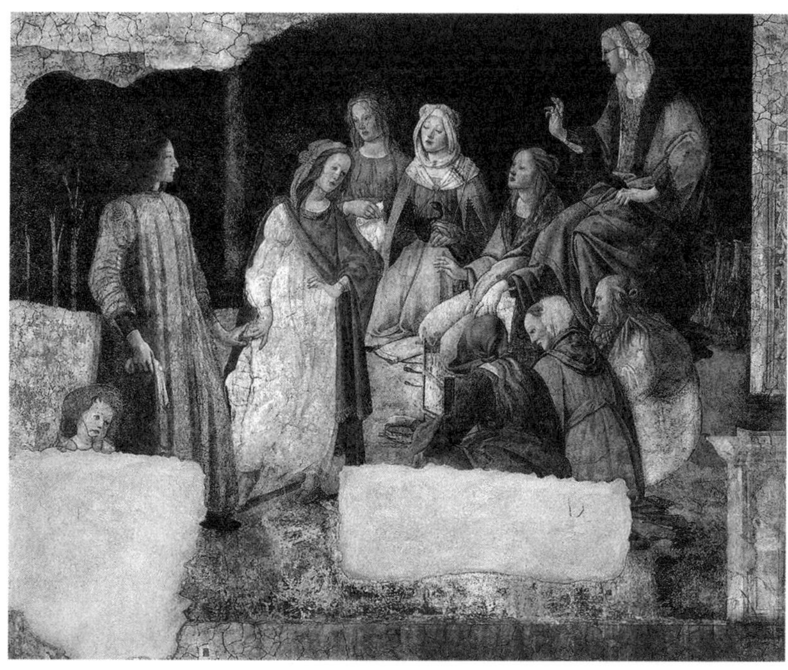

FIG. 6 Sandro Botticelli, *A young man conducted to the Liberal Arts*, Paris, Musée du Louvre

 Gombrich and 'Warburgian' Iconography

associated with the Tornabuoni and Albizzi families, the personification of Grammar
(as it seems, though Gombrich construed her as Venus)[48] conducts the youth in
question towards the other Liberal Arts, and to Philosophy herself, who presides over
them.[49] In fact it is now known that Botticelli's *Primavera* was almost certainly made
for a bedroom, to go above a day-bed (*'letuccio'*) in a Medici house in Florence, and
that it probably celebrated a Medici marriage. So it is unlikely to be about Platonic
love and study. But this information, first published in 1975,[50] was – fortunately for
Gombrich's attempt to save his argument – not known in 1972, and Gombrich could,
with some sleight of hand, present his old article as an example of method: an attempt
to answer the question, which is indeed an interesting and significant one, of why
Botticelli was 'the first to paint mythological paintings of such a monumental kind,
which in their size and in their seriousness vied with the religious art of the period'.[51]

In the interviews with Didier Eribon published in 1993, Gombrich said even
more to justify his republication of the article on the *Primavera*. He explained that
Neoplatonic interpretations were fashionable at the Warburg Institute at the time,
and that many of his colleagues were studying the ideas of Marsilio Ficino, and other
Renaissance philosophers. And his colleagues were also interested in the circle of
Lorenzo de' Medici.[52] This is all true. But there was also, I think, another, personal
aspect to Gombrich's interest in tackling Botticelli's mythologies.

I have already suggested that Gombrich was rather a marginal figure at the
Warburg Institute in his first years there, and that Saxl and Bing were not quite happy
about his approach to Warburg's ideas. When he returned to the Warburg Institute
after the war, it was with a contract for *The Story of Art*. To his surprise, Saxl was not
very pleased about this. He told him that he should not be wasting his time trying to
write a 'popular' book on art. As a result Gombrich produced the book entirely in his
spare time, in the evenings at home.[53] As far as Gombrich was concerned, I would say,
The Story of Art was as much part of his intellectual enterprise as his other books. But
Saxl evidently did not see it this way. Or perhaps he was not really in sympathy with
Gombrich's intellectual enterprise.

In his conversations with Eribon, Gombrich revealed that he was still affected by
Saxl's dismissive attitude to *The Story of Art*. For he said:

> People know me as the author of *The Story of Art*, who have never heard of me as a
> scholar. But many of my colleagues have never read the book. They may have read
> my papers on Poussin and Leonardo, but not that. It is a curious double life.[54]

This, I would say, is a reflection not of the situation in the 1990s, but rather
of Gombrich's perception of his status in the late 1940s. And that the lack of
appreciation shown by Saxl for Gombrich's project for a popular work meant that in
the research he conducted at the Institute at this period Gombrich wanted all the more
to 'prove himself' as a Warburgian, to show that while engaged in a book aimed at a

wide, and unscholarly, public, he could at the same time take on the most Warburgian of subjects, the topic of Aby Warburg's famous dissertation, and produce a more learned and consistently philosophical explanation than Warburg himself had dreamt of. As it happens, we know that Saxl was not convinced. Among his papers Gombrich preserved a letter from Saxl which reveals that, though sympathetic to a Neoplatonic hypothesis, he was very sceptical of Gombrich's detailed arguments, particularly the relevance of Apuleius.[55] He did, however, make some suggestions, which Gombrich incorporated – for example the comparison with the tapestry of 'The Court of Venus' in the Musée des Arts Decoratifs in Paris[56] – and he was evidently happy enough that the revised version be published in the *Journal*.[57]

Fortunately Gombrich returned to the interpretation of the *Primavera* in another context in which he felt able to express himself freely and simply, with the wisdom of age, and in the knowledge now of the original context of the picture, in a bedroom. Here too Gombrich found a way of answering the old question that he had posed in the late 1940s, and of justifying his conclusion that Neoplatonic interpretations of ancient myth had been crucial 'in opening up to secular art emotional spheres which had hitherto been the preserve of religious worship'. He did this in a film about the *Primavera*, made for British television in 1996.[58] Remarking 'The *Primavera* is a wonderful painting. I like it very much', he goes on:

> It is about the realm of Venus … the kingdom of Venus is a realm in which love
> and grace predominate, and which is important to human beings as a sublimation
> of their animal instincts …. Finished.'

     Gombrich and 'Warburgian' Iconography

Appendix

Warburg Institute Archive, Archive of E.H. Gombrich, Selected Letters II, Saxl, Fritz to
Gombrich, Ernst H. 20/04/194[?6]
[Selected Letters II, Corr S, Saxl]

Dear Gombrich,

I have read the 'Primavera' with enthusiasm. Astute, subtle, full of invention & I would very
much like to believe that Apuleius is the text. But you say that early Renaissance images are
mostly illustrations and cite a splendid array from Bott[icelli] to Titian. The 'Primavera'
certainly does not fit into that array. You do not think that the traditional title is false, but
it remains unexplained. Nor is the Judgement of Paris illustrated. On the one hand you try
to save the link with Apuleius (emendations for Zephyr and Flora, Mercury's senseless
gesture, senseless, since he is not delivering Jupiter's request to Paris, which however one
would expect to see from the text of Apuleius), on the other hand Bott[icelli]'s overall theme
has nothing to do with Apuleius. I fear Apuleius is not the text which served as the unique
source. The source must have as its upshot the idea of Primavera and the grove of delight.

Since apparently we do not yet know the source, we probably have to fall back on the old
method of a *combinatio* of sources & then Apuleius will have his place, without our having to
force the interpretation.

I should think that we have another element to add: typology. If I am not mistaken I
have made exactly the same comparison as you, in comparing the Venus pose with the
Baldovinetti Virgin in the Annunciation. And I still think that a 'comparison' like this gives
crucial indications for the interpretation of content. The figure above whom Amor is floating
with the bow is found, as is well known, in woodcut book illustrations and it seems to me
doubtful, that the group can only be interpreted as deriving from Apuleius. But you would
probably agree with me, that typological motives should be worked into the interpretation.

The second part is brilliant up to the conclusion – when it does not strike me as necessary
that Primavera is here dancing [just] because in Apuleius Venus dances after her victory over
Pallas and Juno.

Gombrich my dear friend, I would have preferred a thousand times over to write that I
believe you perfectly, especially given the fact that the reading of your piece has given me such
pleasure. Yet I cannot rid myself of the thought that your method of omitting the essential
(i.e. the Judgement of Paris) from one text, and virtually ignoring the main theme of Spring,
is better than the old method of explaining everything piece by piece. In your method you are
surely right, but the text has not yet been found.

What next? I wouldn't know what else to do, than to rephrase and say – that [*i.e.*
Apuleius's text] was probably known in Florence, and influenced the unknown author of the
programme. I have in the past found in manuscripts a few representations of spring and had
them photographed. They bore no close relation. I had more success in comparisons with
wall tapestries (Court of Love, Paris Musée des Arts Decoratifs?), but that is just the method
of bad historiography, which you rightly would not want to adopt. I would publish the thing
but with changes.

     Elizabeth McGrath

Allow me to take this opportunity to say how much I anticipate from your vol. 1 and how happy I am about your being with us again.

With friendship as ever, and greetings to you and Ilse,

Your F.S.

Lieber Gombrich,

Ich habe die „Primavera" mit Begeisterung gelesen. Klug, scharfsinnig, voll Phantasie & ich möchte gerne glauben, dass Apuleius der Text ist. Aber Sie sagen, Früh-Renaissance Bilder sind meistens Illustrationen & zitieren eine glänzende Reihe von Bott[icelli] bis Tizian. In die Reihe paßt die „Primavera" sicher nicht. Sie glauben nicht, dass der traditionelle Titel falsch ist, der bleibt aber unerklärt. Ebensowenig ist das Paris Urteil illustriert. Einerseits versuchen Sie den Zusammenhang mit Apuleius zu retten (Emendationen für Zephyrus & Flora, Mercur's sinnlose Gebärde, sinnlos, weil er nicht Jupiter's Wunsch an Paris überbringt, soll doch aus dem Apuleius Text stammen), andererseits hat das Gesamtthema Bott[icelli]s nicht mit Apuleius zu tun. Ich fürchte, Apuleius ist nicht der Text, der als ausschließliche Quelle gedient hat. Die Quelle muss doch wohl von der Primavera Idee & dem lustvollen Hain ihren Ausgang genommen haben.

Da wir offenbar die Quelle noch nicht kennen, müssen wir wohl auf das alte Mittel der Combinatio von Quellen zurückkommen & dann wird Apuleius an seine Stelle kommen, ohne dass wir die Interpretation zu forcieren haben.

Ich würde glauben, dass wir noch ein Element hinzuzunehmen haben, die Typologie. Wenn ich mich nicht irre habe ich genau denselben Vergleich gemacht den auch Sie machen, die Venus-Pose mit der der Baldovinetti Maria in der Verkündigung zu vergleichen. Und ich glaube noch immer, dass so ein „Vergleich" wichtige Anhaltspunkte für die inhaltliche Deutung gibt. Die Figur über der Amor mit dem Bogen schwebt gibt es bekanntlich im Buchholzschnitt & es scheint mir zweifelhaft, ob man die Gruppe allein aus Apuleius deuten kann. Aber darin wären Sie ja wohl mit mir einig, dass die typologischen Motive in die Interpretation eingearbeitet werden müssen.

Der zweite Teil ist brillant bis auf den Schluss – denn es leuchtet mir noch nicht als notwendig ein, dass die Primavera hier tanzt, weil in Apuleius Venus tanzt nach ihrem Sieg über Pallas & Juno.

Lieber Freund Gombrich, ich hätte tausend mal lieber geschrieben, ich glaube Ihnen vollkommen, besonders, da mir das Lesen so grosses Vergnügen gegeben hat. Aber ich kann nicht darüber weg, dass Ihre Methode aus einem Text das wesentliche wegzulassen (i.e. Paris Urteil) und das Hauptthema „Frühling" fast nicht zu berücksichtigen, besser ist als die alte Methode stückweise zu erklären. In der Methode haben Sie sicher recht, aber der Text ist noch nicht gefunden.

Was tun? Ich wüßte nichts anderes, als umstilisieren & sagen – das war in Florenz wohlbekannt & hat auf den unbekannten Autor des Programms eingewirkt. Ich habe in früheren Jahren in Handschriften ein oder die andere Darstellung des „Frühlings" gefunden & photographieren lassen. Sie hatten keinen direkten Bezug. Besser war, was ich durch Vergleich mit Wandteppichen erreichen konnte (Minnehof, Paris Mus. des Arts Dec.?), aber alles das ist die Methode der Geschichtsklitterung, die Sie mit Recht nicht anwenden wollen. Ich würde die Sache drucken aber mit Änderungen.

Darf ich bei dieser Gelegenheit sagen, wie viel ich mir von Ihrem vol. I erhoffe & wie froh ich darüber bin, dass Sie wieder bei uns sind.

In alter Freundschaft, mit vielen Grüssen an Sie & Ilse

Ihr F.S.

    Gombrich and 'Warburgian' Iconography

* I am most grateful to Rembrandt Duits, Chiara Franceschini, Charles Hope, Berthold Kress and Hiroko Takahashi for their helpful comments.

1 Its genesis, content and fate are considered below, pp. 42-45.

2 E.H. Gombrich, *Art and Illusion: a Study in the Psychology of Pictorial Representation*, London, 1960, p. 4, quoting H. Wölfflin, *Kunstgeschichtliche Grundbegriffe. Das Problem der Stilentwicklung in der neueren Kunst*, Munich 1915, p. 11: '*Nicht alles ist zu allen Zeiten möglich*'.

3 See, for example, below, n. 18.

4 See E.H. Gombrich and D. Eribon, *A Lifelong Interest: Conversations on Art and Science*, London 1993, p. 152.

5 E.H. Gombrich, 'Tobias and the Angel', in Gombrich, *Symbolic Images: Studies in the Art of the Renaissance II*, Oxford 1972, pp. 26-30. Gombrich's insight was developed and applied to other images of saints by Charles Hope in 'Altarpieces and the Requirements of Patrons', in *Christianity and the Renaissance: Image and Religious Imagination in the Quattrocento*, eds. T. Verdon and J. Henderson, Syracuse, NY 1990, pp. 535-71. See also J. Stumpel, *The Province of Painting: Theories of Italian Renaissance Art*, Utrecht 1990, pp. 27-58. The discussion in G. Kaftal, *Iconography of the Saints in Tuscan Painting*, Florence, 1952, p. XVIII, is also important, though the first publication of Gombrich's essay predated it.

6 For these see below, pp. 45-48.

7 E. Panofsky, *Studies in Iconology*, New York 1939, pp. 3-31; *Meaning in the Visual Arts*, Garden City, NY 1955, pp. 26-54 (here the 1939 chapter appears with some additions and alterations). Richard Woodfield has noted, with surprise, that reviews of Gombrich's *Symbolic Images* failed to pick up on his reference to Panofsky. See R. Woodfield, 'Gombrich and Panofsky on Iconology', *International Yearbook of Aesthetics*, XII, 2008, pp. 151-64. Gombrich in fact printed, under the title of the Introduction, Panofsky's words about the danger that iconology might be to iconography what astrology is to astrography .

8 For Panofsky's regrets about the excesses of his followers see below, n. 15. Gombrich's particular scepticism about Panofsky's *Iconography of Correggio's Camera di San Paolo*, published as volume XXVI in the Studies of the Warburg Institute in 1961 when he was both Director and Editor of the series, was expressed at the time in courteous and slightly deferential Latin letters (there was apparently no question of rejecting the text, which had been solicited from the author), and subsequently – after Panofsky's death – in plain English in *Topos and Topicality in Renaissance Art*, London 1975 (Annual Lecture of the Society of Renaissance Studies, 1974; available online in The Gombrich Archive) reproducing passages from the correspondence with Panofsky. Gombrich's own proposal, presented there, that the guiding principle for Correggio's varied programme was reference to the goddess Diana (Luna) is indeed far more plausible, even if it fails to account for every element in the decoration. A revised Italian version of the argument is included in M. dell'Acqua, ed., *Il Monastero di San Paolo*, Parma 1990, pp. 189-93.

9 Dieter Wuttke has listed and analysed occurrences of the words iconological and iconology in the writings and discussions of Warburg: 'Nachwort' in Aby M. Warburg, *Ausgewählte Schriften und Würdigungen*, ed. D. Wuttke, Baden-Baden 1992, pp. 625-38. See esp. the citations from Warburg's notes and writings on pp. 630-33. It appears to me particularly interesting that Warburg employed the epithet 'ikonologisch' for his *Bilderatlas* in 1928 (Wuttke, as above, p. 633, quoting a letter of 1 December 1928 to the Director of the Hertziana, Ernst Steinmann); this project, to which he gave the name Mnemosyne, and which he intended to publish as a book, was concerned not so much with iconographic themes as the transformations of motifs in history. For the *Bilderatlas* see notably E.H. Gombrich, *Aby Warburg: an Intellectual Biography*, London 1970, pp. 283-306, and M. Warnke, ed., *Der Bilderatlas Mnemosyne* (Aby Warburg, *Gesammelte Schriften: Studienausgabe*, II.1.2), edn Berlin, 2008; also K. Mazzocco, 'The work of Ernst H. Gombrich on the Aby M. Warburg fragments', *Journal of Art Historiography*, 5, December 2011 (available online). For the references to iconology in writings on images before Warburg see

     Elizabeth McGrath

T. Heck, 'The Evolving Meanings of Iconology and Iconography: Toward Some Descriptive Definitions' in *Picturing Performance: The Iconography of the Performing Arts in Concept and Practice*, Rochester 1999, pp. 7-41, esp. 8-13.

10 In a draft of a light-hearted letter of 1903 to the historian of medieval art Adolph Goldschmidt, Warburg had made it clear he did not belong to the category of iconographers, whom he characterised as dealing with 'restricting conditions due to iconographic tradition'; see Gombrich, *Warburg* (n. 9 above), pp. 141-45. He placed himself in the peculiar category (of which he is, unsurprisingly, the sole representative) of those concerned with 'restricting conditions due to the nature of man's expressive movements (*Bedingtheiten durch die Natur des mimischen Menschen*)'. Playful as his categorisation of art historians undoubtedly is here, it is important, as Gombrich has observed (Gombrich, *Warburg* (n. 9 above), p. 144) that Warburg did not consider himself a student of iconography.

11 A. Warburg, 'Italienische Kunst und internationale Astrologie im Palazzo Schifanoia zu Ferrara', in *Italia e l'arte straniera*, Rome 1922, p. 191; cf. Aby Warburg, *The Renewal of Pagan Antiquity*, trans. D. Britt, p. 585; Wuttke (n. 9 above), p. 632. See also W. Heckscher, 'The Genesis of Iconology', *Acts of the 21st International Art Historical Congress in Bonn, 1964*, Berlin 1967, III, pp. 239-62, pronouncing, 'Iconology was born in the month of October in the year 1912'.

12 As Gertrud Bing once put it: 'Asking himself under what conditions and by what means one civilisation was apt to appear at a later time and under utterly different circumstances, Warburg recognised symbols to be the vehicles of transmission ...'. See G. Bing, *The Warburg Institute, The Library Association Record*, V, 1935, p. 3.

13 As Gombrich has remarked: '[Warburg] liked to contrast the same theme in its degraded and its appropriate rendering, and to re-live vicariously the liberation of a content from alien accretions'. See Gombrich, *Warburg* (n. 9 above), p. 313. Towards the end of his life, in his Notebook of 1927-28, Warburg wrote:

'We attempt to grasp the spirit of the age as it moulds style by comparing the same subject as it is treated in various periods in various countries' ('*Wir suchen den Geist der Zeiten in seiner stilbildenden Funktion dadurch persönlich zu erfassen, dass wir den gleichen Gegenstand zu verschiedenen Zeiten und in verschiedenen Ländern vergleichend betrachten*'). Gombrich, *Warburg* (n. 9 above), pp. 268, 269. But see e.g. pp. 313-14 for Warburg's criticism of the idea of the spirit of the age.

14 See above, n. 7.

15 See Panofsky, *Studies in Iconology*, 1939 (n. 7 above), esp. p. 8; cf. *Meaning in the Visual Arts* (n. 7 above), pp. 40-41; also p. 50. Somewhat ironically, it was only towards the end of his life, at a time when he felt the desire to distance himself from the rising tide of far-fetched 'iconological' readings of works of art which he acknowledged he had inspired – and perhaps looking for someone with whom to share the blame for his 'school' – that Panofsky explicitly referred his notion of iconology back to Warburg, and the study of the frescoes in Ferrara. See his comments in *Essais d'Iconologie*, trans. C. Herbette and B. Teyssèdre, ed. B. Teyssèdre, Paris 1967, p. 3.

16 See notably E.H. Gombrich, 'In Search of Cultural History' (The Philip Maurice Deneke Lecture, Oxford, 1969) in E.H. Gombrich, *Ideals and Idols: Essays on Values in History and in Art*, Oxford, 1979, pp. 24-59. Much later Gombrich wrote of Panofsky: '... iconology was only one aspect of the method he had absorbed from the German tradition of art history, one which was deeply rooted in German intellectual history, but relatively new to American academic life. What distinguished this tradition was the claim to hold the key to the history of artistic styles as an expression or manifestation of changing "world views", or *Weltanschauungen*. To this approach, which ultimately goes back to the Romantic philosophy of Georg Friedrich Hegel (1770-1831), the course of human history resembles a clockwork of wheels within wheels activated by the unfolding spirit of mankind, a spirit that animates art, no less than science, law or religion, in a precise and determined way'. See E.H. Gombrich, review of Panofsky, *Three Essays on Style* and *Perspective as Symbolic*

Form, *The New York Review of Books*, 15 February 1996, p. 29 (available online in The Gombrich Archive). For Warburg's use of the term 'spirit of the age' see above, n. 13. For some contradictions in Gombrich's attitude to such ideas see Peter Burke's and Paul Crossley's contributions to this volume.

17 E.H. Gombrich, 'Introduction: Aims and Limits of Iconology', in Gombrich, *Symbolic Images* (n. 5 above), pp. 1-25 (7).

18 Gombrich, *Symbolic Images* (n. 5 above), preface, p. vii. He adds that this is 'a study often and very one-sidedly equated with the activities of the Warburg Institute. It found its most influential representative in the great Erwin Panofsky, who made this new, luxuriant branch of study known under the name of Iconology'. In *Art and Illusion* (n. 2 above, p. 7) he had also associated iconology with the study of symbolism, commenting that it 'investigates the function of images in allegory and symbolism and their reference to what may be called "the invisible world of ideas".' He does not seem to have developed the parallel he suggested, in a review of Charles Morris's *Signs, Language and Behavior* (*The Art Bulletin*, xxxi, 1949, pp. 68-73, esp. 72), between iconology and linguistics. On this subject see R. Woodfield, 'Ernst Gombrich: Iconology and the "linguistics of the image"', *Journal of Art Historiography*, 5, December 2011 (published online), esp. p. 2.

19 Gombrich, 'Aims and Limits' (n. 17 above), p. 6. Earlier, he had characterized iconology as the search for 'texts and contexts to restore the original meaning to works of art': E.H. Gombrich, 'Art and Scholarship' (Inaugural Lecture at University College, London 1957), in Gombrich, *Meditations on a Hobby Horse and Other Essays on the Theory of Art*, London 1963, pp. 106-19 (p. 116); see also his passing reference to iconology as the 'fitting of texts to images' in 'Focus on the Arts and Humanities', *Bulletin of the American Academy of Arts and Sciences*, xxxv, 4, 1982), pp. 5-24 (p. 10). At around the same time, however, in a review of a book by Panofsky and his wife Dora (*Pandora's Box: The Changing Aspects of a Mythical Symbol*, New York 1956), he made a rather odd distinction between iconography and iconology, in relation to their relevance to works of art: 'Iconography was, or is, the handmaiden of art history. Iconology is not. It may and does use works of art as evidence, but no more so than works of literature, oratory or propaganda. The art lover, therefore, has no right to be disappointed if he finds no great paintings reproduced in this book devoted to the changing aspects of a mythical symbol' (*The Burlington Magazine*, xcix, 1957, p. 280).

20 E.H. Gombrich, 'Raphael's *Stanza della Segnatura* and the Nature of its Symbolism', in Gombrich, *Symbolic Images* (n. 5 above), pp. 85-101. In fact the scheme is especially appropriate in the context of a library, which, it is generally believed, was the original function of the room. See J. Shearman, 'Raphael's Unexecuted Projects for the Stanze', in *Walter Friedlaender zum 90. Geburtstag*, eds. G. Kauffmann and W. Sauerländer, Berlin 1965, pp. 159-80; and P. Taylor, 'Julius II and the Stanza della Segnatura', *Journal of the Warburg and Courtauld Institutes*, lxxii, 2009, pp. 103-41.

21 E. Wind, *Pagan Mysteries in the Renaissance*, edn London 1967, p. 238: 'There are historians, many of them admirable, who stress the importance of the commonplace in history. Their work is salutary and indispensable, because the commonplace is a relentless force. But in so far as their method is specially contrived to examine that particular subject, it is not suited to deal with the exceptional in history, the power of which should also perhaps not be underrated.'

22 See esp. Gombrich, '*Stanza della Segnatura*' (n. 20 above), p. 101.

23 For Gombrich's relationship with Kris see 'Reminiscences of Collaboration with Ernst Kris', in E.H. Gombrich, *Tributes: Interpreters of Our Cultural Tradition*, London and Ithaca, NY, 1984, pp. 221-33. On Kris and Kurz see also E. Levy, 'Ernst Kris and National Socialism: Political Subtexts of Kris's late Viennese Art Historical Works (1933-1935)', in *Im Dienst des Ich: Ernst Kris Heute*, ed. T. Haarmann, S. Krüger and T. Röske (forthcoming).

24 On this project, the *Bilderatlas*, which existed only as photographs of screens with images pinned to them in different configurations and diffuse notes and fragments of commentary, see above, n. 9.

    Elizabeth McGrath

25 Cf. the comments in Gombrich and Eribon, *A Lifelong Interest* (n. 4 above), p. 50. Also Gombrich, *Warburg* (n. 9 above), pp. 2-3.

26 The problems Gombrich had, particularly with Gertrud Bing, in presenting his conviction (arrived at in the 1940s) that he should renounce a full publication of Warburg's papers in favour of an account of Warburg's ideas and their development, are described, with some understatement, in Gombrich, *Warburg*, (n. 9 above), pp. 4-6, where the difficult birth of the *Intellectual Biography* of 1970 is also explained.

27 Gertrud Weiss, born in Vienna in 1909 (d. 1981), arrived in London in 1936; two years later she emigrated to the US, where she had a distinguished career in medicine. She married the physicist Leo Szilard in 1951.

28 The tributes to Kurz written by Gombrich after his friend's death eloquently testify to the bond of affection between the two: E.H. Gombrich, 'Otto Kurz', *Burlington Magazine*, CXVIII, 1976, pp. 29-30 (reproduced in slightly adapted form as the Preface to Otto Kurz, *Selected Studies*, London 1977, pp. i-iii); idem, 'Otto Kurz, 1908–1975', *Proceedings of the British Academy*, 65, 1979, pp. 718-35 (reprinted as the introduction to Otto Kurz, *Selected Studies Vol. II*, London 1982, pp. i-xvi); also included under the title 'The Services to Scholarship of Otto Kurz' in Gombrich, *Tributes* (n. 23 above), pp. 234-49.

29 This applies even to certain studies which centre on a specific work of art: they were often provoked by the implausibility of an earlier interpretation. See Gombrich's own comments in Gombrich and Eribon, *A Lifelong Interest* (n. 4 above), p. 141.

30 E.H. Gombrich, 'Bosch's "Garden of Earthly Delights": A Progress Report', *Journal of the Warburg and Courtauld Institutes*, XXXII, 1969, pp. 162-70.

31 Gombrich, 'Bosch' (n. 30 above), p. 166, n. 15.

32 Gombrich, 'Otto Kurz', 1979 (n. 28 above), pp. 732-33.

33 This was the basement of Thames House, Millbank. The Institute was able to move into the Imperial Institute Buildings, South Kensington, in 1937.

34 For Gombrich's account of this see Gombrich and Eribon, *A Lifelong Interest* (n. 4 above), pp. 54-55; also Gombrich, 'Otto Kurz', 1979 (n. 28 above), p. 727.

35 Now in the Warburg Institute Archive.

36 'Dr. Kurz has written the book at the request of the Courtauld Institute of Art, and its form and scope have been planned throughout as a result of consultation between members of the Warburg and Courtauld Institutes.'

37 The text includes the sentence: 'It is hoped in a second volume to deal with problems of profane iconography along similar lines.' But brackets are pencilled around it.

38 E. Panofsky, *Korrespondenz 1910 bis 1968: eine kommentierte Auswahl*, ed. D. Wuttke, 5 vols., Wiesbaden, 2001-11, II, p. 141. The footnote here (p. 142) misidentifies this as probably the Kris-Gombrich caricature book. The book referred to in the same letter as Praz's 'Emblematik' is the third in the series of Studies of the Warburg Institute: M. Praz, *Studies in Seventeenth-Century Imagery*. The first volume of this work was published in 1939, but the accompanying second volume, a bibliography of emblem books, had to wait until after the war, appearing in 1947.

39 This job came to him through Kris, who had already been analysing German propaganda broadcasts for the Service; see Gombrich, *Tributes* (n. 23 above), p. 231.

40 As far as the other items in the list (fig. 3) are concerned, Terborch's work is the picture designated 'Paternal Advice' after the inscription on the 18th-century engraving by J.B. Wille; 'Aer' refers to a 12th-century miniature featuring the Four Winds, Muses etc. in Rheims (Bibliothèque municipale, MS 672, fol. 1); 'Charles I' designates John Singleton Copley's *Charles I demanding the five impeached members* (Boston Public Library); Vermeer's picture is *The painter in his studio* (Kunsthistorisches Museum, Vienna). 'Tebaldeo' refers to four little paintings, in the National Gallery, London, which were controversially attributed to Giorgione when they were acquired in 1937; Gombrich cleverly identified the iconographic source in the Eclogues of the Ferrarese poet Antonio Tebaldeo, though with the demotion of the pictures (now attributed to Antonio Previtali), the identification of their subject matter has aroused relatively little interest. See N. Penny,

National Gallery Catalogues. The Sixteenth Century Italian Paintings, I: Paintings from Bergamo, Brescia and Cremona, London 2004, no. 4884, pp. 291-99.

41 Two case-studies were, however, adapted for publication as articles. One, about Reynolds' *Ladies adorning a term of Hymen*, was treated in 'Reynolds's Theory and Practice of Imitation', *Burlington Magazine*, LXXX, 1942, pp. 40-45; 'The Subject of Poussin's Orion' also appeared in the Burlington Magazine (LXXXIV, 1944, pp. 37-41). Along with the drafts of the iconography book is a plan for a different, though not entirely unrelated, book by Gombrich, entitled 'The Realm and Range of the Image'. This is the project Gombrich refers to in Gombrich and Eribon, *A Lifelong Interest* (n. 4 above), p. 105, where he also comments that *Art and Illusion* and *The Sense of Order* were 'only fragments' of a projected 'general book on images and the different function of images. It was to include illustration, symbolism, emblems and decoration.' Richard Woodfield has pointed to ways in which the plan for *The Realm and Range of the Image* foreshadows *Art and Illusion*: 'Iconology ...' (n. 18 above), pp. 9-10.

42 E.H. Gombrich, '*Icones Symbolicae*: The Visual Image in Neo-Platonic Thought', *Journal of the Warburg and Courtauld Institutes*, XI, 1948, pp. 163-92.

43 'Neoplatonism and the Arts', Taylor Institution, Oxford, February 1948.

44 C. Giarda, *Bibliotecae Alexandrinae icones symbolicae elogiis illustratae*, Milan 1626 and 1628. Gombrich found the text in J. G. Graevius and P. Burmannus, *Thesaurus antiquitatum et historiarum Italiae*, 9 vols., Leiden, 1704, IX, 6.

45 E.H. Gombrich, 'Botticelli's Mythologies: A Study in the Neo-Platonic Symbolism of his Circle', in *Symbolic Images* (n. 5 above), pp. 31-81.

46 'Botticelli's Mythologies: A Study in the Neoplatonic Symbolism of his Circle', *Journal of the Warburg and Courtauld Institutes*, VIII, 1945, pp. 7-60. Correspondence in the *Journal* Archives (Warburg Institute) indicates that the volume was published only in the spring of 1947.

47 In the second version of his article Gombrich concedes that he did not help his hypothesis by 'suggesting the possibility that the programme may have rested on a misunderstanding of the text': Gombrich, 'Botticelli's Mythologies' (n. 45 above), p. 34.

48 Gombrich pointed to a similarity with a figure of Venus in the corresponding Villa Lemmi mural of a young woman ('Botticelli's Mythologies' (first version) (n. 46 above), pl. 16a-b), probably the bride of the young man, receiving gifts (flowers?) from Venus and the Graces. But it is an exaggeration to say that the supposed Venus with the young man is dressed 'exactly like' that with the woman; and Grammar is otherwise missing from the Liberal Arts. On these paintings, see R.W. Lightbown, *Sandro Botticelli: Life and Work*, 2 vols., London, 1989, II, pp. 62-63; and F. Zöllner, *Sandro Botticelli*, Munich and London, 2005, pp. 120-24, and pp. 225-00, nos 49a-b.

49 Zöllner (n. 48 above) calls this presiding figure Phronesis, mother of Philology, referring to Martianus Capella. But Gombrich was surely right to see her as Philosophy (or Sapientia), who is regularly shown as the mother of the Liberal Arts. That she is carrying a bow is, however, unexplained by any interpretation. There is a curious irony in the fact that it is the contrasting and non-philosophical female scene, presumed to be for the bride of the young man, which has a real iconographic relationship with the *Primavera*, since here we have a clothed Venus accompanied by the Graces.

50 J. Shearman, 'The Collections of the Younger Branch of the Medici', *Burlington Magazine*, CXVII, 1975, pp. 12-27 (p. 25, no. 38); W. Smith, 'On the original location of the *Primavera*', *Art Bulletin*, LVII, 1975, pp. 31-40. The idea, so widespread in the older literature, that the *Primavera* was some kind of pendant to the *Birth of Venus* (even though the two works were executed in different media) derives from the fact that they are described together in the 1540s in the Medici Villa of Castello in Vasari's *Vite*. In the preface to his revised 'Botticelli's Mythologies' (n. 5 above), p. 33) Gombrich still assumes the paintings were both made for Castello. In the 'Bibliographical Note' that prefaces the third edition of *Symbolic Images* (1984, pp. IX-x), Gombrich

acknowledges the new evidence about the location of the *Primavera*, and mentions some other recent literature, though he still suggests that Neoplatonism may be relevant.

51 Gombrich was pleased to report that Panofsky (who disputed elements of his interpretation) 'quoted and endorsed' his suggestion that 'it was the Neo-Platonic approach to ancient myth which succeeded "in opening up to secular art emotional spheres which had hitherto been the preserve of religious worship" ': Gombrich, 'Botticelli's Mythologies' (revised version) (n. 5 above), p. 35. See E. Panofsky, *Renaissance and Renascences in Western Art*, edn London 1970, p. 188, citing Gombrich, 'Botticelli's Mythologies' (first version) (n. 46 above), p. 43.

52 See, for example, Gombrich and Eribon, *A Lifelong Interest* (n. 4 above), pp. 148-49.

53 Cf. Gombrich and Eribon, *A Lifelong Interest* (n. 4 above), p. 64.

54 Gombrich and Eribon, *A Lifelong Interest* (n. 4 above), p. 65.

55 I thank Veronika Kopecky for drawing this letter to my attention and Eckart Marchand for help with the transcription. It is included below in the Appendix.

56 This appears as fig. 29 in the article.

57 Saxl was not at the time an Editor, but it is hard to imagine that anything, above all on the *Primavera*, would have been published by the Institute without his approval.

58 'Botticelli's *Primavera*: Myths and Fingerprints', directed and produced by Agnieszka Pietrowska and shown on British television (Channel Four) in 1996. At the time of writing it is available in segments on the Internet.

'Style' in the Archive
of E.H. Gombrich*

VERONIKA KOPECKY

IN HIS WILL, Ernst Gombrich left first pick of the books in his personal library to the Warburg Institute, but he made no mention of what should happen to his papers. A rather private man with no interest in what he called 'gossip', one suspects that he might have preferred these to be treated as Michelangelo is said to have treated his drawings: that is, to burn them. Luckily, no such thing happened and the sizeable estate is now looked after at the Institute. In more than 300 archival boxes are housed his correspondence, lecture notes, over 200 notebooks, as well as his collection of diaries (complete for the years 1940 to 2000, but starting as early as 1918).

I was given the task of filing away these items when they arrived at the Institute, and in this paper I would like to give some idea of the kinds of material the Gombrich Archive contains, and what that material can tell us about Gombrich's working method. Rather than providing a dry overview of its contents, I shall focus on a test case, that of Gombrich's recurrent interest in the concept of 'style'. I do not intend in what follows even to attempt to say the last word on this rich and important theme of Gombrich's thought; my aim is simply to use it as a way of delving through his literary remains.[1] I hope this brief introduction to the contents of the Archive will encourage others to use it more extensively in future.

I

One of Gombrich's earliest attempts publicly to analyse the subject of style was a review of Millard Meiss' book *Painting in Florence and Siena after the Black Death* (1951).[2] Meiss argued that the Florentine and Sienese artists succeeding Giotto rejected his narrative style to give expression to their own social and spiritual values – drastically changed by the epidemic – by turning back to more hieratic and archaic modes of representation. Gombrich interpreted this as a regression of art and started with a quotation from Leonardo:

> Leonardo da Vinci held it up as a warning example of what happens to Art when
> the study of Nature is neglected: "After him [Giotto] Art suffered a relapse
> (*ricadde*), for everyone imitated paintings already made and so it went on from

century to century [sic] till ... Masaccio demonstrated by his perfect work how those who had taken as their authority anything but Nature had laboured in vain.

Of course, Gombrich states, everyone including the author will find the art of Andrea Orcagna, Andrea da Firenze or Barna da Siena wanting if measured by the Renaissance standards of Leonardo's naturalism. He continues that:

> ... one might even accept Prof. Meiss' historical interpretation of the influence of the Black Death and yet side with Leonardo by saying that the catastrophe brought about a lowering of standards, be it among the painters who failed to master the complexities of naturalistic rendering or the public who failed to appreciate the autonomous artistic values of Giotto's style .... It might then be said that this art 'expresses' the crisis of the Black Death less by its emotive content than by the symptomatic character of regression, true to the old dictum that 'devout pictures are often bad pictures'.[3]

Gombrich allowed for the disharmonies of such 'bad pictures': they may very well have given evidence of aesthetic intention but, he concluded: 'If inconsistencies are no evidence of a falling off of standards what criterion of quality remains?' Finally, he wished that Meiss had placed the Tuscan period into the wider context of contemporary European art, where similar tendencies had been established in fourteenth-century German painting and sculpture.

Meiss found this assessment puzzling. What Gombrich had implied was that several artists at the time of, and following, Giotto were qualitatively better masters than those of the subsequent generation. Also, the American scholar could not agree with his reviewer's wish to place the problem within the bigger picture of European art. In a letter to Gombrich of 29 June 1953 Meiss questioned this further:

> Is there disagreement between us about the quality of the painting of the period?
> ... a 'falling off of standards' implies also that the painters who surrounded Giotto or who immediately followed him, such as Pacino, Taddeo Gaddi, Daddi, were stronger masters than Orcagna, Andrea da Firenze, and Giovanni da Milano.
> I think few would agree that they were .... After 1520 there wasn't a painter in Florence of the stature of Raphael, but does this mean that the formal innovations of Pontormo and Rosso are to be attributed, as they once were, to vagrancy or incompetence? If not, why did you raise the problem of style versus incompetence with regard to Orcagna? Havent [sic] you loaded the dice by transforming my concepts of disharmony, tension and conflict into 'inconsistency?' ... I did not undertake a discussion of the relationship of Italian and Northern or German painting because the dissimilarities between the styles seem far greater than the likenesses, so that the discussion would inevitably become highly abstract. To deal with this matter would lead one into the rarefied atmosphere of those endless debates about neo-Gothic or late-Gothic-baroque in the Trecento .... The implications of even your brief beginning of this realm spins my head.[4]

 'Style' in the Archive of E.H. Gombrich

For Meiss, Gombrich went too far; not because he was wrong, but because the
issue he raised in the review distorted the intention of the book. Meiss had written it
to explore if and how the events during the Black Death affected the art of its time.
Gombrich, however, tried to hint at the larger framework, the relationship of one
aspect of a culture to another, such as art to literature or, in this case, art to religion.
In his review Gombrich in fact suggested the scope of his interest in the status of style
in cultural history. He was trying to understand the historical relationships of artistic
styles in the widest possible context.

From around the same time, 1953-54, originates a privately circulated single-page
peer-review of Meyer Schapiro's *Essay on Style* (1953). Gombrich expressed his high
esteem for the work and recommends it for publication:

> Professor Schapiro has provided a most admirable and up-to-date guide through
> the theoretical edifice of our untheoretical discipline ... what is now needed is
> a fresh interest in fundamentals. There is hardly a paragraph in this rich essay
> which could not be made to further this aim if it were made accessible to students.
> Expanded, and made less abstract by the multiplication of concrete examples it
> could be of immense service to students and teachers alike.[5]

Bearing in mind that the review was meant to help the publication of Schapiro's
essay one must take its enthusiastic tone with a pinch of salt, but the fact that
Gombrich had closely studied the piece is of importance. Schapiro began his twenty-
five page essay with a working definition of the term, then introduced and commented
on the key theories and their problems. He found these issues represented in the
works of several seminal figures in the history of art, among them Heinrich Wölfflin,[6]
Alois Riegl,[7] Emanuel Löwy,[8] Max Dvořák,[9] and even Arnold Hauser.[10] Schapiro, just
like Gombrich, was trained in a school of thought where the publications of these men
played a vital part in the discussions of style and expression. Gombrich had studied
at Riegl's and Löwy's alma mater in Vienna – the latter also having been his teacher –
and he must have felt this influence even more strongly. In his essay Schapiro defines
the concept of style as follows:

> ... style is, above all, a system of forms with a quality and a meaningful expression
> through which the personality of the artist and the broad outlook of a group
> are visible. It is also a vehicle of expression within the group, communicating
> and fixing certain values of religious, social, and moral life through the
> emotional suggestiveness of forms. It is, besides, a common ground against
> which innovations and the individuality of particular works may be measured.
> By considering the succession of works in time and space and by matching the
> variations of style with historical events and with the varying features of other
> fields of culture, the historian of art attempts, with the help of common-sense
> psychology and social theory, to account for the changes of style or specific traits.[11]

     Veronika Kopecky

If Meiss's book on the Black Death was too restricted in its approach, Schapiro's extended notion of style and its similarities to his own thoughts certainly found much of Gombrich's approval. The paragraph touched on his own research, which he had been pursuing since working for the BBC Monitoring Service during the war years. He had already written several commentaries on the different styles and characteristics of propaganda in 1941: the aim was to provide monitors with guide lines for their own translations and summaries of German broadcasts so as to identify clearly the differences between actual news and the emotional propaganda of the Nazis.[12] From 1947 survives an important synopsis for a book to which the scholar gave the working title *The Realm and Range of the Image*. This is the first surviving draft of ideas of what will crystallize into *Art and Illusion*, and it already contains layouts for chapters on style and 'the symbolism of relation'.[13] From 1952 we have another outline for the same project in which he states:

> Painting has to be learned. This is an aspect of the matter which was once a truism and now tends to be forgotten. Yet we shall never get beyond the certain 'mystique' which surrounds the idea of 'style' in most books on Art (especially those written in the German tradition) unless we analyse the concrete way in which the vocabulary of forms was actually acquired and handed on and what was its psychological and artistic relevance.[14]

Further correspondences with Schapiro's essay must have struck Gombrich in particular. His American colleague commented on a number of points which would be of central concern to Gombrich's arguments for *Art and Illusion*:

- the relationships of forms and colours within a painting;
- the inter-relationship of works of art throughout 'time and space';
- the interest in the art of primitive cultures;
- the method of representation as a progression from a concept or 'schema' to a naturalistic system including perspective;
- art as a skill acquired through 'trial and error'.

What the author could only hint at in the essay, due to its nature and purpose, would serve as some of Gombrich's strongest and best developed arguments in *Art and Illusion*. Schapiro shaped and sharpened Gombrich's views on several issues raised in that book.[15] Gombrich also reacted to Schapiro's evaluation of 'theories of cyclical development of art' in the late 1960s, to which I shall return later.

II

From Gombrich's point of view, the request to review his colleague's article must have seemed perfectly timed, coming at just the moment when he was testing his own theories in several lectures. His way of investigating this subject for more than ten years from the late 1940s until the publication of *Art and Illusion* can be traced in a number of notebooks and the lectures that followed.

Gombrich considered it a given that 'style' related to concepts in many different disciplines, and even between different disciplines. In his Andrew Mellon Lectures, delivered in Washington in 1956, Gombrich introduced his audience to the entertaining party game of 'ping' and 'pong': if in art, music, sculpture, architecture or, indeed, life we only had a language of two words by which we could understand the relationship of objects to one another, then -- for Gombrich-- ice cream would be ping and hot soup pong; Mozart in comparison to Beethoven would be ping, a Rembrandt next to a Watteau painting would be pong, and so on. This game of categorization doesn't always work, Gombrich concedes, since the route a viewer had chosen to walk through a museum, for example, might have influenced the perception of certain paintings. But the principle becomes sufficiently apparent: 'ping pong' demonstrates that certain artistic styles relate to one another in one way or another.[16]

Gombrich developed his ideas about style by hunting down passages which supported or challenged his ideas on the topic. A collection of quotes in an undated notebook, probably from *c.* 1957-58, shows him at work. An excerpt from Johann Joachim Winckelmann's *History of Ancient Art* (1764) about the 'expressive style' of actors in the Greek amphitheatre is followed by three definitions of 'style' from art dictionaries from 1792 to 1830. From the *Dictionnaire des arts de peinture* (1792) by Claude-Henri Watelet, Gombrich extracts that Velázquez is mentioned as having a 'style naturelle', while his quote from Aubin Louis Millin's *Dictionnaire des Beaux arts* (1806) is a reference to styles of architecture. On the next few pages he covers styles of poetry and art criticism, indirectly arriving at a first note on Charles E. Osgood's *The Measurement of Meaning*, via a quote from Ernest Chesneau's *L'art et les artistes modernes en France et en Angleterre* (1864), that he will eventually deal with in *Meditations on a Hobby Horse* (1963) (fig. 1).[17] Gombrich's notebooks are full of first, second and more attempts to find the correct words for an argument, but a comment like this, directly linked to a primary source, is quite rare among his bibliographical excerpts.

In four general folders Gombrich collected passages from books which were directly or indirectly linked to one of his arguments. They were his pool of indispensable knowledge and comprehensively brought together everything that Gombrich considered useful, from rhetoric to the decline of painting according to Carlo Cesare Malvasia to different styles of skiing.[18] There are passages relating to the classical background, quoting from Cicero's *De oratore* and Longinus' *On the Sublime,*

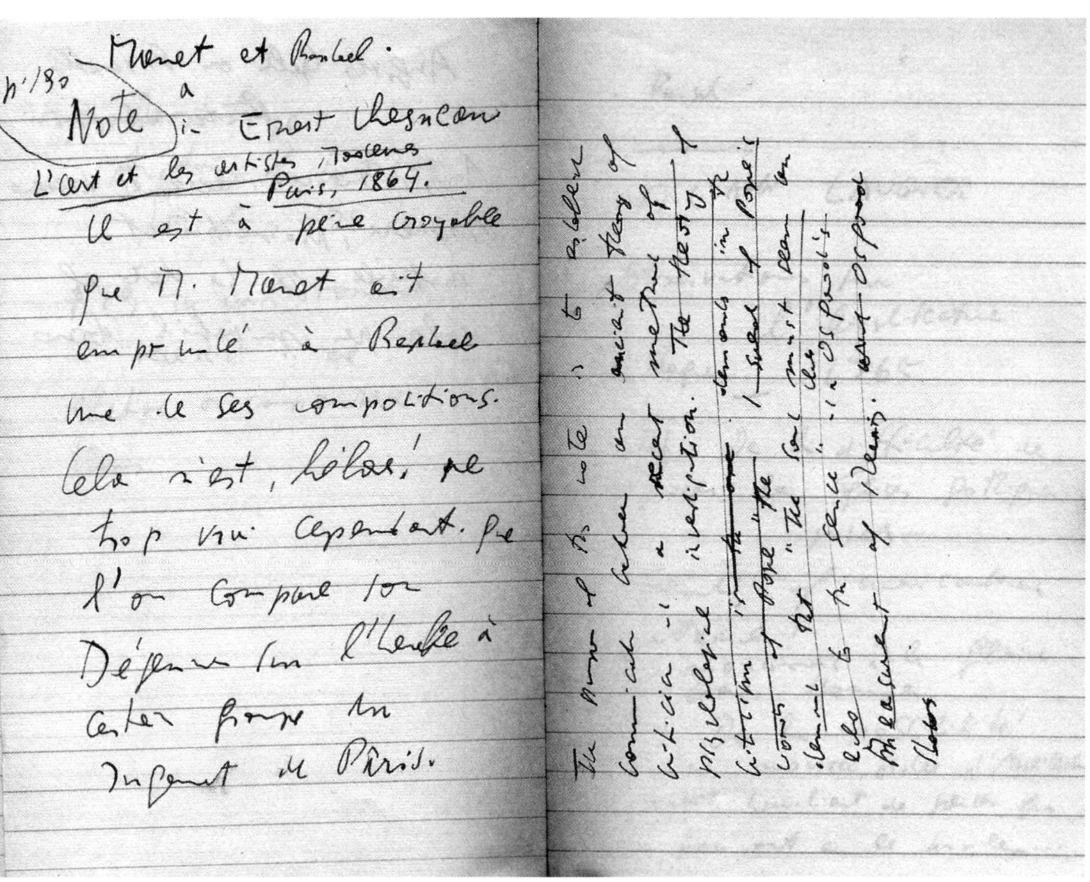

FIG. 1 E.H. Gombrich, Undated notebook (*c.* 1957-58?), quoting E. Chesneau, *L'art et les artistes modernes* (1864)

and moving on to Alberti's *De architectura* on social style. From Fréart de Chambray's *Idee de la Perfection de la Peinture* (1662) he copied the five parts of criticism (invention, proportion, colour, expression and disposition), and he added a few lines from Jonathan Richardson's *Essay on the Theory of Painting* (1715) about the correct use of colour for grave, melancholic or terrible subjects. Following the time line he arrives at Alois Riegl's arguments for the change in style of the acanthus leaf from his *Stilfragen* (1893). Among all of these excerpts there features, last but not least, a paragraph from Heinrich Höhn's *Deutsche Holzschnitte bis zum 16. Jahrhundert* (1925) displaying the notorious nationalism of its author.

Gombrich did not sort the contents of these folders, but the folders themselves did follow a system of classification. His subjects of interest are sorted by topic – e.g.

Neoplatonism, International Style, Perception, Perspective, Image, Ornament – his
lectures by place and date, and his correspondence by alphabet.

From this material Gombrich produced no less than six similar drafts for
different occasions. They belong to lectures on: 'Art and Fashion' (1957);[19] 'Style and
Fashion'(1958);[20] 'Style and Expression' (1958);[21] 'Expression and Communication'
(1960);[22] 'Mannerism' (1961) and 'Literary Style of the Renaissance' (1961).[23]

For the lecture on 'Style and Fashion' at Oberlin College Gombrich produced a
long list of examples to illustrate and underline his arguments, from the duc de Berry's
Très Riches Heures via secular art, Giotto and Lorenzetti to the 'Spirit of the Age'
and its sweet and lyrical moods (fig. 2). On two further pages for the same lecture,
he goes into more detail and tells the story of style in ten chapters. Under chapters 5
and 6 he uses the expressions 'no innocent eye' and 'from making to matching' which
will become such important arguments in *Art and Illusion* (fig. 3). On yet another
separate page Gombrich gives a very condensed sketch of the 'stylistic categories and
their origin in the ancient world', starting the introduction with an explanation of
the word 'stilus' (fig. 4). Both drafts have advantageous qualities and hold valuable
information that the other omits, so it is not necessarily true that the more condensed
and theoretical draft came first. Eventually their purpose is the same: they combine
certain elements of the same subject depending on the main focus of his talk. Another
demonstration of how Gombrich was able to bring light to a subject from a different
angle is in 'Style and Expression', delivered in the same year to Members of the
Cleveland Psychoanalytic Society. It deals with the notion of artistic choice, which he
called 'the language of alternatives'. Gombrich used his favourite example, the art of
John Constable, to discuss the conventions of eighteenth-century landscape painting
and Ruskin's art theory.

In the following year, 1959, he was invited to teach at Harvard, and one of his two
seminars was called 'The Concept of Style in the History of Art'. His visit lasted from
February to April and this gave him sufficient time to discuss the subject in nineteen
sessions. We still have a set of lecture notes that he distributed among the students of
the seminar.[24] These notes convey his thoughts at the time and help us to understand
the many other pages and lists of keywords on which he does not comment. The
Harvard lectures focus on what he summarizes under 'Psychological Evolutionism'. In
the introductory session he developed the following ideas:

> Style as mode and style as skill .... In interpreting the styles of the past the student
> of history must try to separate mode from skill since only a developed skill allows
> of a free choice between various modes. A third element to be considered is that
> of social habits or mores. A 20th-century tubular chair is different in style from a
> 19th-century piece of 'period imitation' but this change is meaningful only because
> both serve the same purpose. Where people generally sit cross legged on the floor,
> chairs 'mean' something different anyhow. Expression demands a context. There

     Veronika Kopecky

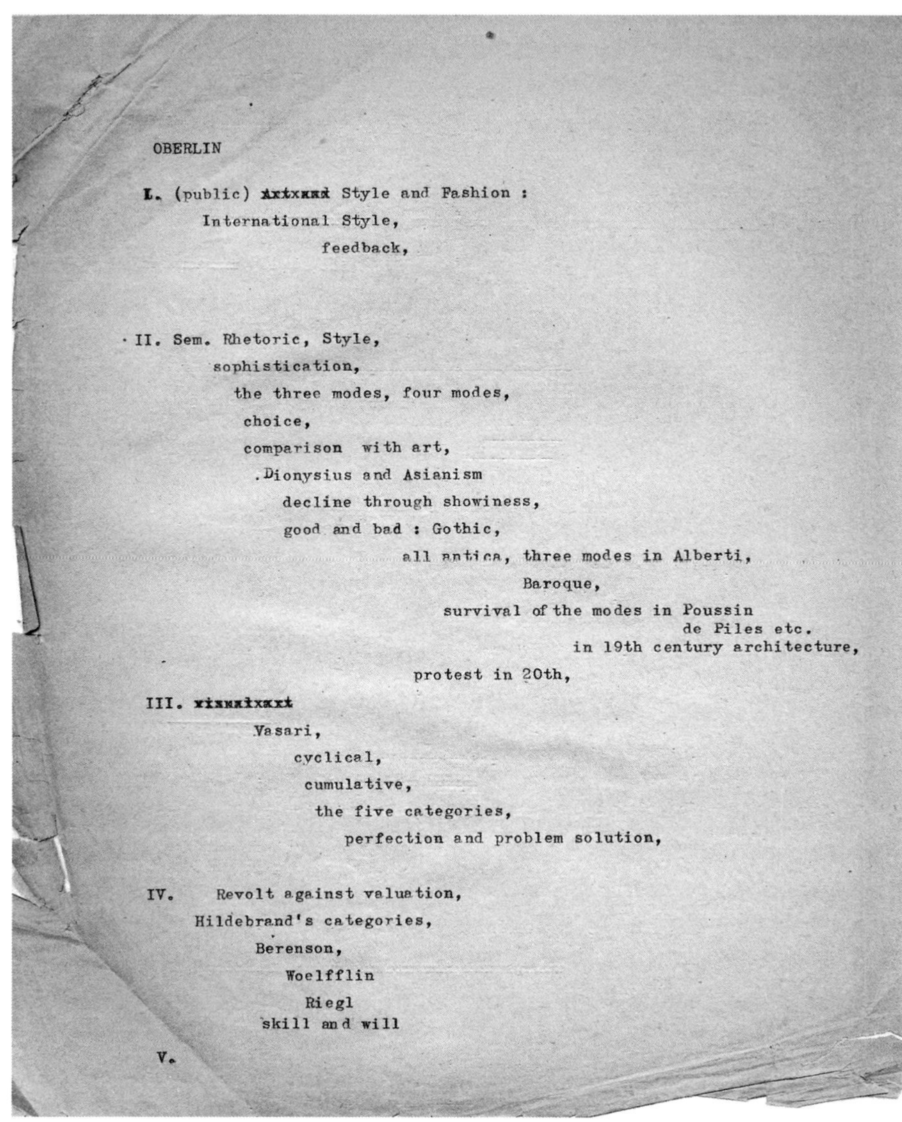

FIG.2 E.H. Gombrich, Lecture notes for 'Style and Fashion', Oberlin College, 1958

are no 'non-smokers' before the introduction of tobacco. The uncritical acceptance of the idea that we can read off the 'spirit of the age' from the styles of the past has given way to increasing scepticism (Examples of discussions e.g. on the usefulness of the term "Baroque" as expressing the total character of a period are given on the first reading list). Yet the historian of art knows that he can work with and only with the assumption of period styles, hence the need for a reassessment.[25]

```
V.    Evolutionism considered,

           Seeing and Knowing
               Loewy,
                 its value,

                 itxxiim
                   the primitive,
                       the study of copies etc.
                   its limitations :
                       Thouless problem,
                         no innocent eye
                             but no cubist vision
                             ─────────────

                             ─────────────
   VI.
               The iconological approach,
                   comparison with language,
                     from making to matching
                       the stereotype im and simile,
                         Villard's lion,
                             the patternbook
                         teaching how to,
                 Malraux

   VII.    The personal style,
               khaixmxxitkimi    connoisseurship,
               Oxdmmxñxxkxx         emergence of form
                                     Michelangelo and Raphael,
                                     Daumier and Ingres,
                                     more personal ?
                                     choice

   VIII. Critique of Geistesgeschichte : Mannerism
                     the story,
                         furm follows function
       IX. The feedback :
                 Cubism
                 Totalitarianism
       X. (Public : ) Immmmtimm Style and Discovery : texture and structur
```

FIG.3 E.H. Gombrich, Lecture notes for 'Style and Fashion', Oberlin College, 1958

From this prologue, which echoes his review of Schapiro's essay, Gombrich proceeds to introduce the 'all'antica style' of the Italian Renaissance, immediately linking it to Heinrich Wölfflin's notion of polarities between Renaissance and Baroque.[26] He argues that the styles which the Swiss scholar had identified were generalizations or abstractions at which one arrives by studying what all works of

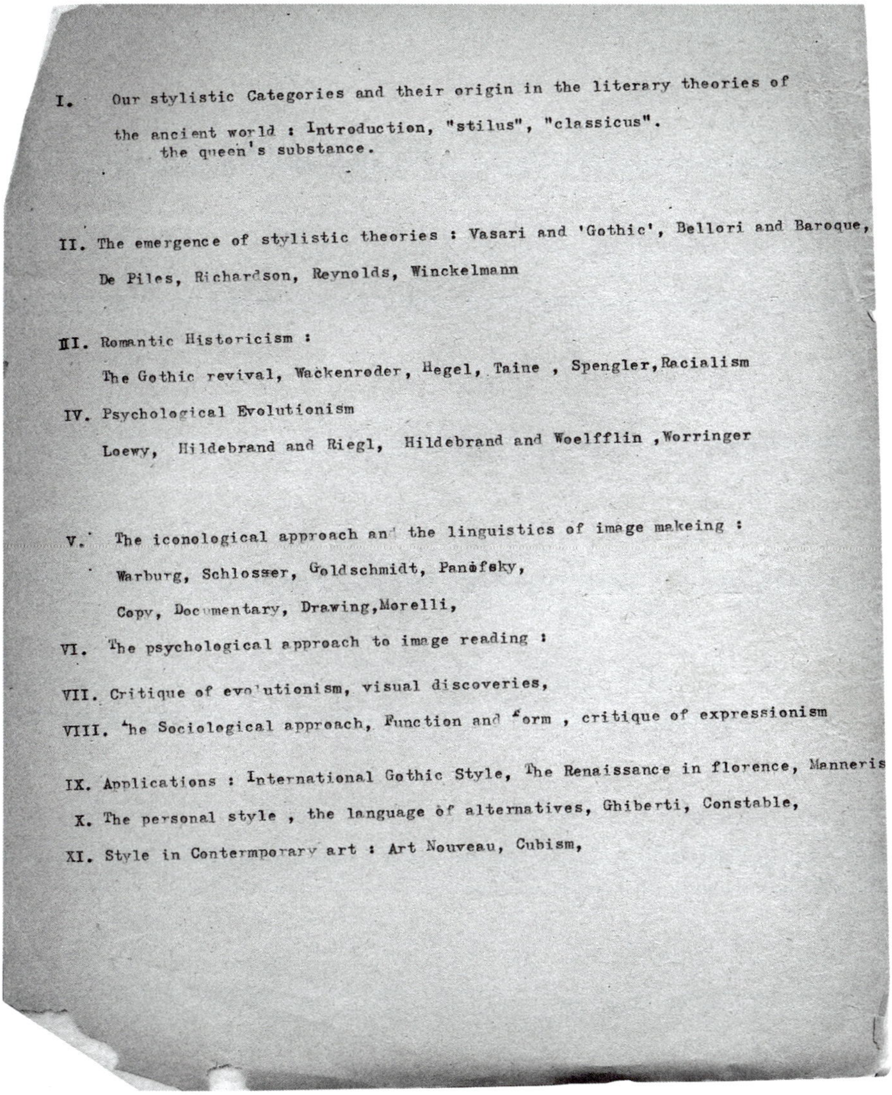

I. Our stylistic Categories and their origin in the literary theories of

    the ancient world : Introduction, "stilus", "classicus".
            the queen's substance.

II. The emergence of stylistic theories : Vasari and 'Gothic', Bellori and Baroque,

    De Piles, Richardson, Reynolds, Winckelmann

II. Romantic Historicism :

    The Gothic revival, Wackenroder, Hegel, Taine , Spengler,Racialism

IV. Psychological Evolutionism

    Loewy, Hildebrand and Riegl, Hildebrand and Woelfflin ,Worringer

V. The iconological approach and the linguistics of image makeing :

    Warburg, Schlosser, Goldschmidt, Panofsky,

    Copy, Documentary, Drawing,Morelli,

VI. The psychological approach to image reading :

VII. Critique of evolutionism, visual discoveries,

VIII. The Sociological approach, Function and Form , critique of expressionism

IX. Applications : International Gothic Style, The Renaissance in florence, Manneris

 X. The personal style , the language of alternatives, Ghiberti, Constable,

XI. Style in Contermporary art : Art Nouveau, Cubism,

FIG.4 E.H. Gombrich, Lecture notes for 'Stylistic categories', *c.* 1958

art produced in certain periods 'have in common'. This technique of inclusion and
exclusion favoured quick categorizations, for example 'classical' or 'non-classical'. This
concept, to Gombrich, in itself is not altogether wrong, because:

> There is no reason to think, however[,] that these categories are 'inherent'
> in the works themselves. They 'work' so well because they are based on our

'physiognomic' reactions. We know a good deal more about such reactions since Charles Osgood and his collaborators in their book *The Measurement of Meaning* has shown that we are ready to scale or grade almost any random object or concept along any scale of contrast.[27]

Of course, one is reminded here of the game of 'ping pong' to which I referred above. Gombrich reverts to his notes on Osgood's book as well as having his excerpt from Heinrich Höhn in mind: in the following sentences he makes sure to point out that the incorrect application of such categorisations can be highly inappropriate, as in their misuse in the name of nationalist propaganda.

His next lectures concentrated on the complete scope of the subject: starting with 'the ideal of the classic' and Aristotle's poetics, he took a short cut to rhetoric, Cicero, Quintilian and others. His link back to art is Winckelmann and he includes Hegel and Marx to move to a longer discussion of Riegl and Löwy. The last lectures are reserved for examples, as seen in the condensed chapter layout (fig. 4): the International Style around 1400, the Renaissance in Florence, and Mannerism. By following Gombrich's effort to produce this historical assessment it almost goes unnoticed that he provided his listeners with a compendium of relations and distinctions rather than with his explanation of artistic styles. This he would reserve for *Art and Illusion*, published a few months later.

III

In 1968 Gombrich came full circle and returned to Schapiro's essay by writing an entry on 'Style' in the *Encyclopedia of the Social Sciences*.[28] Schapiro, too, had addressed the difficulty of accounting for the social components in art. He was sceptical of the psychological approach to art, and had observed that general ways of feeling and thinking are certainly influential for an artist's style, but projecting personal and individual feelings into a style that should be representative of a period was an argument difficult to defend. Besides the individual traits of an artist, one had to account for education, profession and environment; social life, ideas and customs of the artist's surrounding and society. So far Gombrich would have agreed. At this late point in the essay and without further explanation, however, Schapiro had introduced Karl Marx's theory of economics and society. Investigated and applied systematically, he claimed, it could potentially clarify the changing relationships between a society and the art it creates, because

> ... [b]etween the economic relationships and the styles of art intervenes the process
> of ideological construction, a complex imaginative transposition of class roles
> and needs, which affect ... religion, mythology, or civil life – that provides the chief
> themes of art.[29]

     Veronika Kopecky

In 1953 Gombrich had just written his review of Arnold Hauser's *The Social History of Art* arguing against a Marxist theory of art,[30] and this last paragraph in Schapiro's essay must have been difficult to stomach. Interestingly, as far as I can see, Gombrich never commented on it directly.[31] The entry for the encyclopaedia in 1968 would have provided an ideal setting to disagree with Schapiro, but the nature of the entry only allowed for a general account of the subject and implicit criticism. Gombrich's typescript of 20 pages, naturally, makes extensive use of all the aforementioned material, and he elaborated on the links between social stratifications and manners of speech. Leaving the orators behind, he discusses the social implications of architecture, starting with Vasari and the history of artistic styles or *maniere*, but avoiding the morphological approach to the arts, that is styles of paintings, sculpture or other. Here for the first time he develops an argument extensively drawing on Karl Popper's *The Poverty of Historicism* (1957). Like his close friend Popper, Gombrich warns the reader not to jump to Hegelian and Marxist conclusions about any individual or group via their speech, dress or writings.[32]

> The way a person speaks, writes, dresses and looks merge for us into the image of his personality. We therefore say that all these are expressions of his personality. And we can sometimes rationalise our conviction by pointing out supposed connections. But the psychologist knows that it is extremely hazardous to make inferences from one such manifestation to all the others even where we know the context and conventions extremely well. Where this knowledge is lacking, nobody would venture on such a diagnosis and claim to be able to tell the character of a Chinese from his handwriting. Yet it is this paradoxically which the diagnosticians of group styles claim to be able to do .... More often than not they are simply arguing in a circle and inferring from the static or rigid style of a tribe that its mentality must also be static or rigid. The less collateral evidence there is, the more easily will this kind of diagnosis be accepted – particularly if it is part of a system of polarities in which, for instance, dynamic cultures are opposed to static ones or intuitive mentalities to rational ones .... There is no necessary connection between any one aspect of a group's activities and any other.[33]

On the other hand, Gombrich points out that the principle of choice is a helpful 'pointer', a quality to describe a particular culture:

> For without choice a certain principle does not apply. (…) Eskimo igloos cannot be interpreted as a sign of simple ideals. Though they are certainly most closely connected with the Eskimo's mode of life it is not helpful to speak of their style as an expression of Eskimo culture.[34]

This last quotation was omitted from the published version, but it drives home the point about the importance of choice, and this is where Gombrich reiterates his 'theory of art' as promoted in *Art and Illusion*: style is dependent on the possible choices the artist, architect, etc. has and makes, and these not only include, but inherently are environmental and psychological choices. Since the entry was for an encyclopaedia of the social sciences Gombrich exchanged the Eskimo example for a different one more suitable for the year 1968. To demonstrate the political implications of style the Eskimos were substituted with an anticommunist man from Poland of the late 1960s 'who would like to paint a brawny, happy tractor driver', and, of course, he could paint his tractor 'but one would have to tell him that this subject and style has been pre-empted by his political opponents'.[35]

IV

In September 1981 Thomas DaCosta Kauffmann sent Gombrich a letter asking if he could dedicate one of two attached essays to him. In the essay 'The Eloquent Artist: Towards an Understanding of the Stylistics of Painting at the Court of Rudolf II' he used 'iconographic and cultural historical evidence to approach a problem of stylistic synthesis' and calls for a 'revision of our notions of Mannerism'.[36] Gombrich read it and replied with a comment:

> As I said, I read your essays with interest and I shall certainly be flattered if you decide to dedicate one of them to me. Perhaps I am even more of a sceptic concerning discussions about 'style' than you are, but I don't disagree with what you say. If I may be quite frank, though, I am not sure that your proposal solves the problem. No doubt the term 'style' could also be applied, and was often applied, in the context of the theory of decorum where it is synonymous with modus or genus dicendi. The possibility of various such 'modes' being available to artists is also discussed in Baxandall's latest book,[37] and I don't doubt its relevance, after all, music almost lives on these distinctions, symphonia Eroica, pastorale, etc., and within the symphony or suite the allemande, the scherzo, the "alla danza tedesca" (in Beethoven's quartette). But this multiplicity of available 'styles['] does not preclude that the limewood sculpture of Germany discussed by b. [Baxandall] has 'a' style, or that Beethoven has one. The term simply has a variety of meanings, logically, though not, perhaps, historically you could imagine many substyles being all subordinate hierarchically to an overarching style. I believe that what art historians hoped to find has always been such a hallmark, a characteristic which distinguishes every work of art produced in a particular school or period. Now if you admit what I have called 'principles of exclusion' as well as of inclusion it is undeniable that the works produced in Prague in 'your' period neither look like Egyptian nor like 20th century paintings. People conversant with the milieu recognise them for what they are. How they do it is a different matter. Is it just 'inductively' by remembering the masters and works, or do they still share a more elusive flavour not easily verbalised? I don't profess to know, but I would not

    Veronika Kopecky

exclude this possibility simply because they also exemplify the various categories of style. After all we believe we recognise, say, an Englishman though the English upper class differs notoriously very different [sic] from the working class etc. But before one knows where one is one finds oneself confronted with the oldest problem of philosophy, the problem of 'universals'. Art history, to my mind, still treats this in an Aristotelian, 'essentialist' fashion, believing in the efficacy of intellectual in[t]uition to grasp the 'essence' of a style. In science, including the more forward looking social sciences there are statistical methods of trait or fac[t]or analysis which may not offer ideal solutions, but are a little less naïve. But enough of these quibbles. What I feel you will not and should not be able to avoid in the long run is the problem of value, of quality. It seems to me to be the weakness of the stylistic-Aristotelian approach that it wants to bypass it.[38]

The letter to Kaufmann is certainly representative of Gombrich's struggle with the elusiveness of the term. His approach to 'style' was as multifaceted as he claimed the subject to be in the letter. On the one hand the letter presents most clearly how Gombrich advocated Popper's critical rationalism and his hopes that a more scientific approach to art would help to solve some of its problems. On the other hand mentioning Aristotle and the problem of 'universals' is ambiguous: in *Art and Illusion*, twenty years earlier, he had tied together the philosopher's 'universals' with his notion of 'schema', and in that context the connection had worked very well for him.[39] If one had asked Gombrich for his definition of style, he certainly would have said that there was no definitive answer. In his endeavours to tie up the loose ends on the topic Gombrich realised that style – as the category of the highest order – could hardly ever be investigated in isolation from its parts.

     'Style' in the Archive of E.H. Gombrich

* I would like to thank Leonie Gombrich and her family who are funding the cataloguing of the Gombrich Archive papers. On behalf of the Gombrich family I also wish to thank the Warburg Institute and Charles Hope for housing the papers and vitally assisting the progress of the cataloguing at the Institute. Special thanks go to Dorothea McEwan, who has given important support to my work at the Gombrich archive. In what follows I frequently use the following abbreviation, EHG, WIA, which denotes E.H. Gombrich archive, Warburg Institute Archive. Other abbreviations within square brackets refer to archival classmarks.

1 Since I am more interested in the unpublished than the published I shall say nothing about one of Gombrich's most important statements on style, the chapter 'The Psychology of Styles' in E.H. Gombrich, *The Sense of Order: a Study in the Psychology of Decorative Art*, Oxford, 1979, pp. 195-216.

2 From a surviving announcement poster we know that Gombrich's last Slade Lecture of the term in May 1952 was called 'Reflections on Style'. The notes to this lecture currently resist discovery. With luck, however, they are hiding in one of the archival boxes amongst another lecture or publication for which he used them.

3 Italics by Gombrich; E.H. Gombrich, 'The Impact of the Black Death', in Gombrich, *Reflections on the History of Art: Views and Reviews*, ed. R. Woodfield, Oxford, 1987, pp. 42-45; originally published as a review of M. Meiss, *Painting in Florence and Siena after the Black Death*, Princeton, 1951, *Journal of Aesthetics and Art Criticism*, 11, 1953, pp. 414-16.

4 Millard Meiss to E.H. Gombrich, 29 June 1953; EHG, WIA [Corr M (Meiss)].

5 E.H. Gombrich, 'Review. Style, by Meyer Schapiro, Reprinted for private circulation from Kroeber, ed., *Anthropology Today*, University of Chicago Press, 1953', 1 p.; EHG, WIA [RevC&Fr (Style)].

6 H. Wölfflin, *Renaissance und Barock. Eine Untersuchung über Wesen und Entstehung der Barockstil in Italien*, Munich, 1888; idem, *Kunstgeschichtliche Grundbegriffe: das Problem der Stilentwicklung in der neueren Kunst*, Munich, 1915.

7 A. Riegl, *Stilfragen. Grundlegungen zur einer Geschichte der Ornamentik*, Berlin, 1893; idem, *Die spätrömische Kunstindustrie*, Vienna 1901.

8 E. Löwy, *Die Naturwiedergabe in der älteren griechischen Kunst*, Rome, 1900 (E. Loewy, *The Rendering of Nature in Early Greek Art*, London, 1907).

9 M. Dvořák, *Die Entstehung der Barockkunst in Rom*, Vienna 1908.

10 A. Hauser, *The Social History of Art*, New York, 1951; E.H. Gombrich, review of A. Hauser, *The Social History of Art*, New York, 1951, *The Art Bulletin*, 35, 1953, pp. 79-84; reprinted in E.H. Gombrich, *Meditations on a Hobby Horse and Other Essays on the Theory of Art*, London, 1963, pp. 86-94.

11 M. Schapiro, 'Style', *Anthropology Today*, ed. A.L. Kroeber, Chicago, 1953, pp. 287-312 (p. 287).

12 EHG, WIA [BBC War reports (Style, Style Sobering)].

13 MS 'The Realm and Range of the Image'; [EHG, WIA (Early A&I)].

14 Image Book Synopsis, 4 pp., together with a letter of E.H. Gombrich to B. Horovitz, 27 September 1952 [EHG, WIA (Early A&I)].

15 E.H. Gombrich, *Art and Illusion: a Study in the Psychology of Pictorial Representation*, London, 1960, p. 19 and notes to pp. 19, 22.

16 EHG, WIA [L&T 50-59, Mellon MS, pp. 215-16]; Gombrich, *Art and Illusion* (note 15 above), pp. 370-71.

17 Note book, *c.* 1958 [WIA EHG, NB undated].

18 EHG, WIA [RevC&Fr (Psychology Lectures); LN 1973 (Leeds); LN USA 50s (Harvard 1959); UAM (Seattle)].

19 'Art and Fashion', Reading University, 1957.

20 'Style and Fashion', Oberlin College, 1958.

21 'Style and Expression', Cleveland Psychoanalytic Society, April 1958.

22 'Expression and Communication', lecture given at the Victoria and Albert Museum, March 1960; published in *Hobby Horse* (n. 10 above), pp. 56-69.

23 Both read at the International Congress of the History of Art, New York 1961. The title 'Mannerism' remained the same; 'Literary Style of the Renaissance' would later be called 'The Style all'antica. Imitation and Assimilation', and appeared in Gombrich, *Norm and Form: Studies in the Art of the*

Renaissance I, London, 1966, pp. 99-106; 122-28.

24 EHG, WIA [LN USA 50s (Harvard 1959)]

25 Lecture Notes, session of 3 Feb 1959, p. 1; EHG, WIA [LN USA 50s (Harvard 1959)].

26 H. Wölfflin, *Renaissance and Baroque*, Munich, 1888.

27 Lecture Notes, session of 7 February 1959, pp. 2-3; EHG, WIA [LN USA 50s (Harvard 1959)]; C.E. Osgood, G. Suci and P. Tannenbaum, *The Measurement of Meaning*, University of Illinois Press, 1957. This passage exists more or less unchanged in both the Mellon Lectures and Gombrich, *Art and Illusion* (note 15 above), pp. 370-71.

28 MS Style, 20 pp. EHG, WIA [RevC&Fr (Style)]; E.H. Gombrich, 'Style', in *International Encyclopaedia of the Social Sciences*, ed. D.L. Sills, 18 vols., New York, 1968, vol. 15, pp. 352-61.

29 Schapiro, 'Style' (n. 11 above), pp. 287-312 (p. 311).

30 Gombrich, Review of Hauser (n. 10 above).

31 Alan Wallach suggested that Schapiro did not go further into the Marxist theory of art because of the political situation in the United States at the time. It would speak for Gombrich's integrity towards his colleague that he chose not to criticize Schapiro on that account. See A. Wallach, 'Meyer Schapiro's Essay on Style: Falling into the Void', *The Journal of Aesthetics and Art Criticism*, 55, 1997, pp. 11-15.

32 In regards to Karl Bühler, who was the teacher of both Popper and Gombrich, see 'Achievement in Medieval Art' and 'Art and Scholarship' in *Hobby Horse* (n. 10 above). My thanks go to Richard Woodfield, who drew my attention to this.

33 MS Style, p. 17; Gombrich, 'Style' (n. 28 above), p. 358.

34 MS Style, p. 18; for a similar Eskimo example see Gombrich, 'Art and Scholarship', in *Hobby Horse* (n. 10 above), p. 112.

35 Gombrich, 'Style' (n. 28 above), p. 359.

36 T. DaCosta Kauffmann, 'The Eloquent Artist: Towards an Understanding of the Stylistics of Painting at the Court of Rudolf II', *Leids Kunsthistorisch Jaarboek*, 1, 1982, pp. 119-48. T. DaCosta Kaufmann to E.H. Gombrich, 9 September 1981, EHG, WIA [L&T 78-82 (WC)].

37 M. Baxandall, *The Limewood Sculptors of Renaissance Germany*, New Haven and London, 1980.

38 E.H. Gombrich to T. DaCosta Kaufmann, 1 October 1981; EHG, WIA [L&T 78-82 (WC)].

39 Gombrich, *Art and Illusion* (n. 15 above), pp. 146-78.

       'Style' in the Archive of E.H. Gombrich

Gombrich and the
Middle Ages

PAUL CROSSLEY

GOMBRICH'S CONTRIBUTION TO THE ART HISTORY of the Middle
Ages is notable by its absence: a slight paper on late Gothic and early Renaissance
altarpieces;[1] a short overview of the International Style;[2] a late consideration of the
Romanesque as a branch of the 'preference for the primitive';[3] passing references in
larger articles or books on non-medieval topics; and (the one exception to which I
shall return) a review article published in 1937 on a study of medieval artistic theory.[4]
Otherwise, the longest coherent examinations of medieval art that I can find in
Gombrich's work are in his two books for children and adolescents – forty-five pages
in *A Little History of the World*,[5] and sixty pages in *The Story of Art*.[6]

Yet anyone surveying Gombrich's student days in Vienna in the late 1920s and
early 1930s would have been forgiven for predicting a brilliant career for him as a
medievalist. In his Autobiographical Sketch, published in 1991, the reminiscences of
his youth are dominated by the experience of medieval art. As a teenager he had already
found a refreshing alternative to connoisseur-type art history in the new wave of
Expressionism in Germany, which centred on the discovery of late medieval imagery:
Grünewald and Veit Stoss, folk-like wooden Pietas, and the crude woodcuts and
popular prints of the fifteenth century.[7] And as a student, Gombrich's regular classes
in the Kunsthistorisches Museum with his tutor and future *Doktorvater*, Julius von
Schlosser, introduced him to medieval objects from the barbarian migrations to the
International Style.[8] His written work was dominated by the extensive rehabilitation
of medieval art initiated by the so-called Vienna School of Art history from the 1890s
onwards. He read (approvingly) Franz Wickhoff's study of Late Antique and Early
Christian narrative in his *Vienna Genesis* of 1895.[9] He was profoundly influenced by
the new historicist approach to barbarian ornament in Alois Riegl's *Stilfragen* (1893)
and, at the promptings of Schlosser, he wrote a paper on it.[10] He 'devoured' Max
Dvořák's book on naturalism and idealism in Gothic art 'as soon as it came out' in
1924 – 'one of the most impressive books I had ever read'.[11] Gombrich's 1966 study of
ritualized gesture owed its inception to a Schlosser seminar of over thirty years earlier
on the *Sachsenspiegel*, a north German legal manuscript of the fourteenth century,
where communication through gesture plays a critical role.[12] Gombrich's teachers

74

and contemporaries included Hans Sedlmayr (later the author of the longest and most ambitious book ever written on the Gothic cathedral),[13] Karl Maria Swoboda (an authority on Bohemian medieval art and architecture); Hans Tietze (the leading specialist on the history and construction of the cathedral of St Stephen in Vienna) and Hans Hahnloser, the editor of Villard d' Honnecourt's thirteenth-century portfolio.[14] And the classic work on *Kunstliteratur* published in 1924 by the most influential figure of his Vienna years, his revered *Doktorvater* Julius von Schlosser, introduced Gombrich to medieval texts about art and artists in the rigorous detail characteristic of Schlosser's scrupulous scholarship.[15] Schlosser's history of medieval art (*Die Kunst des Mittelalters*, 1923) established for the first time the decisive role that the formula or *simile* plays in medieval art – a concept central to Gombrich's *Art and Illusion*.[16]

Yet for all this early exposure to the art and art history of the Middle Ages, Gombrich never became a specialized 'medievalist', despite his admission, in his Autobiographical Sketch, that around 1933 'he had started to be a medievalist'.[17] Answers to the obvious question 'why did he not continue to be a medievalist?' are both speculative and prosaic. A welcome distraction from the Middle Ages was his doctoral dissertation on the quintessentially Mannerist Palazzo del Tè, submitted in 1933, while his move to the Warburg Institute in London in 1936 strengthened his preoccupation with Italian Renaissance and post-Renaissance art and directed his interest towards the 'after life' of the classical tradition.[18] At the Warburg his work with Ernst Kris on art and psychoanalysis opened up an old interest in the Freudian joke and its nearest visual equivalent, the caricature.[19] His Autobiographical Sketch also hints at other reasons for his defection. He found medieval art, especially in its early centuries, too obscure, too little documented, to pursue with the kind of historical and scientific accuracy demanded by the rigorous Schlosser.[20] Indeed,the problem seems to have been neatly encapsulated in one of Gombrich's Kunsthistorisches Museum classes with Schlosser, where his teacher had asked him to lecture on a supposedly late classical ivory pyx in the Applied Arts Department. Gombrich put forward the original idea that it was not Antique at all but a Carolingian copy. Schlosser thought the piece should be published, and it appeared, as Gombrich's first publication, in the *Jahrbuch der Kunsthistorischen Sammlungen* in 1933.[21] But the whole exercise only sharpened Gombrich's frustration at the lack of evidence surrounding early medieval objects. He was struck by 'the arbitrariness and the many blank patches on the map of seventh- and eighth-century art history', and he became 'a little sceptical about the possibility of finding exactly when and where this particular ivory carving was made'. 'This,' he stated, 'was one of the reasons why I gradually turned away from medieval studies.'[22]

But there were other, I suspect more important, reasons to avoid the Middle Ages, reasons to do less with dearth of data than with the young Gombrich's cast of mind. If medieval art history offered little material for wider study, it also promoted interest in the kind of art – the angular expressionism of German Late Gothic – which

   Gombrich and the Middle Ages

Gombrich found aesthetically and ideologically unsympathetic, not least in the nationalistic and racist overtones of its interpreters.[23] Moreover, Dvořák's seductive analyses of the Gothic in terms of explanatory 'spirits of an age' were soon seen by the young Gombrich as promoting the kind of collectivist post-Hegelian cultural theory that he was to oppose for much of his life. 'Art history as the history of the Spirit' – the title of Dvořák's collected papers – was a cliché in need of revision.[24] Furthermore, his early experience of medieval art was too implicated in the world of museums and connoisseurship, a world he found dull. He never really wanted to become what he called, with a certain disingenuous modesty, 'a proper art historian'. He wanted, as he said later, to *explain* art and its development, to become 'a kind of commentator on the history of art'.[25] It was no coincidence that the last extended essay that the eighteen-year-old Gombrich completed for his final school exam was a commentary, on changes in art appreciation from Winckelmann to the present day. 'I have sometimes thought' he admitted, 'that this is all I have ever done – pursued my interest in this particular subject'.[26] By 'subject' he meant not only the period of this investigation – from the Enlightenment onwards – but the whole explanatory and theoretical approach to all periods which will characterize his work.

It is not therefore surprising that Gombrich's one serious foray into the Middle Ages should occur in this medievalizing Viennese environment, and that its topic engaged with matters of general explanation, not connoisseurship or archival discovery. The work in question consisted of a long review in the intellectually progressive *Kritische Berichte* of 1937, and was devoted to a critique of Ernst von Garger's slightly earlier paper in the same journal on the difficulties of evaluating medieval art.[27] Gombrich's paper was entitled 'Wertprobleme und mittelalterliche Kunst' – *Wertprobleme* possibly best translated as 'problems concerned with the qualities or characteristics' of medieval art, and not just as 'Achievement in Medieval Art', the title given it by Michael Podro in his invaluable translation of the review.[28] For the young Gombrich is here evaluating not just the achievements of medieval art but its fundamental nature; and he is couching his arguments in the lucid rhetorical polemic which will be a hallmark of his later work. Garger had tried to explain the non-mimetic nature of medieval art in terms of artistic incompetence. Medieval artists intended, he argued, to represent the natural world, but failed actually to do so. There was a shortfall between aim and effect. Gombrich dismissed this Platonic division between intending and achieving, between the mind and the hand, as inappropriate to medieval creativity. The medieval artist did not entertain ideas which he could not realize, nor did he – unlike his Renaissance and post-Renaissance successors – follow his inner voice, his primary conception, and then struggle to realize it. Instead he obeyed a real model existing outside himself – a *simile* – which he had to master and do justice to. Like a musician or an actor, his achievement was not to invent new forms, or realise his own inner vision, but to respect his exemplar, perform his task with skill, and charge his text with meaning. Skill, not originality, was the prized asset. As far as representation of the real world was concerned, skill involved matching the artist's given model with the image to be depicted so as to 'attain the required degree of recognizability'.[29]

Gombrich's emphasis here on the formula is indebted to Schlosser's study of types and stereotypes in numismatics, but it also anticipates, to an uncanny degree, the main argument of his *Art and Illusion* twenty years later: namely that the complex process of pictorial representation is not simply a matter of copying what we see, but involves projection and substitution: projecting on to the depicted object what we already know about it in our consciousness, our schema, and then, to use his famous phrase, 'making and matching' – adjusting, correcting and modifying that schema to the natural object that is being depicted ('attain the required degree of recognizability'). Medieval art introduced the young Gombrich to the power of the schema – the presence of knowing in the act of seeing – with a clarity that post-medieval representations as yet could not.

At least two other aspects of 'Achievement' anticipate *Art and Illusion*. In Gombrich's emphasis on skill we are introduced to another of his favourite notions, one in which he was later to find some confirmation in Karl Popper's understanding of scientific method: that artistic achievement is a process akin to scientific discovery – that your hypothesis is the artist's task and the solution to it is the artist's skill. As Popper put it, 'there is no difference in principle between explanations in history and in science; the difference is in the direction of our interest'.[30] The second notion in 'Achievement' is an early warning: it is the one that looms largest in *Art and Illusion* and is most identified with Gombrich and his conception of history: his antipathy to collective spirits – particularly Hegelian ones – as sources of stylistic change.[31] Garger had had the temerity to suggest, in the manner of early twentieth-century German expressionist art theory, that the constraint of medieval forms in schematic shapes expressed feelings of constraint on the part of the artist and of his whole society towards the world and nature. Gombrich pounces on this hypostasized collective social personality, condemning such inferences from forms to states of mind as collective fictions, removed as much from real history as from the untidy individuality of the artist and his patrons. Here, in embryo, is Gombrich's attack on Hegel, and on the romantic philosophy of history as a collective and holistic Mind, manifesting itself in all aspects of a culture.[32] This 'negative' cultural theory will be one of the leitmotifs of *Art and Illusion*.[33] Yet we are faced here with a paradox. We find at least two of the central ideas of Gombrich's later work – the schema, and the dangers of Hegelian 'historicism' – precociously mapped out in the unlikely setting of an exploratory article on medieval art. It is medieval art which defines, in Gombrich's terms, its opposite: the long tradition of Western naturalism. Gombrich himself sees this. Referring to the 1963 re-publication of the article he noted: 'on re-reading [the article] after so many years I realized how frequently I have since returned to the questions which irked me at the age of twenty-six.'[34]

     Gombrich and the Middle Ages

If *Art and Illusion* expands critical notions already broached in 'Achievement', Gombrich's second great study, the *Sense of Order* of 1979,[35] a complement to *Art and Illusion*, also grew out of his student confrontation with the Middle Ages, and most particularly with Alois Riegl's masterpiece, *Stilfragen*, a study of the migration of ornamental patterns across two millennia.[36] *Stilfragen* (a book on which Schlosser had asked Gombrich to prepare a paper) is a diachronic history of a single motif, while Riegl's later book, *Spätrömische Kunstindustrie* of 1901, is a synchronic analysis of all art forms in the era of change from Roman to Early Christian and 'barbarian' cultures.[37] Riegl's marriage of these stylistic changes with the psychological notion of 'modes of perception'[38] formed the basis for Gombrich's similar interests in the psychology of ornament, just as the influence of Schlosser and the early appearance of Gestalt theory in Vienna opened up to him questions of psychology and representation addressed in *Art and Illusion*. Once again, 'Achievement' anticipates some of the themes of *The Sense of Order*, particularly those concerning the expressive nature of scripts and linear patterns. Gombrich introduces us, in this early article, to his by now familiar principle of the 'art of the possible' – the normal range of possibilities of meaning open to an artist at any given period. He warns us that expressiveness of ornament may not be a direct communication of 'innocent' forms but a matter of convention: the spikiness of Gothic script is just a given formula of communication, not the sign of an aggressive or neurotic scribe. One needs a standard of comparison, a norm, by which to measure the strength or weakness of the convention over and against the expressive force of the individual.[39] This early suspicion of expression and Expressionism will blossom in *The Sense of Order* into an explicit attack on the popular expressionist writings of Wilhelm Worringer. 'Achievement' also anticipated Gombrich's important concept of 'fields of force' in ornament, which give meaning and focus to decoration. The example he gives in *A Sense of Order,* that of a medley of lines transformed into a writhing knotwork of dragons by the addition of eyes and tails,[40] is prefigured in examples of the same phenomena discussed in 'Achievement': 'scrolls and palmettes, and even letters and sacred symbols are transformed into zoomorphic shapes by the addition of eyes, beaks and claws … and the *horror vacui* of these styles extended from the crowding of motifs to the superimposition of ever fresh meanings'.[41]

If intimations of *Art and Illusion* and *The Sense of Order* appear in 'Achievement' it is not surprising that Gombrich's last book, posthumously published, his *Preference for the Primitive* of 2002, also takes up a number of themes from 'Achievement'. The 'primitive' had engaged him, on and off, since his youth; and of all Gombrich's major categories of art historical commentary – representation, pattern-making, and expression – it was with the expressive and anti-mimetic language of the 'primitive' that he most closely associated medieval art. Hence 'Achievement' often refers to aspects of 'the primitive' that closely anticipate the concepts that Gombrich deployed in his last book. Thus the notion of the primitive child-like representation-substitute

     Paul Crossley

(most famously the hobby horse) which plays a defining role in *Art and Illusion,* and reappears in *The Preference for the Primitive,* is prefigured in 'Achievement' in its brief but telling discussion of 'primitive' image making. In his critique of Garger's confusion between incompetence and primitiveness in medieval art, Gombrich searches for a definition of the 'primitive' which includes what he calls 'the conceptual image', namely, the predilection of the 'primitive' for picture writing, its interest in the symbol and the sign, its preoccupation with clarity of content over verisimilitude of form and its kinship with child art.[42] Schlosser's interest in child art and its 'primitive' images had already alerted Gombrich to the importance of the formula in 'primitive' art, and now, in 'Achievement', he is collecting together a set of other tendencies in art which, in *Art and Illusion* and in *The Preference for the Primitive,* he will expand into a full identification with the 'primitive' inclinations of medieval art. Thus the art of Duccio and Sassetta displays elements of 'child art', with its 'toy trees' and 'toy boats' and its reliance on limited schema to 'make' a boat or a tree.[43] As he noted in 'Achievement', 'the question as to the respects in which medieval art belongs to what we broadly term "primitive image-making" does not appear senseless'.[44] Indeed, 'Achievement' goes on to argue that medieval art was 'a return to the primitive', and with it what Gombrich called 'the emancipation of formal values'. Provided medieval art discharged its primary function, of conveying content through signs, rather than illusions via mimesis, then it could indulge in free and 'primitive' forms – bright and precious colours, ornamental elaboration and a raw, striking purity of image.[45] Gombrich was to elaborate on this concept when he came to discuss the 'primitive' effects of flat, brightly coloured stained - glass windows.[46] Besides providing opportunities for a new formal and 'primitive' artistic language, Gombrich noted at this early stage how the primitive also opened up to medieval art new possibilities of ordered meaning in the form of pictograms and image patterns which potentially manifested, in their flat and schematic patterning, the whole system of hierarchic medieval thought.[47] And finally, 'Achievement' recognizes the expressive, spiritual and irrational aspects of the primitive in medieval art, though Gombrich here, and much later, voices his suspicions of irrational 'expression' as emotionally excessive. In an anticipation of Wollheim's notion of intransitive modes of expression (expression that simply 'expresses'), the young Gombrich warns us that 'primitive masks may appear expressive, although we know that some of their lines are not intended as part of a facial expression'.[48] Here, in 1937, he is already prophetically aware of the dangers of an ahistorical admiration for the primitive, as if (to quote from his last book) 'all the spectator had to do was to surrender to the impression that the art of the past made on him to gain an intuitive contact with the life of bygone centuries'.[49] Such 'presentism' is obvious in the ahistorical juxtaposition of Cycladic doll and Brancusi sculpture in the timeless isolation of the museum.[50]

Why have I spent so much time tracing the origins of Gombrich's mature thinking to a small review in a defunct periodical? Because it is here that Gombrich, possibly

     Gombrich and the Middle Ages

for the first time, reveals his tendency to use medieval art as an explanatory foil: to define, as if by its opposite, the principles of Western naturalism in art. This thinking via dialectic (I will return to this concept later) is especially obvious in *Art and Illusion*, where the Middle Ages on one side and Renaissance and post-Renaissance art on the other are brought together in confrontation: skill versus invention; the schema of the simile versus representation; meaning and expressive distortion versus mimesis. *Art and Illusion* presents medieval art as the shadow side, the failed experiment, in the western tradition of the conquest of appearances. Medieval art belongs, he claims, to 'the pathology of representation', a pathology which will give us a unique 'insight into the mechanisms which enabled the masters [Renaissance artists] to handle this instrument [mimesis] with such assurance'. A little earlier, Gombrich had suggested that medieval art could be described as a 'failure', one that fruitfully defines the successes of post-Renaissance representation: 'In the study of art no less than in the study of man, the mysteries of success are frequently best revealed through an investigation of failures'.[51]

It is easy to see how this antipathy – allied to this polarity of attitude – can overplay the contrasts between Middle Ages and Renaissance. The medieval artist's conformity to the schema was not always the order of the day. We now appreciate that the later medieval artist had to master another skill: to make studies from nature and apply them to pictures. Invention as well as skill was prized by medieval patrons. The architects of the High Gothic cathedrals were commemorated in mazes on the nave floor, signalling them out as latter-day Daedaluses, noted for their ingenuity and invention.[52] William of Sens, architect of the Gothic choir of Canterbury cathedral, was praised in the late twelfth-century chronicle of Gervase of Canterbury as 'inventive in wood and stone', his modern Gothic choir praised by Gervase for its richness and subtlety, in contrast to the crudities of the Romanesque nave.[53] Gombrich himself notes, in *The Story of Art*, that much of High and Late medieval art exhibited a new spirit of individuality and realism, particularly in cathedral sculpture.[54] In his 1989 paper, 'Images as Luxury Objects', Gombrich admitted that schema and skill in the courtly richness of the International Style in the later Middle Ages had now to run alongside an understanding of the natural world, even if it was only a 'selective naturalism'.[55]

The Sense of Order, concerned with ornament and pattern, was bound to offer more insights into the structures and decorations of medieval art than the representational thrust of *Art and Illusion*. But like *Art and Illusion*, *The Sense of Order* is an account of artistic responses to our deepest psycho-biological instincts. Organic life – runs Gombrich's argument – is governed by hierarchical structure and by ordered rhythms of events (waves, cornfields, rhythms and time) which lock into our projections of order and, like a process of adjustment, sink below the threshold of our attention. Any change in these regularities leads to an arousal of attention. The environment of order we create for ourselves satisfies this dual demand for adjustment and arousal.

    Paul Crossley

Too much harmonic adjustment and we become bored and inattentive; too many changes, too much arousal, and we cease to have a grasp of the whole. The book, long, discursive, and crammed with Gombrich's familiar global range of examples, enumerates the various refractions and modifications which these basic tendencies have undergone in the history of art. Fruitful for medieval art in this context is Gombrich's mental mechanism, the 'break spotter', which complements our mental assumption of regularity and 'adjustment' by articulating undifferentiated ornament with framing devices and structures, thus creating an ordered hierarchy which guards the mind against the confusions of multiple and continuous ornament by chopping up the decoration into containing structures (he gives as an example the Mirador de Lindaraja, in the Alhambra). Gombrich calls this process of 'Laws and Orders' 'the balance of regularity and variation'.[56]

There are many other categories of ornament and order which throw light on medieval art, especially architecture and its ornaments. There is 'the challenge of constraints', where virtuoso craft confections (choir stalls, sacrament houses) push against the structural limits of their materials.[57] There are the 'variations on simple themes' (usually window tracery and its essential geometries).[58] There are 'ornaments as fields of force', where a seeming medley of writhing lines and knotworks – amounting to no more than a set of complex abstract patterns – is transformed into meaningful (and animal) shapes by the addition of heads and tails (for example a carpet page of the Hiberno-Saxon Book of Durrow).[59] There is 'the language of architecture' which, characteristically, discusses only what John Summerson famously called the 'Classical Language of Architecture'.[60] On the very different language of medieval architecture, bound up with the copy, the dedication and the liturgical function, Gombrich is silent, perhaps because there have been far fewer commentators on the crude approximations of medieval copies than on the subtle grammatical disciplines of classical buildings.[61] *The Sense of Order* is permeated with commentary on commentators. It is as much a study of the historiography of ornament as of ornament itself. Indeed, the two phenomena often overlap, even collide. Under the rubric of 'the Force of Habit' and 'the Psychology of Style' (the tenacity of ornamental forms and their tendency to modify but not to innovate) Gombrich calls in Riegl's *Stilfragen* (which he calls the greatest of ornamental etymologies) to suggest that the naturalistic leaf carving of the High Gothic cathedrals (e.g. Rheims, Southwell) may not be copies of nature after all, but part of a long tenacious tradition which could well find its origins in Riegl's distant acanthus and its modifications. Ornament grows out of ornament.[62] This speculation on the nature of Gothic naturalism, based on no evidence, ignores the probable origins of these leaves in spheres beyond the architectural capital: in nature itself, but also in manuscript illumination and herbals.[63] His long discourse on 'the pervasiveness of style' – the tendency of all ornamental Gothic forms to pervade every aspect of medieval life, from altarpieces to furniture and implements – is treated as yet another

     Gombrich and the Middle Ages

opportunity to mount a charge against Hegel's holism, as exemplified particularly in
Panofsky's *Gothic Architecture and Scholasticism* of 1951.[64] Yet is it only 'the force of habit'
which explains the mystery of the pervasiveness of style in a given period?

The most confusing intersection of historiography and medieval architectural
history in *The Sense of Order* comes in the section on 'Purity and Decadence'.[65] As
the title suggests, it deals with theories of decline in Gothic architecture advanced
by Ruskin, Thomas Rickman and Henri Focillon. All of them share the conviction
(though Focillon gave it a more art-historical context) that Gothic architecture
went through a pseudo-biological process of experimental birth, classic maturity
and impure decline. According to all three writers, the 'decline' in its late phase
was due to an imbalance between structure and ornament: its ornaments began
to conceal and suffocate its structure, to such an extent that the structure actually
became ornamental. Focillon went beyond Ruskin in seeing this 'loss of purity' as
an inevitable process, common to all late styles, from Baroque to *Jugendstil* – an all-
pervasive law which drove styles to their dissolution, from which state of collapse they
initiated a new cyclic phase.[66]

It is extraordinary that Gombrich, with his antipathy to historical 'laws' and
'patterns', should concur with this explanation for the decline and death of styles;
but he does, albeit in his own elusive and nimble rhetoric. Borrowing from Viollet-le-
Duc's analysis of Gothic as a skeletal system, he defines the 'ornaments' of a Gothic
elevation – its shafts, arches, colonnettes – as what he calls 'explanatory articulation':
they facilitate our grasp of the structure of the object they articulate – they form a kind
of surface shorthand for the real gravitational forces in the weight and structure of the
walls behind them.[67] So far pure Focillon and pure Viollet; and so far unexceptional in
its correctness. But then, in pursuit of a general principle of Gothic decline, Gombrich
begins to derail himself. He advances a notion of 'classic' Gothic that places him in the
company of most German art historians of the inter-war period: the 'classic' cathedrals
of Amiens and Rheims, he argues, embody a perfect but short-lived balance between
the structural clarity of the explanatory articulation and its ornamental variety; and
that balance is precarious because the ornamental elements involved are, he argues,
bound to become more and more complex, and their reconciliation more difficult.
Gombrich at this point invokes another of his conceptual categories, one borrowed
from Karl Popper, 'the logic of situations': the course of action a logical being would
choose in pursuit of a particular aim. In the case of Gothic architectural decline
Gombrich identifies the logic of situations as a set of historical facts which apply to
the development of all ornaments, including Gothic ones: ornaments tend (he argues)
to get more and more complicated, as patrons and artists single out a particular set
or type as 'critical issues' (the shaft arch system in architecture or the interlace in
Insular art). Then, equally inevitably, this process of enrichment is accelerated by
competition, by the needs of patrons and artists to overtop each other. In the history

    Paul Crossley

of Gothic architecture this enrichment has far-reaching effects on the whole building: the explanatory articulation, increasing in decorative density and complication, ceases to explain the structure behind it and becomes a semi-autonomous scaffolding, until the whole structure is smothered by elaboration (e.g. Henry VII's chapel, Westminster Abbey). At this point, when the process has reached an extreme, the style, according to Gombrich, 'has run its course of development and can go no further'. The satiety of forms is matched by 'aesthetic fatigue': the style has gone on too long to prevent boredom; it has to be replaced.[68]

I have followed Gombrich's argument here in great detail, because it represents a tendency in his scholarship to elusiveness, even to a certain logical slipperiness. What he is advancing in this narrative is a formal and biological determinism, combined with a schematic model of cultural context (competition among artists and patrons). Ornament aspires to dominance, and through dominance reaches satiety, from which state, in its exhaustion, it can only die. For Gombrich to espouse such a mechanical evolution, and combine it with a schematic cultural history, is extraordinary, given that a few pages earlier in *The Sense of Order* he had taken to task Panofsky's *Gothic Architecture and Scholasticism* as just such a deterministic explanation of architectural style.[69] The contradictions are evident to us, and probably to himself, in the tentative, highly qualified style of writing which marks out these sections. He advances the idea of stylistic saturation, of extremes going no further, but then rightly draws back: 'But is it only hindsight that makes us call it an extreme?'[70] On the same page he states that 'the idea that a style becomes 'exhausted' must always be somewhat suspect', yet on the following page he writes: 'there is no need to dismiss altogether the explanation of 'aesthetic fatigue' first proposed by Adolf Göller, for it is based on the undeniable psychological fact that the familiar tends to register less than the unfamiliar, and that the public therefore demands ever stronger stimuli.'[71] The development of ornament is 'a gradual process of accumulation brought about by creative individuals', yet he presents it here as a super-personal pathway. Under these conditions, the physical history of Gothic ornament cannot escape from Gombrich's elaborate theoretical commentary.

'Commentary' is the central subject of his last book, posthumously published, on the subject of primitive art – the *Preference for the Primitive* (2002). The book amounts to a remarkably broad and useful collection of texts and comments, from antiquity to modernity, on the visual art of the 'primitive', indeed on all antidotes to cloying charm and bland perfection. The 'primitive' embodies qualities of freshness, expressive vigour, moral purity, visual distortion and sincerity. Gombrich's history of these qualities, from Cicero to Picasso, from Greek vases to Quattrocento painting, from tribal sculpture to children's art, is dazzlingly and deliberately wide, for it amounts to another of his 'negative definitions', one that opposes kitsch or schmaltz or, indeed, the easy mastery of three-dimensional mimesis represented by High Renaissance and

Baroque art. Primitivism, like medieval art, is a foil to Gombrich's Western tradition
of illusionistic representation. Not surprisingly, medieval art figures prominently
in the book, though Gombrich is careful to acknowledge that generalizations about
'medieval art' – an art that lasted over half a millennium and comprised a vast range of
monuments and styles – 'are bound to be superficial if not misleading'.[72] Gombrich's
discussion of the 'primitive' Middle Ages begins with the espousal of flat decorative
patterning (and all its moral and spiritual implications) in the art of the nineteenth-
century neo-Gothicists, especially Ruskin and Viollet-le-Duc. And these evangelists
of a moral art were in turn drawing our attention to the flat, non-mimetic decoration
of medieval stained glass, hangings and painted ornament. As Gombrich had shown
in *The Sense of Order*, the acceptance of distortion as a means of art needed the
intermediary stage of decoration and ornament.[73] From this background Gombrich
addresses three particular issues, all of them the subject of much argument and
discussion during his student days: medieval architectural sculpture; expressionism
and German art; and the 'rediscovery of the Romanesque'. In a juxtposition that is
still stimulating, Gombrich places, firstly, Wilhelm Vöge's famous analysis of the west
front sculpture at Chartres of 1894 side by side with, secondly, *japonisme* and, thirdly,
the cultural primitivism of Gauguin. All three, he argues, had avoided suppressing
the nature of their materials in the interests of mimesis; on the contrary, they had
submitted themselves to the inherent formal values of those materials – had 'listened'
to their demands. On the west front of Chartres cathedral, figural decoration and
architectural structure are two sides of the same artistic process: the figure must never
be allowed to obscure the architectural organization of the whole.[74]

Expressionism, particularly its medieval and German variant, left Gombrich
in at least two minds. As a boy he was fascinated by its high-minded spirituality,
particularly as propounded by Dvořák's book on medieval art; but he showed a
consistent aversion to its more nationalistic manifestations, especially in Wilhelm
Worringer's popular *Abstraktion und Einfühlung* (Abstraction and Empathy) of
1908.[75] In Gombrich's eyes, Worringer's expressionism traded on chauvinism, on
emotional excess, and on a meaningless anthropomorphic definition of style, in which
all forms of medieval German art, in their linearity and restlessness, were supposed
to express the collective psychology of 'Nordic Man'. For a scholar of Gombrich's
sophisticated humanism, one who believed in art as a civilizing act, the nationalist
effusions of expressionist German artists like Nolde and Macke were anathema. They
denied intention in art, excluded rational forms of communication, and marginalized
traditional notions of skill.[76] Yet Gombrich admitted in his Autobiographical Sketch
of 1991 to an early love of Grünewald, and acknowledged the 'expressionistic' power
of a photograph of the thirteenth-century prophet Jonah in Bamberg cathedral,
with his hypnotic stare and tumultuous drapery.[77] That Gombrich, the sceptic of
expressionistic excess, could be so affected by the force of this figure is a measure of

the extraordinary power German Gothic sculpture of the early thirteenth century
(e.g. the Bamberg Rider, the Naumburg *Stifterfiguren*) exerted over the chauvinistic
imagination of inter-war German art history.[78]

If Gothic was the talisman of German expressionism, Romanesque was the
touchstone of religious art for the French and the Catalans. Romanesque fascinated
Gombrich towards the end of his life: it loomed large in his Primitivism book, and
he wrote a lengthy article on the rediscovery of the Romanesque in 1990 for Sixten
Ringbom.[79] As in his treatment of the style in *The Preference for the Primitive*, the article
is about the nineteenth- and twentieth-century reception of Romanesque, and it
opens stimulating vistas into the distortions of museum display. In André Malraux's
'Imaginary Museum', primitive objects could be stripped of their original functional
and historical identity and admired for their purely expressive formal values. With
the aid of modern lighting and careful positioning, 'primitive objects' of all kinds,
from Cycladic dolls to early Romanesque sculptures, could be brought together in the
museum to form a notional unity – a unity informed by that mysterious spirit, 'the
primitive'. All one had to do, in order to gain an intuitive contact with the life of these
images of bygone ages, was to surrender to their power. Yet, as Gombrich reminds
us, how sure could we be that our experience corresponded to the intentions of their
makers? We must not, he argues, confuse expression with communication.[80]

Gombrich's ambivalence towards the Middle Ages is especially clear in *The
Preference for the Primitive*. In the last pages of the book he returns to the theme of
Art and Illusion, and, behind it, to 'Achievement'. He distinguishes art with skilful
rendering of natural appearances to art which is in any of his many senses 'primitive',
and argues that there is a 'law of gravitation' at work, 'which pulls the untutored
artist away from the higher zones of mimetic representation towards the piecemeal
and the schematic', towards what he calls 'the base line' of image-making. The 'base
line' is the primitive, in particular children's art and medieval art, in its 'frontality'
and 'simplicity', its standardized relationships of scale and distance, its reduction in
depth. By contrast, the 'high flier', with its visual language of 'intricate complexity',
is the Western tradition of representation.[81] He makes the point in *The Preference
for the Primitive* by means of language, an analogy based on a linguistic insight of
Roman Jakobson, though it is no less denigratory: the complex range of emotion,
relationship and expression in Renaissance and post-Renaissance art is paralleled
in the rich markers of time, colour, feeling and space to be found in the languages
of native, predominantly European, speakers. In contrast, the abrupt simplicity of
the foreigner's language reminds us of the crudities of child art or the simplicities
of 'primitive' images.[82] Gombrich exemplifies this process of downward gravitation,
from naturalism to the primitive, by a comparison between the Liège font of the
early twelfth century, with its classical, individualistic and 'eye-witness conception'
of the human figure, over and against the 'primitive' Romanesque font from Castle

Frome parish church of c. 1170, the latter an abstracted mass of writhing interlace.[83] Asked if his concentration on the Western tradition of naturalism implied that he thought naturalistic art more valid than other kinds of art, Gombrich vehemently denied the charge; yet these categorizations hardly bear him out. In fact, mimesis had the qualities of the heroic for him: 'the more we become aware of the enormous pull in man to repeat what he has learned', he notes in *Art and Illusion*, 'the greater will be our admiration for those exceptional beings who could break this spell and make a significant advance on which others could build'.[84] It was this sacred discontent, this desire to break with tradition, which was, for him, 'the leaven of the Western Mind since the Renaissance, and which pervades our art no less than our science'.[85]

It would, however, be a caricature of Gombrich's writing to dismiss him, as some recent commentators have done, as having a largely negative attitude to the Middle Ages – as seeing the period as an obstacle in the history of painting, 'rolling inexorably towards Constable and naturalism'.[86] On the contrary, Gombrich's astonishing range of understanding opened to him the achievements of the Middle Ages with a clarity unmatched by even the most professional medievalist. The schema of the Middle Ages threw into sharper relief the originality of post-Renaissance art. The skill of the high flier might no longer have been needed or practised in seventh-century Britain, but skill of another kind was not lost, namely the marvellous abstractions of the Insular carpet page. And skill in 'selective naturalism' – making studies from nature and applying them to pictures – characterizes the burgeoning realism of later medieval art. The medieval conceptual image helped to emancipate new formal values, conveying supernatural and didactic truths. The abstractions of medieval art express impulses and ideas more readily than naturalistic images. Formal and psychological novelties were shaped in the High Gothic cathedrals; and it was out of the 'medieval' realities of Trecento sculpture that Giotto fashioned his revolution. Between these two phenomena, the medieval primitive and the Renaissance explorer, there is little sense of negotiation, at least in Gombrich's work. He was content to lay them out and leave them there, for others, like ourselves, to separate or join. In a conversation with Hayden White at Cornell in 1971 Gombrich was asked whether he had a 'dialectical' conception of the interaction between different stylistic traditions. Hating the word 'dialectic', Gombrich's reply categorically distanced itself from the metaphysical, Hegelian notion of 'dialectic' and also from its logical meaning, as that which reconciles two contradictions. He preferred, he told White, to use the musical word 'symphonic': every theme that turns up in the history of Western art has a relation to what goes before it and sometimes to what comes after it. The theme acquires its meaning partly from this symphonic relation within the history of art.[87] The Middle Ages performs exactly this function in Gombrich's vision of art history – the modest enabler which enlightens, by its opposition, the achievements of Western art, and which threads its way into that naturalistic tradition as both an enemy and an ally.

1 E.H. Gombrich, 'Paintings for Altars. Their Evolution, Ancestry and Progeny', in Gombrich, *The Uses of Images: Studies in the Social Function of Art and Visual Communication*, London, 1999, pp. 48-79; first published in *Evolution and its Influence*, ed. Alan Grafen, Oxford, 1989, pp. 107-25.

2 E.H. Gombrich, 'Images as Luxury Objects. Supply and Demand in the Evolution of the International Gothic Style', in *Uses of Images* (n. 1 above), pp. 80-107.

3 E.H. Gombrich, 'From Archaeology to Art History. Some Stages in the Rediscovery of the Romanesque', in *Icon to Cartoon: A Tribute to Sixten Ringbom*, ed. M. T. Knapas and A. Ringbom, *Kunsthistorikar Studier*, 16, 1990, pp. 91-108.

4 E.H. Gombrich, 'Achievement in Medieval Art', in Gombrich, *Meditations on a Hobby Horse and Other Essays on the Theory of Art*, London, 1963, pp. 70-77; tr. Michael Podro of 'Wertprobleme und mittelalterliche Kunst', *Kritische Berichte zur kunstgeschichtlichen Literatur*, 6, 3-4, 1937, pp. 109-16.

5 E.H. Gombrich, *A Little History of the World*, New Haven and London, 2005, pp. 110-14, 123-162; tr. Caroline Mustill of *Eine kurze Weltgeschichte für junge Leser: von der Urzeit bis zur Gegenwart*, Cologne, 1985 (1st edn *Weltgeschichte von der Urzeit bis zur Gegenwart*, Vienna, 1936).

6 E.H. Gombrich, *The Story of Art*, London, 1950, pp. 91-98, 109-60.

7 E.H. Gombrich, 'An Autobiographical Sketch', in *The Essential Gombrich*, ed. R. Woodfield, London, 1996, pp. 21-36 (p. 24).

8 Ibid., pp. 24-25.

9 F. Wickhoff, *Die Wiener Genesis*, Vienna 1895. See also Gombrich's comments on 'the great Franz Wickhoff' in E.H. Gombrich, *Art and Illusion: a Study in the Psychology of Pictorial Representation*, London, 1960, p. 15 and note, p. 337.

10 A. Riegl, *Stilfragen. Grundlegungen zu einer Geschichte der Ornamentik*, Berlin 1893, tr. E. Kain as *Problems of Style: Foundations for a History of Ornament*, Princeton, 1992. For Gombrich's views on the interrelationship between Wickhoff, Heinrich Wölfflin and Riegl see his 'Kunstwissenschaft', in *Das Atlantisbuch der Kunst. Ein Enzyklopädie der bildenden Künste*, Zurich, 1952, pp. 653-63. See also Gombrich's discussion of the importance of psychology during his student days in Vienna, in E.H. Gombrich, 'Kunstwissenschaft und Psychologie vor fünfzig Jahren', *Akten des XXV Internationalen Kongresses für Kunstgeschichte*, Vienna, Cologne, Graz, 1984, pp. 99-104; tr. Gombrich as 'Art History and Psychology in Vienna Fifty Years Ago', and published online at *The Gombrich Archive*, ed. Richard Woodfield, http://www.gombrich. co.uk. Gombrich refers to his student paper on Riegl's *Stilfragen* in Gombrich, 'Autobiographical Sketch' (n. 7 above), p. 26.

11 M. Dvořák, *Kunstgeschichte als Geistesgeschichte. Studien zur abendländischen Kunstentwicklung*, Munich, 1924; tr. R.J. Klawiter as *Idealism and Naturalism in Gothic Art*, University of Notre Dame, 1967. Gombrich, 'Autobiographical Sketch' (n. 7 above), p. 23.

12 Gombrich, 'Autobiographical Sketch' (n. 7 above), p. 26. See E.H. Gombrich, 'Ritualized Gesture and Expression in Art', *Philosophical Transactions of the Royal Society of London*, 251, 1966, pp. 393-401; republished under the same title in Gombrich, *The Image and the Eye. Further Studies in the Psychology of Pictorial Representation*, Oxford 1982, pp. 63-77.

13 H. Sedlmayr, *Die Entstehung der Kathedrale*, Zurich, 1950. For Sedlmayr's place in the so-called Second Vienna School see C. Wood, ed., *The Vienna School Reader. Politics and Art Historical Method in the 1930s*, New York, 2003, pp. 35-72.

14 Gombrich, 'Autobiographical Sketch' (n. 7 above), p. 27.

15 J. von Schlosser, *Die Kunstliteratur: ein Handbuch zur Quellenkunde der Neueren Kunstgeschichte*, Vienna, 1924. See Gombrich's obituary of his teacher in *The Burlington Magazine*, LXXIV, 1939, pp. 98-99.

16 J. von Schlosser, *Die Kunst des Mittelalters*, Berlin 1923. Gombrich, *Art and Illusion* (n. 9 above), p. 19.

17 Gombrich, 'Autobiographical Sketch' (n. 7 above), p. 25.

18 E.H. Gombrich, *Giulio Romano als Architekt*, PhD dissertation, University of Vienna; partly published as 'Zum Werke Giulio Romanos', *Jahrbuch der kunsthistorischen Sammlungen in Wien*, N.F. 8, 1934 and 9, 1935. Gombrich,

'Autobiographical Sketch' (n. 7 above), pp. 27-30.

19 For a summary of his work with Kris, see Gombrich, 'Kunstwissenschaft und Psychologie' (n. 10 above), and Gombrich, 'Autobiographical Sketch' (n. 7 above), p. 30. See also E.H. Gombrich, 'The Study of Art and the Study of Man: Reminiscences of Collaboration with Ernst Kris (1900-1957)', in Gombrich, *Tributes: Interpreters of our Cultural Tradition*, Oxford, 1984, pp. 220-33.

20 Gombrich, 'Autobiographical Sketch' (n. 7 above), pp. 25-26.

21 E.H. Gombrich, 'Eine verkannte karolingische Pyxis im Wiener Kunsthistorischen Museum', *Jahrbuch der kunsthistorischen Sammlungen in Wien*, N.F. 7, 1933, pp. 1-14, and Gombrich, 'Autobiographical Sketch' (n. 7 above), p. 25.

22 Gombrich, 'Autobiographical Sketch' (n. 7 above), pp. 25-26.

23 Gombrich, 'Achievement' (n. 4 above), p. 72: 'Quite enough has been written by interpreters of mediaeval art about expressive lines, giving, that is, a graphological interpretation'. In E.H. Gombrich, *The Sense of Order: a Study in the Psychology of Decorative Art*, Oxford, 1979, p. 202, Gombrich criticizes the way Riegl's perceptive study of early medieval linear ornament had become 'vulgarized and sensationalized' in the writings of Wilhelm Worringer, and Oswald Spengler. The latter was adopted by National Socialism as a prophet of nationalistic resurgence, the former became the guru of German expressionism and one of the most influential apologists for medieval expressionist art and its supposedly nationalist character. For Worringer's influence on inter-war German art history see *Invisible Cathedrals. The Expressionist Art History of Wilhelm Worringer*, ed. N. H. Donahue, Pennsylvania, 1995. Gombrich's most extensive polemic against Worringer and the Expressionists can be found in E.H. Gombrich, *The Preference for the Primitive: Episodes in the History of Western Taste and Art*, London, 2002, pp. 219-33.

24 For the German title of Dvořák's book, see n. 11 above. Gombrich, 'Autobiographical Sketch' (n. 7 above), pp. 28-30. Dvořák's work also comes in for criticism on just this point in Gombrich's classic anti-Hegelian broadside:

E.H. Gombrich, *In Search of Cultural History*, the Philip Maurice Deneke Lecture, Oxford, 1969; reprinted in E.H. Gombrich, *Ideals and Idols: Essays on Values in History and in Art*, Oxford, 1979, pp. 24-59 (p. 44).

25 Gombrich, 'Autobiographical Sketch' (n. 7 above), pp. 34-35.

26 Ibid., pp. 23-24.

27 E. von Garger, 'Über Wertungsschwierigkeiten bei mittelalterlicher Kunst', *Kritische Berichte zur Kunstgeschtlichen Literatur*, 1932-33.

28 Gombrich, 'Achievement' (n. 4 above).

29 Gombrich, 'Achievement' (n. 4 above), p. 74.

30 K. Popper, *The Poverty of Historicism*, London, 1959, p. 28.

31 Gombrich, *Art and Illusion* (n. 9 above), pp. 16-18.

32 Gombrich, 'Achievement' (n. 4 above), pp. 75-76.

33 Gombrich, *Art and Illusion* (n. 9 above), especially pp. 16-25.

34 E.H. Gombrich, 'Preface', in *Hobby Horse* (n. 4 above), p. XI.

35 Gombrich, *Sense of Order* (n. 23 above), passim.

36 Riegl, *Stilfragen* (n. 10 above).

37 A. Riegl, *Spätrömische Kunstindustrie*, Vienna, 1901; tr. R. Winkes as *Late Roman Art Industry*, Rome, 1985.

38 M. Podro, *The Critical Historians of Art*, New Haven and London, 1982, pp. 71-97.

39 Gombrich, 'Achievement' (n. 4 above), 72-73; Gombrich, *Sense of Order* (n. 23 above), pp. 197-204. The issues are discussed in relation to 20th-century abstraction in E.H. Gombrich, 'Expression and Communication', in *Hobby Horse* (n. 4 above), pp. 56-69.

40 Gombrich, *Sense of Order* (n. 23 above), pp. 155-59 (p. 158).

41 Gombrich, 'Achievement' (n. 4 above), p. 75.

42 Ibid., pp. 73-74.

43 Gombrich, *Art and Illusion* (n. 9 above), pp. 248-50. See also Gombrich, *Story of Art* (n. 6 above), p. 118: 'when the medieval artist of this period had no model to copy, he drew rather like a child'.

44 Gombrich, 'Achievement' (n. 4 above), p. 74.

45 Ibid., pp. 74-75. For Gombrich's other examples of this process – Japonisme, folk art and the 'intrinsic values of the Romanesque' – see Gombrich, *Primitive* (n. 23 above), pp. 177-94.

46 Gombrich, *Primitive* (n. 23 above), pp. 188-89.

47 Gombrich, 'Achievement' (n. 4 above), p. 75, and nn. 8 and 9, p. 75.

48 Gombrich, 'Achievement' (n. 4 above), p. 76. R. Wollheim, *Art and its Objects,* 2nd edn, Cambridge, 1980, pp. 93-96.

49 Gombrich, *Primitive* (n. 23 above), p. 233.

50 Ibid., pp. 195, 214-33 (p. 229).

51 Gombrich, *Art and Illusion* (n. 9 above), p. 67, see also pp. 247-49.

52 P. Binski, '"Working by Words Alone". The Architect, Scholasticism and Rhetoric in Thirteenth-century France', in M. Carruthers, ed., *Rhetoric Beyond Words. Delight and Persuasion in the Arts of the Middle Ages,* Cambridge, 2010, pp. 14-51.

53 F. Woodman, *The Architectural History of Canterbury Cathedral*, London, Boston and Henley, 1981, pp. 87-117 (p. 92).

54 Gombrich, *Story of Art* (n. 6 above), pp. 137, 147.

55 E.H. Gombrich, 'Images as Luxury Objects. Supply and Demand in the Evolution of the International Gothic Style', in *Uses of Images* (n. 1 above), pp. 80-107.

56 Gombrich, *Sense of Order* (n. 23 above), pp. 82-3, 145-8.

57 Ibid., pp. 63-94.

58 Ibid., pp. 82-3, 145-48.

59 Ibid., pp. 155-58, 175-80.

60 J. Summerson, *The Classical Language of Architecture*, London, 1963.

61 The classic study of medieval architectural copies is R. Krautheimer, 'Introduction to an Iconography of Medieval Architecture', *Journal of the Warburg and Courtauld Institutes,* v, 1942, pp. 1-33.

62 Gombrich, *Sense of Order* (n. 23 above), pp. 171-216 (pp. 188-89).

63 The nature of 'Gothic naturalism' is discussed in J. Givens, *Observation and Image-Making in Gothic Art*, Cambridge 2005, especially pp. 5-36.

64 Gombrich, *Sense of Order* (n. 23 above), pp. 197-200.

65 Ibid., pp. 206-09, 211.

66 Ibid., pp. 205-06, where Gombrich quotes extensively from H. Focillon, *The Art of the West in the Middle Ages*, ed. and intr. J. Bony, tr. D. King, London, 1963 (1st edn, H. Focillon, *Art d'Occident: le moyen âge, roman et gothique*, Paris, 1938).

67 Gombrich, *Sense of Order* (n. 23 above), pp. 209, 211, and p. 199 for Viollet-le-Duc.

68 Ibid., p. 209.

69 Ibid., pp. 199-200.

70 Ibid., pp. 211-12.

71 Ibid., p. 211.

72 Gombrich, *Primitive* (n. 23 above), p. 291.

73 Ibid., pp. 188-89.

74 Ibid., pp. 188-90, 191-95.

75 W. Worringer, *Abstraktion und Einfühlung: ein Beitrag zur Stilpsychologie*, Munich, 1908. See above n. 23. For Dvořák see above, n. 24.

76 Gombrich, *Primitive* (n. 23 above), pp. 221-29.

77 Gombrich, 'Autobiographical Sketch' (n. 7 above) pp. 23-24. Gombrich, *Primitive* (n. 23 above), p. 229.

78 For the political uses of this 'Staufer' sculpture in Germany, exploited especially by National Socialism between the world wars, see K. Brush, 'The Naumburg Master: a Chapter in the Development of Medieval Art History', *Gazette des Beaux-Arts,* 6th series, 122, 1993, pp. 109-22. Also W. Sauerländer, ' Die Naumburg Stifterfiguren. Rückblick und Fragen', in *Die Zeit der Staufer. Geschichte, Kunst, Kultur. Katalog der Ausstellung,* Stuttgart, 1979, pp. 169-245.

79 See above, n. 3.

80 Gombrich, *Primitive* (n. 23 above), pp. 229-33.

81 Ibid., pp. 280-91 (p. 280).

82 Ibid., pp. 280-81.

83 Ibid., p. 291.

84 Gombrich, *Art and Illusion* (n. 9 above), p. 20.

85 Ibid., p. 148.

86 C. Wood, 'Introduction', in *Otto Pächt. The Practice of Art History. Reflections on Method,* tr. D. Britt, London 1999, pp. 9-18 (p. 12).

87 'Interview: Ernst Gombrich', *Diacritics*, I, 1971, pp. 47-51; available online at *The Gombrich Archive* (n. 10 above).

Gombrich and the Idea of Primitive Art*

PAUL TAYLOR

THE CONCEPT OF 'PRIMITIVE ART' acts as a kind of frame to Gombrich's career as an art historian. The first chapter of his first art historical book, *The Story of Art*, was devoted to 'Prehistoric and Primitive Peoples',[1] while his last, posthumous volume, *The Preference for the Primitive*, was an historical account of the growing appreciation for 'primitive art' in the nineteenth and twentieth centuries.[2] And in his two intervening major works, *Art and Illusion* and *The Sense of Order*, Gombrich returned frequently to 'primitive art' and the related subject of evolution in the arts. In *The Sense of Order* the designs of 'primitive' peoples are treated incidentally, in the context of discussions of the meanings of decorative motifs;[3] but in *Art and Illusion* the idea that some art can be called 'primitive' underpins much of the central argument of the book. In his discussion of the stereotype and the schema, Gombrich stresses the difficulty which an illusionist artist must encounter as he tries to free himself from the sway of 'primitive' modes of representation.[4]

In the course of his career Gombrich employed the term 'primitive art' in three different but, as he saw it, related senses. In *The Preference for the Primitive*, much of his attention was devoted to early Renaissance and medieval art. He argued that the interest in non-European art which grew up at the end of the nineteenth century would have been unlikely to have taken place if earlier collectors had not developed a taste for 'i primitivi'; that 'just as the appreciation of pre-Renaissance art began with the immediate predecessors of Raphael, and led slowly through Perugino to Fra Angelico and Giotto, so Japanese masters of the colour print led art lovers gradually to the more authentic styles of Asia, before arriving in Oceania and Africa.'[5]

Besides using the word 'primitive' to refer to Trecento and Quattrocento masters, Gombrich also used the word to refer to the art of pre- and proto-literate peoples. The edges of this category were inevitably blurred in his writings, as in the writings of other authors. While acknowledging that the Maya were a literate, urban people with a sophisticated grasp of astronomy, he nevertheless thought it worthwhile to compare their art to the works of other 'primitive' cultures, perhaps because of the 'mysterious', 'gruesome', 'weird', 'unnatural', 'strange', 'uncanny' nature of their decoration – I take these adjectives from the three pages of *The Story of Art* which describe the arts of pre-Columbian Mesoamerica and Peru.[6] But while he was not entirely sure if the Maya and the Aztecs should be called primitive, he clearly felt that the native peoples of sub-Saharan Africa, Oceania, Australia, and North America could justly be characterized in this way.

At the same time, Gombrich repeatedly stressed that he did not mean his talk of primitivism to imply any kind of mental inferiority. He dismissed the notion that the 'mental equipment of primitive man' is 'distinct from that of civilized man',[7] observing that 'there are few historians today, and even fewer anthropologists, who believe that mankind has undergone any marked biological change within historical periods'.[8] In making such statements he wished strongly to dissociate himself from the theories of racial evolutionism which had been common in intellectual circles in his youth, and which, as Gombrich put it, had 'weaken[ed] resistance to totalitarian habits of mind.'[9]

The third meaning which Gombrich attached to 'primitive art' was more closely associated with the theories of *Art and Illusion*. Gombrich held the view that 'the works of untutored adults, children and primitives', hold certain features in common, and that any art, such as the art of ancient Greece, that wishes to progress towards illusionism must learn to overcome these features.[10] For Gombrich, untutored adults, children and primitives depict the world using schemata, or conceptual modes, and the conquest of naturalism takes place as artists gradually accumulate corrections to these primitive schemata by observing reality.[11] Or, as Gombrich put it in *The Preference for the Primitive*, 'What I propose to argue is that mimetic art shares certain characteristics with the skill of flying. It involves surmounting the natural pulls that have dominated image-making in all "primitive" cultures.'[12]

Primitives, children and untutored adults, in Gombrich's view, do not merely fail to depict reality in an accurate manner. He also claimed that they make very similar mistakes. This was an idea that he had learned when he was a student, during lectures at the University of Vienna from the Professor of Classical Archaeology there at that time, Emanuel Löwy.[13] Gombrich thought that Löwy's book *The Rendering of Nature in Early Greek Art* contained 'most of what is worth preserving in evolutionism'. In this book Löwy observed that, to use Gombrich's words, 'the primitive artist, like the child … will tend to represent the human body frontally, horses in profile, and lizards from above' (see fig. 1).[14]

This is a more concrete, and also a simpler formulation than Löwy's own; Löwy wrote that 'as a general rule the figures are shown to the spectator with each of their parts in its broadest aspect, as we shall express it for the present'.[15] Löwy claimed that this method of representation could be found 'in every primitive art of the present as well as the past'.[16]

Gombrich asserted in *Art and Illusion* that 'Loewy's analysis of these archaic modes is still basically accepted', but cited only one article, by Meyer Schapiro, in support of this claim.[17] Is it then true, to use Gombrich's formulation, that 'the primitive artist,

    Gombrich and the Idea of Primitive Art

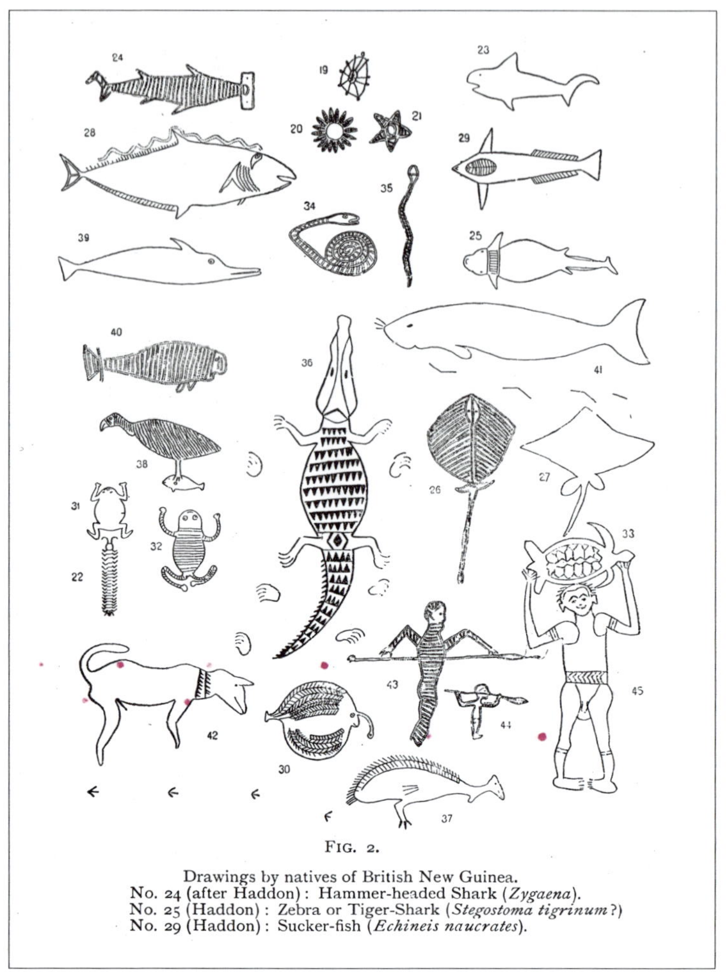

FIG. 2.

Drawings by natives of British New Guinea.
No. 24 (after Haddon) : Hammer-headed Shark (*Zygaena*).
No. 25 (Haddon) : Zebra or Tiger-Shark (*Stegostoma tigrinum*?)
No. 29 (Haddon) : Sucker-fish (*Echineis naucrates*).

FIG. 1 'Drawings by natives of British New Guinea', from Emanuel Loewy,
The Rendering of Nature in early Greek Art, London 1907, fig. 2

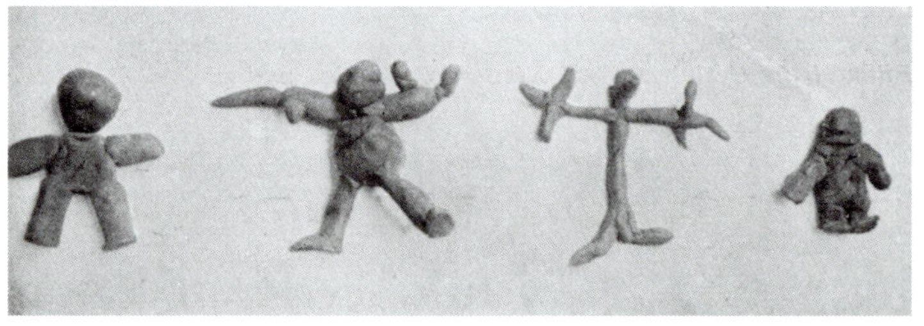

FIG. 2 Sculpture by 4-5 year old children, from Oskar Wulff,
Die Kunst des Kindes, Stuttgart, 1927, plate XIX

     Paul Taylor

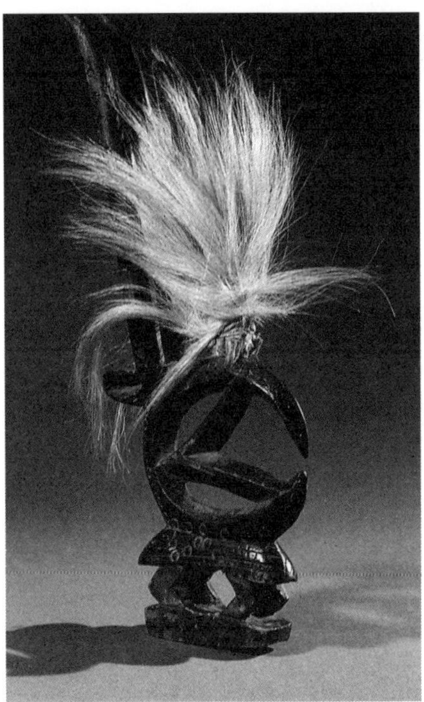

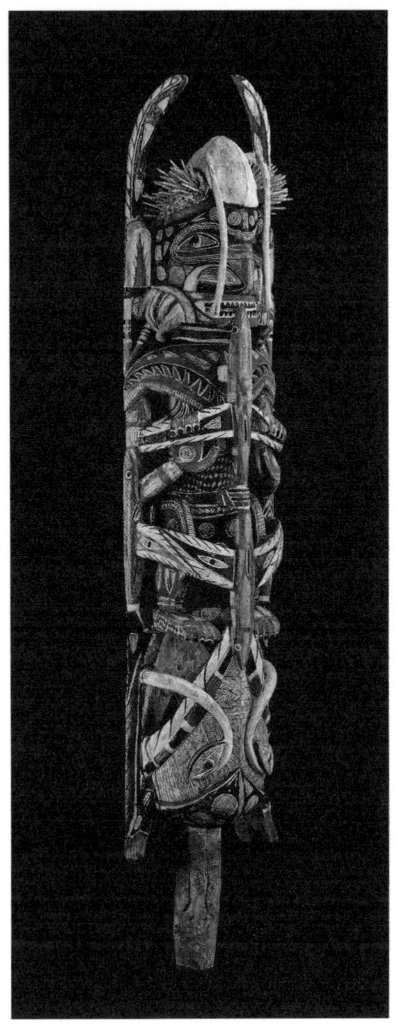

FIG. 3 Bamana, near Ouélessébougou, Mali, Wooden carved upright mask in the form of a stylized antelope or two other animals with long white hair bound on to the horns, 1st half 20th century, 44 cm high, British Museum, Dept of Africa, Oceania and the Americas, Af1953,04.7

FIG. 4 New Ireland, Malagan, Male figure, 19th century, 142 cm high, British Museum, Dept of Africa, Oceania and the Americas, Oc1884,0728.49

like the child … will tend to represent the human body frontally, horses in profile, and lizards from above'?

The first response we might make to this question is that it obviously implies that the representations in question are two-dimensional; and yet the vast majority of surviving 'primitive' art is three-dimensional. In *Art and Illusion* Gombrich did not draw a clear distinction between painting and sculpture, a failing he candidly acknowledged in *The Preference for the Primitive*.[18] This failing is a serious one for the comparison, which he repeatedly makes, between child art and 'primitive' art. There is relatively little child sculpture (fig. 2), and what there is does not look much like 'primitive' sculpture (figs. 3, 4 and 5). Not, of course, that 'primitive' sculpture

     Gombrich and the Idea of Primitive Art

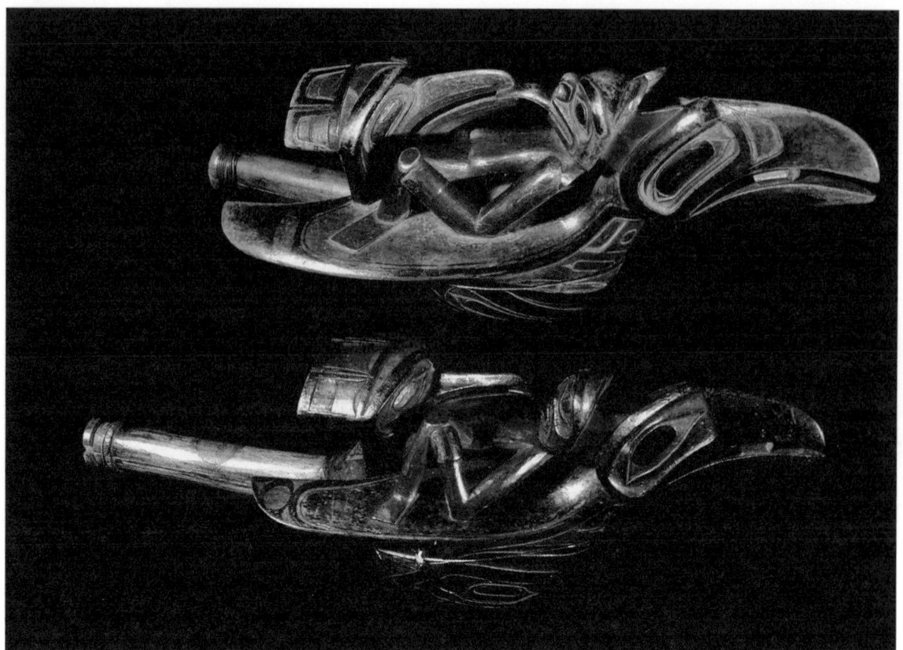

resembles itself very much either; there is quite as much variety in the art of pre-literate
societies as there is in the art of literate societies. The whole category of 'primitive art'
is as formless as the category 'civilized art' would be, if anyone cared to use it.

However, let us accept Gombrich's argument on its own terms, and examine
two-dimensional imagery. Is it the case that 'primitive' draughtsmen and
painters depict humans from in front, horses from the side and lizards
from above?

The claim that in 'primitive art' humans are generally depicted from in front
seems to me highly questionable. For a start, humans are not often represented in
two-dimensional 'primitive' art, but when they do appear in large numbers, as in
certain African rock paintings, they are shown in many different ways. In the San
Bushman painting in fig. 6 we see figures who, as can be seen from the direction of
their feet, are clearly viewed from the side.[19] In another example, a painting made on a
cave wall in the Sahara over 7,000 years ago (fig. 7), we see figures in what appears to
be three-quarter view, and down at the bottom of the image there are also some figures
who appear to be both viewed from the side and swimming.[20] In paintings on ceramics
in Moche Peru (fig. 8), humans are usually shown with their heads in profile, their
legs in profile, but their torsoes seen from in front, although sometimes a full profile

     Paul Taylor

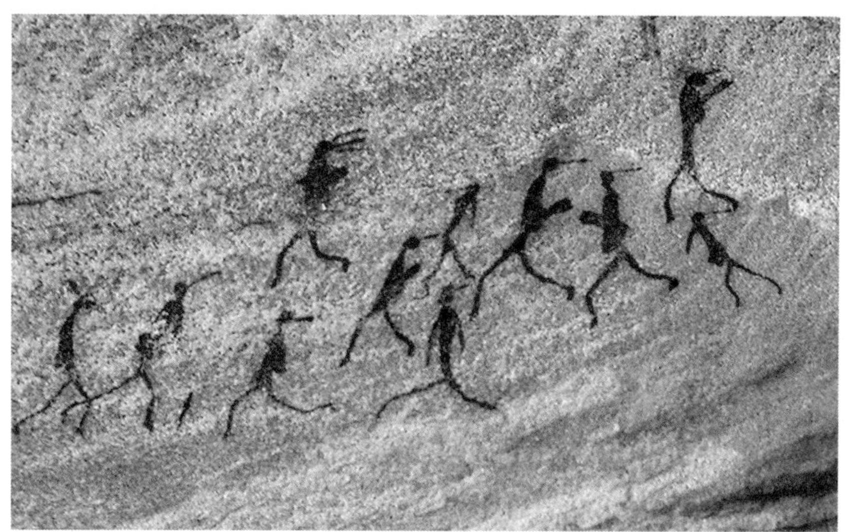

FIG. 6 South Africa, Western Cape Province, Perdekop Farm, near Mossel Bay, Bushman painting. Photo: Andrew Moir

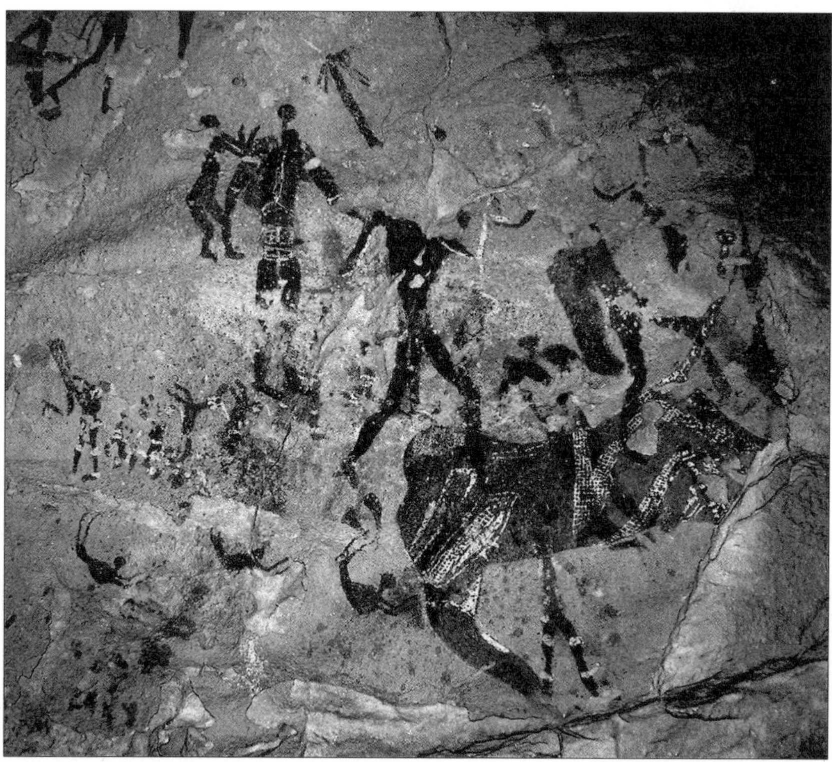

FIG. 7 Gilf Kebir. Photo: Jean-Loic LeQuellec

   Gombrich and the Idea of Primitive Art

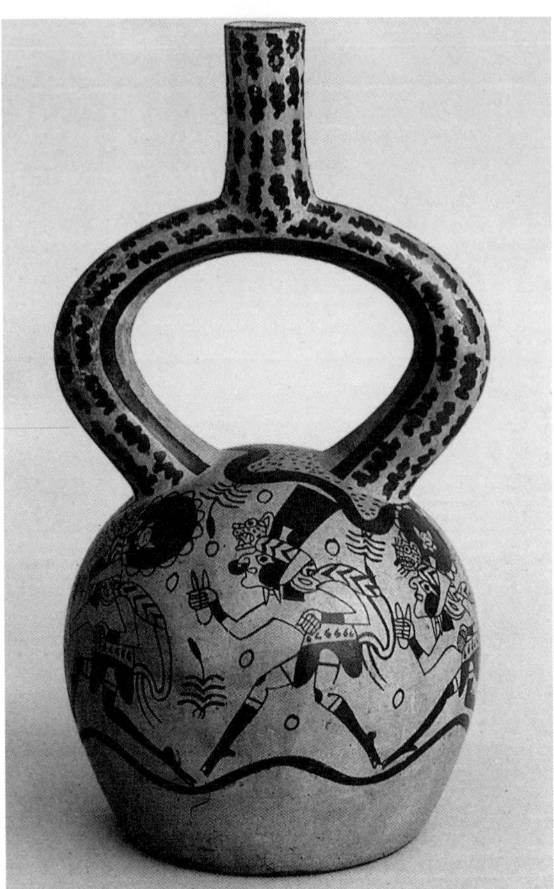

view can be seen.[21] There are no three-quarter views in Moche painting, but there are
almost no depictions from the front, either.[22]

Turning to Gombrich's claim concerning horses: these are vanishingly rare in
the arts of Africa, Oceania and the Americas, for the simple reason that they were
unknown in most parts of these regions until Europeans arrived.[23] Löwy does not
give horses as an example of 'primitive' representation; the idea seems to have been
Gombrich's own. Perhaps he was thinking of the well-known horses of European
Palaeolithic art; and if he was, then indeed he was right that they are invariably
depicted from the side. It is also true that children tend to depict horses from the side,
though many exceptions can be found to this rule: young children in particular can
depict horses in strikingly different ways, some of them barely intelligible (fig. 9).

Nevertheless, the great majority not only of horses but also of other mammals, in
child art as well as in 'primitive' art, *are* depicted from the side. Indeed in European
Palaeolithic painting I know of only one divergence from this general rule, a turning

     Paul Taylor

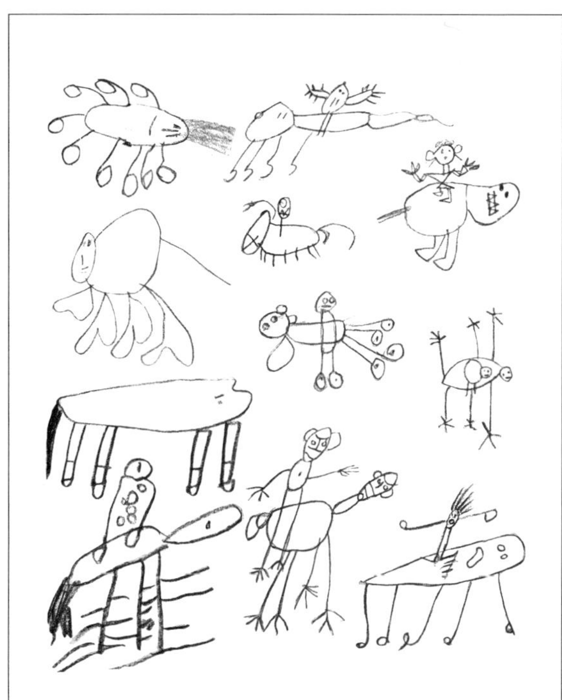

bison in Chauvet cave,[24] although, in the relief ivories of the period, examples can be found of animals turning their heads round on the flat plane.[25]

As for lizards: the great majority of those I have found are indeed seen from above (figs. 10, 11 and 12), although there are a few exceptions (fig. 13).[26] So of Gombrich's three claims concerning 'primitive' two-dimensional art, one seems to me to be dubious, but two to be largely accurate. How are we to explain this apparent uniformity in 'primitive' animal representations across the globe?

Emanuel Löwy argued that the very universality of 'primitive' modes of representation 'rules out of court any theory in which deliberate intent or purpose plays a part'.[27] He maintained that an explanation for the phenomenon must be found in the nature of human psychology, and in particular in what he took to be universal characteristics of memorizing. He argued that 'primitive' artists were representing a condensed mental image that allowed an object to be remembered more efficiently. To express it in his own words, 'As the result of the visual impressions which we have received from numerous examples of the same object, there remains fixed in our minds a memory-picture, which is no other than the Platonic Idea of the object, namely, a typical picture, clear of everything individual and accidental'.[28] It is this 'memory-picture' which the 'primitive' artist, and the child and the untutored civilized artist, attempt to portray.

     Gombrich and the Idea of Primitive Art

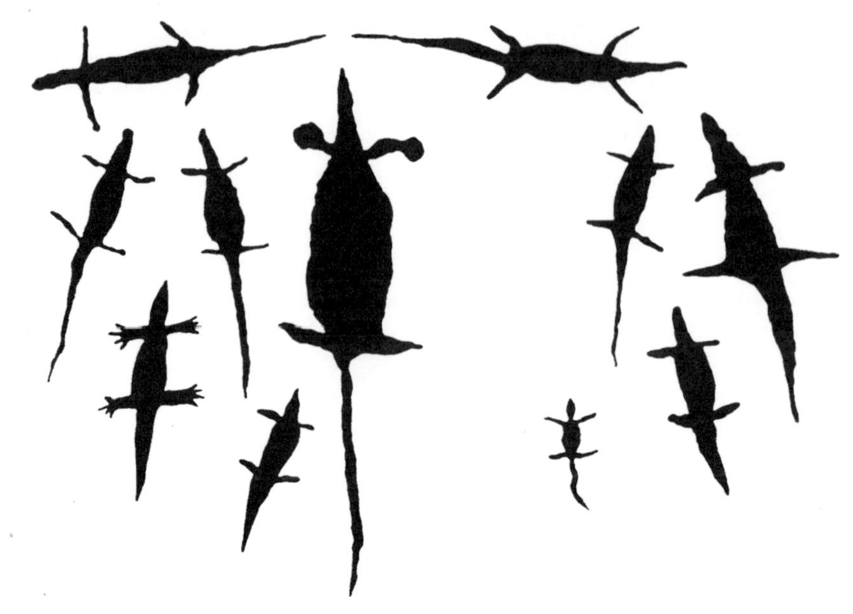

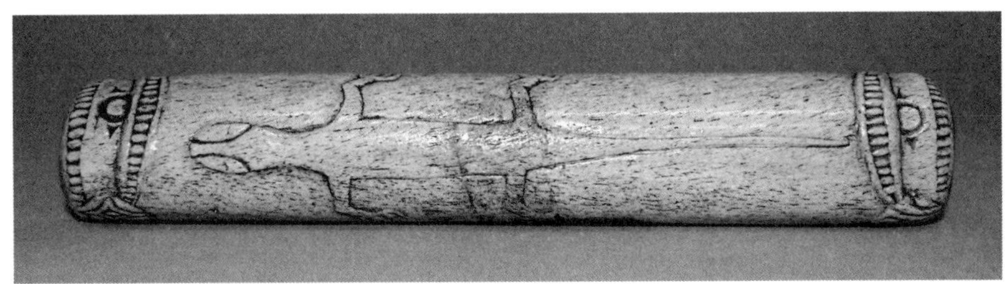

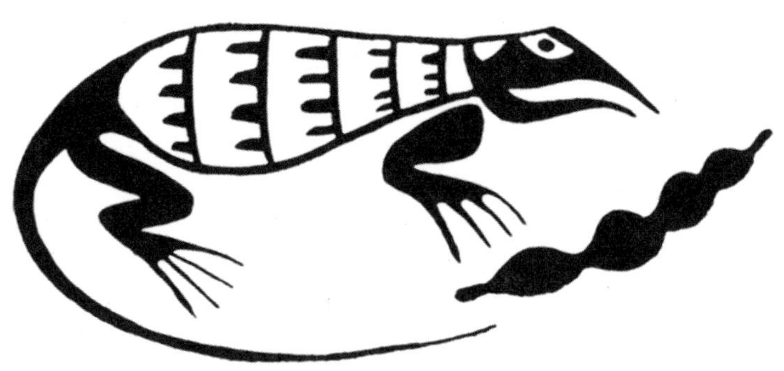

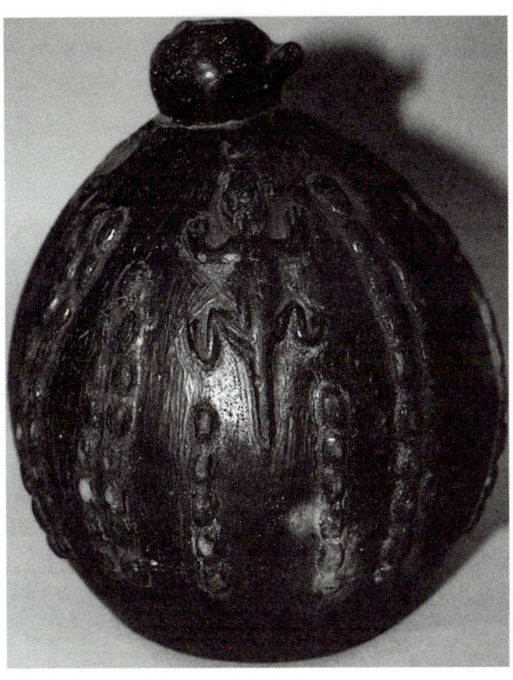

Gombrich was sceptical of this part of Löwy's theory, writing in *Art and Illusion* that 'Loewy's … explanation is really circular: since the primitive artist obviously does not copy the outside world, he is believed to copy some invisible inside world of mental images. For these mental images, in their turn, however, the typical pictures of primitives are the only evidence. None of us, I believe, carries in his head such schematic pictures of bodies, horses, or lizards as Loewy's theory postulates.' Nevertheless, he felt that Löwy had achieved a fundamental insight: 'this criticism cannot detract from the value of Loewy's analysis of those features which the works of children, untutored adults, and primitives have in common. By taking as his subject not the evolution of mankind but the first occasion in history when these features were slowly and methodically eliminated in early Greek art, Loewy taught us to appreciate the forces which have to be overcome by an art aiming at the illusion of reality.'[29]

Talk of 'the forces which have to be overcome' leads us back to Gombrich's own theory that 'primitive' artists are under 'the sway of the stereotype'.[30] As he puts it, 'What is normal to man and child all over the globe is the reliance on schemata, on what is called "conceptual art".'[31] Illusionistic art can only come about after a long, cumulative and necessarily slow series of corrections to these original schemata. And what is more, the schemata are always there, waiting to lure the illusionist artist towards representational error. In Gombrich's words: 'There is a law of gravitation here which pulls the untutored artist away from the higher zones of mimetic

     Gombrich and the Idea of Primitive Art

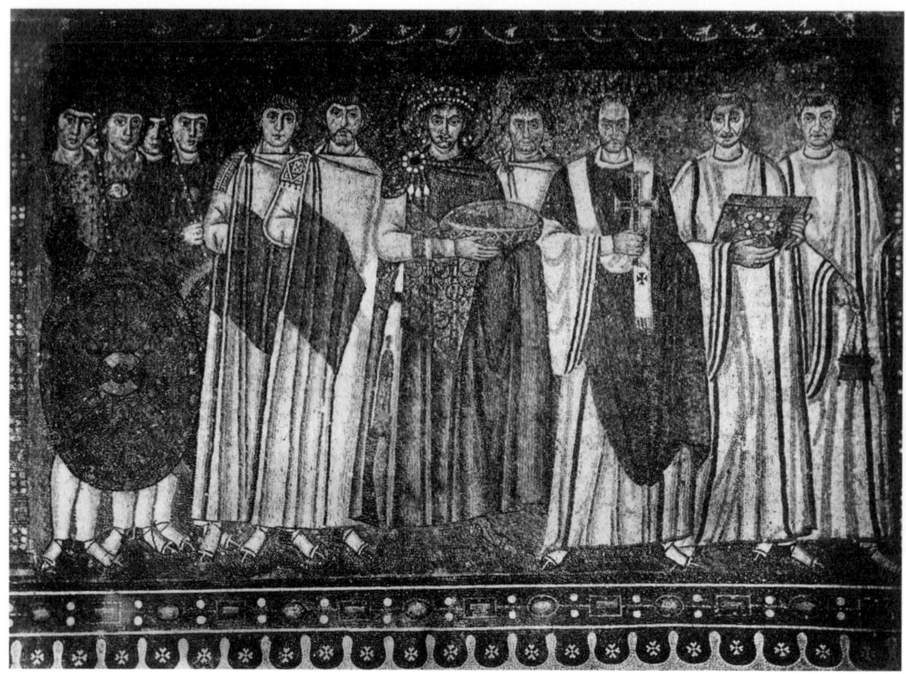

relationships towards the piecemeal and schematic, towards the base line.'[32] In *Art and Illusion*, when discussing the emergence of early Christian art, he writes: 'The schema was not criticized and corrected, and so it followed the natural pull towards the minimum stereotype, the "gingerbread figure" of peasant art.'[33]

He illustrated that remark with the celebrated mosaic of Justinian and his retinue in Ravenna (fig. 14). We may well quibble with his reductive aesthetic judgment;[34] but for now let us ask a more pressing question: what exactly *is* this schema? Gombrich uses the word 'schema' throughout *Art and Illusion*, but what did he mean by it?[35]

Clearly, it cannot be a picture or a mental image in the mind of the artist. As we have just seen, Gombrich criticised Löwy's theory for its circularity; he observed that while Löwy thought that 'primitive' artists were copying mental images, there was in fact no evidence for these mental images beyond the work of 'primitive' artists. He also added, to repeat, 'None of us, I believe, carries in his head such schematic pictures of bodies, horses, or lizards as Loewy's theory postulates'. Clearly then the schema also cannot be construed as a 'schematic picture'.

Gombrich must I think have understood the schema as a kind of mental disposition, of an involuntary or semi-voluntary kind. Quite how such a disposition might work in practice is probably best shown by one of Gombrich's most telling

     Paul Taylor

psychological examples. In *Art and Illusion* he described the celebrated experiment, conducted by Robert Thouless in the early 1930s, which revealed one of the 'perceptual constancies' that distort the way we see the world. Subjects were shown a coin lying at an angle on a table, and were then asked to pick from a sequence of ellipses of different sizes the ellipse which corresponded most closely to the foreshortened circle they had just seen. People, it transpired, invariably picked ellipses which were too circular, a phenomenon which Thouless called 'phenomenal regression to the real object'.[36]

On the face of it, the Thouless experiment provides good support for Gombrich's whole argument about stereotypes; so it is rather surprising that, in the passage where he described it, he did not draw from it the anticipated conclusion. One might have thought that he would compare the 'phenomenal regression to the real object' with the 'natural pull towards the minimum stereotype'; but instead, in one of those remarkable shifts of direction which often characterise his prose, he suddenly put forward a theory of 'primitive' art which runs counter to everything else he had to say on the topic, in both *Art and Illusion* and *The Preference for the Primitive*.

Although Gombrich felt that 'the results of Professor Thouless' experiment are not in doubt', he objected to Thouless's use of the word 'real':

'A penny is not more real when seen from above than when looked upon sideways. But the frontal view happens to be the one which gives us most information. It is this aspect which we call the 'characteristic shape' of the object, the one (or sometimes two) which exhibits most of those distinctive features by which we classify and name the things of our world. It is on these distinctive features, as we have seen, that primitive art will concentrate, not because it draws on knowledge rather than sight, but because it insists on clear classification.'[37]

Gombrich writes 'as we have seen', but in fact we have not seen this argument before in *Art and Illusion*.[38] He may have derived the idea that 'primitive' artists depict objects from characteristic angles from Emanuel Löwy,[39] but the theory is also expressed with great clarity and emphasis in Franz Boas's *Primitive Art*, a book we know Gombrich admired.[40] Just as the modern ichthyologist will tend to depict most fish from the side because this gives more information than a view from above or behind, so the 'primitive' artist, Boas argued, will seek out those views of things that are most characteristic and distinctive.[41]

This is, it seems to me, a good example of what an anthropologist would call an 'if I were a horse' argument;[42] but the interest of it here is that Gombrich seems to be crediting 'primitive' artists with clear, rational reasons for depicting the world in the ways they do. They are not 'under the sway of', or 'following the natural pull towards' the stereotype, they are taking conscious decisions about how to represent the world in a logical way. It may well be significant that this passage should appear precisely at this point in *Art and Illusion*, just after the description of the Thouless experiment. For

     Gombrich and the Idea of Primitive Art

while Gombrich was thinking through the implications of Thouless's ellipses he may
have become uncomfortably aware that he had no more evidence for his 'primitive'
schemata than Löwy had for his memory images. It may be that 'primitive' artists tend
to depict lizards from above; but the only evidence we have that this is a stereotype
towards which 'primitive' artists feel a 'natural pull' is the fact that they tend to depict
lizards from above. Gombrich's argument is just as circular as Löwy's.

It might be possible to construct an experiment similar to that of Thouless, which
would use a lizard instead of a coin. From this it may turn out that we do indeed
have a tendency to regress to the lizard as seen from above. One could construct
similar experiments with horses and other animals, in order to provide support for
Gombrich's theory of 'primitive' art. But without such support, Gombrich's theory of
'primitive' schemata is surely baseless.

As we have seen, Löwy claimed that the universality of 'primitive' modes of
representation made it impossible to explain their appearance in terms of deliberate
intent. Gombrich seems to have been in sympathy with this point of view; talk of the
'natural pull' or the 'sway' of the stereotype provides an image of the 'primitive' mind

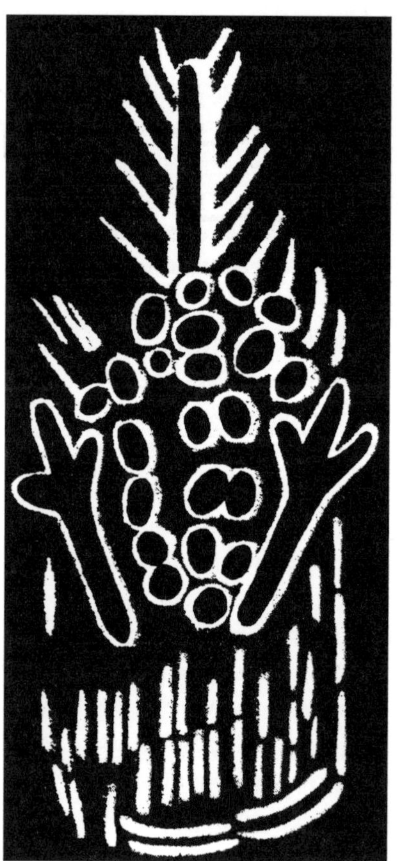

in which purpose and intention are at the mercy
of deeper psychological forces.[43] However it is not
at all clear that 'primitive' artists are as enslaved
by their modes of representation as Gombrich
suggested.

Australian aborigines tend to depict lizards
from above (fig. 10);[44] but one should not deduce
from this that they are incapable of depicting
animals from unusual angles. It would indeed
be difficult to identify the subject of fig. 15 if a
group of Aborigines had not happened to tell the
anthropologist Baldwin Spencer what it depicts:
it shows an emu, sitting on its nest full of eggs, as
seen from below.[45]

This is not a standard depiction in Aboriginal
art. Spencer noted it precisely because it was in his
experience unique. There can therefore have been
no pre-existent schema: the artist decided to draw
this unusual motif, and then drew it. That this was

FIG. 15 Emu, seen from below, drawing of a rock painting at
Reedy Creek, George Gill Range, Watarrka National Park,
Northern Territory, Australia, from Josephine Flood,
Rock Art of the Dreamtime, Sydney, 1997, p. 174

     Paul Taylor

possible is surely not surprising: if artists were incapable of drawing subjects that had never been drawn before, then illusionist art could not have progressed very far. It is unclear to me how Gombrich's theory of schema and correction can deal with this very basic objection. But no matter; we still face the problem: if Aboriginal artists were perfectly well able to draw new subjects whenever they wanted to, why did they almost always draw lizards from above?

Löwy says that they are drawing memory-images; Gombrich says that they are under the sway of the stereotype; Boas says that they are drawing the animals from a characteristic angle. But perhaps they have other reasons entirely, connected to taste, or myth, or religion. Someone might go and ask the Aborigines: armchair theorizing has never produced solid ethnological results.[46]

Löwy, however, would have maintained that this suggestion is an unhelpful one. There is no point in asking the Aborigines, since they would be incapable of providing the true answer. They could perhaps come up with some rationalisation that might seem to explain their own practice, but they would be unable to answer on behalf of those Peruvian peoples who also depict lizards from above. The phenomenon is global, and it requires a global analysis. Ethnology cannot settle the issue.

This seems like a strong argument, but we need to appreciate that there are two separate questions here. The first is: why does it apparently occur to peoples all over the globe to depict animals from the side and lizards from above? And then there is a second question: why do some peoples only depict animals in these ways, when others have gone on to depict them from the front, from three-quarters view and so forth?

The answer to the first question may perhaps be found via research into species-wide aspects of human cognition. But the answer to the second question will I think need to be sought in some more ethnological approach. For consider how white artists might reply if an Aboriginal anthropologist asked them why they never depict emus from below. They might reply that the idea had simply not occurred to them. But if the Aboriginal researcher went on to ask whether, now that they had been given the idea, they would be depicting emus that way in future, they might reply that they would not; and if pressed for their reasons might claim that such a picture would look absurd, or there was no call for one, or they liked their emu pictures as they were, or they could not see the need, and so on.

There is no doubt that the white artist could depict an emu from below. Similarly, there is no doubt that the Aboriginal artist could depict a lizard from the side. But both are comfortable depicting emus and lizards in the way they do, and see no reason to change. Whether or not the idea of change ever occurs to them is in a certain sense unimportant; they are making the art they want to make, and so change is unnecessary.

It is important to appreciate that 'primitive' artists do not go about their work in an oblivious way. When Gombrich saw over-sized heads in tribal sculpture (fig. 16), he assumed a 'systematic misjudgement' on the part of the sculptors.[47] And yet

     Gombrich and the Idea of Primitive Art

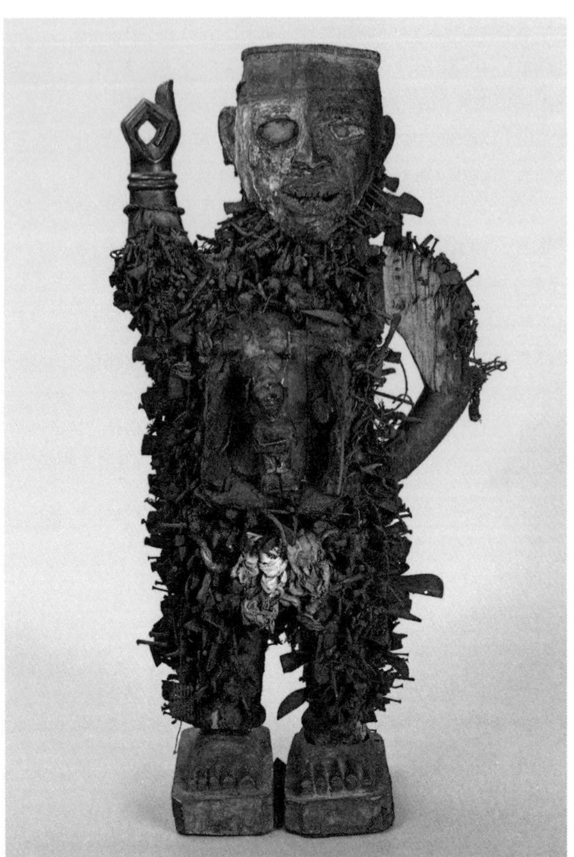 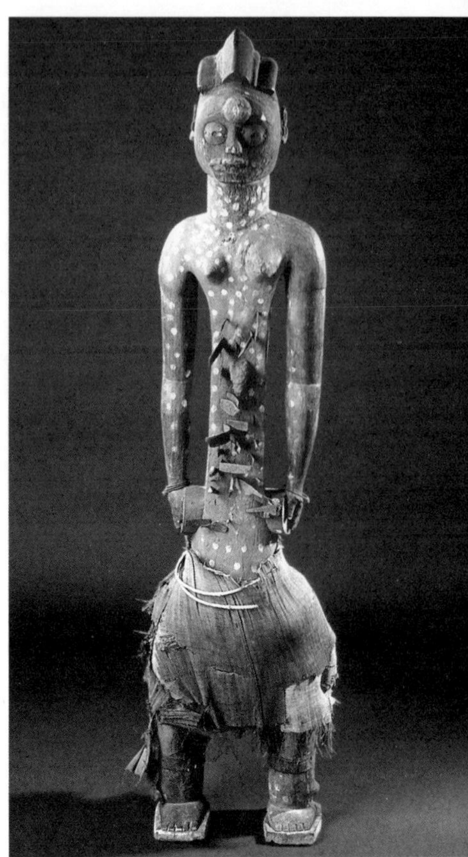

ethnologists of art, from Boas onward, have reported time and again that tribal artists are well aware of such distortions in their work, that they are unrepentant about them, and that they actively seek to include them.[48] There is no question of 'systematic misjudgement'; and in any case, there are many thousands of tribal sculptures with under-sized heads (fig. 17).

Just as European artists seek to use the visual languages they have inherited, with all their potentialities and all their limitations, so too do tribal artists. To read 'primitive art' as no more than a catalogue of stereotypical illusionistic errors is to fail to understand the diversity and complexity of its modes of representation.

In the course of this paper I have allowed Gombrich to set the agenda, and have examined those aspects of 'primitive' art which he considered significant. I hope I have shown that, even on his own terms, his characterisation of 'primitive' art is questionable. As soon as one stops looking for illusionistic errors in the work of 'primitive artists', and starts instead to look at the extraordinary variety of forms and

     Paul Taylor

representational means in their art, then Gombrich's talk of minimum stereotypes and gingerbread men begins to seem hopelessly wide of the mark. Indeed, on examining carvings as inventive as those in figs. 3, 4 and 18, one begins to wonder if it is not European perspectival art that is primitive. Are we sure that Raphael's paintings do not resemble child art rather more closely than these sculptures do? Have children ever made images which play with representation so ingeniously and creatively? Was not Raphael, in his relatively straightforward approach to the depiction of the motif, not then closer in spirit to the child than to the tribal artist?

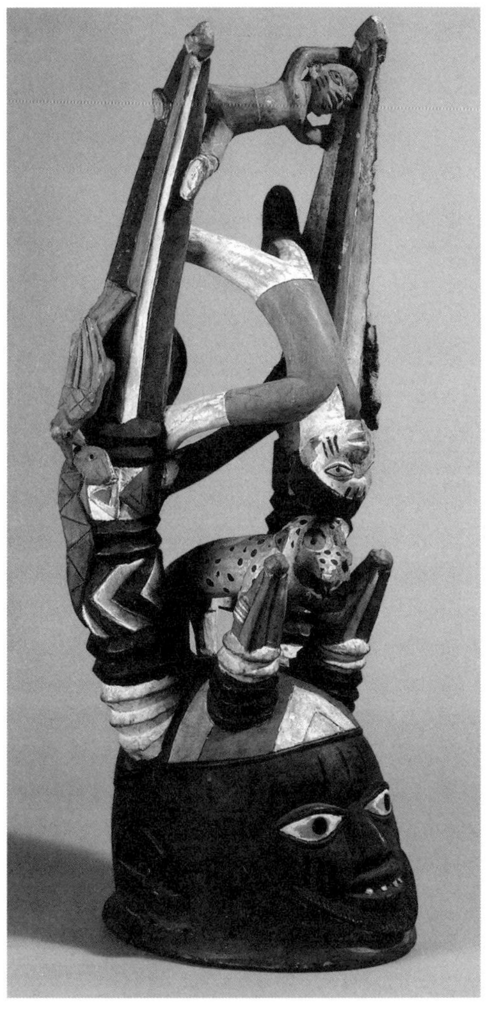

FIG. 16 Bakongo, Human figure (with additional small human figure; ritual) wood, nails (iron), iron, cloth, fibre, cord (vegetable fibre), British Museum, Dept of Africa, Oceania and the Americas, Af1949,46.280

FIG. 17 Bakongo, Male figure (ritual, with blades) wood, nails (iron), iron, shells (cowrie), wire (iron), clay (?), cloth (grass), British Museum, Dept of Africa, Oceania and the Americas, Af1905,0525.2

FIG. 18 Yoruba, Egungun, Mask (horned, with figures) made of wood, British Museum, Dept of Africa, Oceania and the Americas, Af1909,-.118, AN254302

    Gombrich and the Idea of Primitive Art

* I thank Robert Bagley for references and criticism.

1 E.H. Gombrich, *The Story of Art*, London, 1950, pp. 19-30.

2 E.H. Gombrich, *The Preference for the Primitive: Episodes in the History of Western Taste and Art*, London, 2002.

3 E.H. Gombrich, *The Sense of Order: a Study in the Psychology of Decorative Art*, Oxford, 1979, pp. 51-52, 190, 220-24, 264-70.

4 E.H. Gombrich, *Art and Illusion: a Study in the Psychology of Pictorial Representation*, London, 1960, pp. 14, 89-97, 101, 119, 124, 127, 172, 228, 230, 246-50, 255, 265, 289.

5 Gombrich, *Primitive* (n. 2 above), p. 190; see also p. 177.

6 Gombrich, *Story of Art* (n. 1 above), pp. 29-32. By the 16th edition the word 'weird' had been changed to 'remote', p. 53.

7 Gombrich, *Primitive* (n. 2 above), p. 269; Gombrich, *Art and Illusion* (n. 4 above), p. 18; Gombrich, *Story of Art* (n. 1 above), p. 20. F. Boas, *Primitive Art*, Cambridge, Mass., 1927, pp. 1-4.

8 Gombrich, *Art and Illusion* (n. 4 above), p. 18.

9 Gombrich, *Art and Illusion* (n. 4 above), p. 17; E.H. Gombrich and D. Eribon, *A Lifelong Interest: Conversations on Art and Science with Didier Eribon*, London, 1993, pp. 52-53.

10 Gombrich, *Art and Illusion* (n. 4 above), p. 100.

11 Gombrich, *Art and Illusion* (n. 4 above), p. 100; cf. p. 78. The idea that 'the "conceptual image" … dominates child art as well as primitive art' can already be found in Gombrich's early essay, 'Achievement in Medieval Art', in Gombrich, *Meditations on a Hobby Horse and Other Essays on the Theory of Art*, London, 1963, pp. 70-77 (p. 74); tr. Michael Podro of 'Wertprobleme und mittelalterliche Kunst', *Kritische Berichte zur kunstgeschichtlichen Literatur*, 6, 3-4, 1937, pp. 109-16.

12 Gombrich, *Primitive* (n. 2 above), p. 273.

13 Gombrich derived these ideas not only from Löwy but also from Julius von Schlosser, and especially from Schlosser's *Die Kunst des Mittelalters*, Neubabelsberg, 1923: Gombrich and Eribon, *A Lifelong Interest* (n. 9 above), p. 104. For a different analysis of the resemblances between child and 'primitive' art, one that emphasizes the skill and conceptual maturity of the latter, see R. Arnheim, *Art and Visual Perception*, Berkeley and Los Angeles, 1954, pp. 128-9.

14 Gombrich, *Art and Illusion* (n. 4 above), p. 19.

15 E. Loewy, *The Rendering of Nature in Early Greek Art*, tr. J. Fothergill, London 1907; 1st edn, E. Löwy, *Die Naturwiedergabe in der älteren griechischen Kunst*, Rome, 1900, p. 6. This is one of seven 'primitive' methods of representation which Löwy describes on pp. 5-6.

16 In this he was following Julius Lange's 'Gesetze der Menschendarstellung in der primitiven Kunst aller Völker und insbesondere in der Ägyptischen Kunst', which is the introduction (in French, despite its title) to J. Lange, *Darstellung des Menschen in der älteren griechischen Kunst*, Strasbourg 1899, pp. ix-xxxi.

17 Gombrich, *Art and Illusion* (n. 4 above), p. 19 and note to p. 18, p. 337; M. Schapiro, 'Style', in *Anthropology Today*, ed. A.L. Kroeber, Chicago, 1953, pp. 287-312 (pp. 301-02); reprinted in M. Schapiro, *Theory and Philosophy of Art: Style, Artist and Society*, New York, 1994, pp. 51-102 (pp. 76-77).

18 Gombrich, *Primitive* (n. 2 above), p. 271. In Gombrich and Eribon, *A Lifelong Interest* (n. 9 above), p. 99, he stated that 'I prefer to call what we used to call "primitive art", "two-dimensional coding"', but this idea did not resurface in *The Preference for the Primitive*.

19 See too P. Garlake, *The Hunter's Vision: the Prehistoric Art of Zimbabwe*, London, 1995, where the great majority of the depictions of humans are presented from the side.

20 J.-L. LeQuellec, *Rock Art in Africa: Mythology and Legend*, tr. P. Bahn, Paris, 2004, pp. 38-40; idem, 'Can One 'Read' Rock Art? An Egyptian Example', in *Iconography without Texts*, ed. P. Taylor, Warburg Institute Colloquia 13, London and Turin 2008, pp. 25-42 (p. 38, fig. 10).

21 C.B. Donnan, *Moche Art of Peru: Pre-Columbian Symbolic Communication*, Los Angeles, 1978, p. 118.

22 Ibid., and C.B. Donnan and D. McLelland, *Moche Fineline Painting: Its Evolution and its Artists*, Los Angeles, 1999.

23 Horses in the Americas became extinct towards the end of the ice age. P. Hämäläinen, 'The Rise and Fall of Plains Indian Horse

     Paul Taylor

Cultures', *The Journal of American History*, 90, 2003, pp. 833-62 (p. 835); A.D. Barnosky et al., 'Assessing the Causes of Late Pleistocene Extinctions on the Continents', *Science*, n.s., 306, no. 5693, 1 October 2004, pp. 70-75 (p. 74).

24 J.-M. Chauvet et al., *Chauvet Cave: the Discovery of the World's Oldest Paintings*, tr. P. Bahn, London, 1996, p. 115.

25 E.g. A. Leroi-Gourhan, *The Art of Prehistoric Man in Western Europe*, tr. N. Guterman, p. 398, figs. 198 and 201.

26 I have been unable to find depictions of lizards by children, and so am unable to assess this part of Gombrich's claim.

27 Loewy, *Rendering of Nature* (n. 14 above), p. 8.

28 Ibid., p. 10.

29 Gombrich, *Art and Illusion* (n. 4 above), p. 19.

30 Ibid., p. 95.

31 Ibid., p. 101; Gombrich and Eribon, *A Lifelong Interest* (n. 9 above), pp. 99 and 104. Gombrich introduced a distinction between the 'conceptual image' and the 'psychologically grounded minimum image' in 'Meditations on a Hobby Horse or the Roots of Artistic Form', in *Aspects of Form, a Symposium on Form in Nature and Art*, ed. L.L. Whyte, London, 1951, pp. 209-24, reprinted in *Hobby Horse* (n. 10 above), pp. 1-11 (p. 8). From the passages of *Art and Illusion* quoted here, he would seem to have abandoned this distinction during the 1950s.

32 Gombrich, *Primitive* (n. 2 above), pp. 283-85.

33 Gombrich, *Art and Illusion* (n. 4 above), p. 124, but cf. p. 125. Gombrich provides a similar argument when discussing Florentine Trecento painting after the Black Death, which he characterises as 'psychologically speaking … more 'primitive', that is to say, closer to the conceptual image than the intellectual achievements that preceded them'. E.H. Gombrich, 'The impact of the Black Death', in Gombrich, *Reflections on the History of Art: Views and Reviews*, ed. R. Woodfield, Oxford, 1987, pp. 42-45 (p. 42); originally published as a review of M. Meiss, *Painting in Florence and Siena after the Black Death*, Princeton, 1951, in *Journal of Aesthetics and Art Criticism*, 11, 1953, pp. 414-16.

34 He suggests a more positive evaluation in 'Achievement' (n. 10 above), p. 74: 'One day it may be possible to describe the development

toward the primitive in late antique art as one of dissolution, but not one of unqualified decline. For the return to the primitive may have brought out aesthetic virtues which would not otherwise have emerged.'

35 See Jeroen Stumpel's paper in this volume for further analysis of this concept.

36 R.H. Thouless, 'Phenomenal Regression to the Real Object, II', *British Journal of Psychology*, XXII, 1931, pp. 1-30; *Art and Illusion* (n. 4 above), pp. 255-56.

37 Ibid., p. 255.

38 He does mention the idea in passing in some of his earlier work: Gombrich, *Story of Art* (n. 1 above), p. 386; 'Hobby Horse' (n. 31 above), p. 9.

39 Loewy, *Rendering of Nature* (n. 14 above), pp. 12-13.

40 Gombrich, *Primitive* (n. 2 above), p. 269: 'that great book'; E.H. Gombrich, 'Tribal Styles', in Gombrich, *Reflections* (n. 33 above), pp. 23-32 (26): 'that classic work'.

41 Boas, *Primitive Art* (n. 7 above), pp. 64-87, esp. pp. 71-72. Gombrich does not cite either Löwy or Boas at this point in *Art and Illusion*.

42 E.E. Evans-Pritchard, *Theories of Primitive Religion*, Oxford, 1965, pp. 108-09: '[Nineteenth- and early twentieth-century interpretations of primitive religion] were also theories of psychological origins … and … could be said to rest ultimately on psychological suppositions of the 'if I were a horse' sort …. If the scholar himself believed what primitives believe, or practised what they practise, he would have been guided by a certain line of reasoning, or impelled by some emotional state, or immersed in crowd psychology, or entangled in a network of collective and mystical representations.' See also ibid. pp. 24, 43, 47. For criticism of Evans-Pritchard's use of this phrase, see G. Macdonald and P. Pettit, *Semantics and Social Science*, London, 1981, pp. 34-35.

43 On some occasions Gombrich acknowledges that 'primitive' – or at least, Egyptian – artists were able to make lifelike images: however, deviations of this sort succumbed to tradition and 'powers of inertia': *Art and Illusion* (n. 4 above), p. 123.

44 An exception to this rule is a drawing of two lizards incised on a baobab nut (British

Museum, Dept of Africa, Oceania and the
Americas, Oc1939,12). Here the lizards' bodies
are depicted from above, but their heads are
depicted from the side.

45 W.B. Spencer, *Wanderings in Wild Australia*,
London, 1928, pp. 64-65; J. Flood, *Rock Art
of the Dreamtime*, Sydney, 1997, pp. 174-76.
Although it is unusual to see the body of the
emu depicted like this, images in which a pair
of emu footprints are shown on either side of a
cache of eggs are more common: see N. Munn,
*Walbiri Iconography: Graphic Representation
and Cultural Symbolism in a Central Australian
Society*, 2nd edn (1st edn 1973) Chicago,
1986, pp. 124-25. They represent the traces of
totemic ancestors, ibid., pp. 21-27.

46 Evans-Pritchard (n. 42 above), pp. 6-10, 64-67,
101.

47 Gombrich, *Primitive* (n. 2 above), p. 279.

48 E.g. Boas, *Primitive Art* (n. 7 above), pp. 155-
56; R. Hottot, 'Teke Fetishes', *Journal of the
Royal Anthropological Institute*, 86, 1956, pp.
25-36 (pp. 27-28); E. Carpenter, 'The Eskimo
Artist', in *Anthropology and Art*, ed. C.M.
Otten, New York, 1971, pp. 163-70; R. Sieber,
'The Aesthetics of Traditional African Art',
in *Art and Aesthetics in Primitive Societies*, ed.
C. Jopling, New York, 1971, pp. 127–31; J.W.
Fernandez, 'Principles of Opposition and
Vitality in Fang Aesthetics', ibid., pp. 356–73;
R.F. Thompson, 'Yoruba Artistic Criticism',
in *The Traditional Artist in African Societies*, ed.
W.L. d'Azevedo, Bloomington, 1973, pp. 18-
61; C. Abel, 'Suau aesthetics', *Gigibori*, 1, 1974,
pp. 34-35; G. Witherspoon, *Language and Art
in the Navajo Universe*, Ann Arbor, 1979,
pp. 151-78; B. Lawal, 'Orí: The Significance
of the Head in Yoruba Sculpture', *Journal of
Anthropological Research*, 41, no. 1, 1985, pp. 91-
103; G.M.G. Scoditti, *Kitawa: a linguistic and
aesthetic analysis of visual art in Melanesia*, Berlin
and New York, 1989, pp. 64-66; F. Willett,
African Art, rev. edn, London 1993, pp. 161-64;
W. Van Damme, *Beauty in Context: Towards an
Anthropological Approach to Aesthetics*, Leiden,
1996, pp. 31-48, 190, 225, 254-55, 291; A.-M.
Boyer, *Baule*, Milan 2008, pp. 69-70, 78-81;
D.A. Binkley and P. Darish, *Kuba*, Milan
2009, p. 24.

      Paul Taylor

Pattern and Portrayal: Remarks on the Concept of 'Schema' in Gombrich

JEROEN STUMPEL

IN GOMBRICH THE TERM 'SCHEMA' is often coupled with the notion of 'correction',[1] and it was Gombrich himself who noted the analogy of 'schema and correction' with the Darwinian 'trial and error'.[2] In Gombrich' s *Art and Illusion* we find another slogan, which has become equally famous: 'making comes before matching'.[3] Both phrases, 'schema and correction', and 'making comes before matching', are closely related, and Gombrich shows in the second chapter of *Art and Illusion* how they can be made to 'dovetail', in order to enlighten certain important features of the history of style.[4] In fact, their role in Gombrich's arguments may seem to be indistinguishable.

'Making comes before matching' is, in fact, the more basic or fundamental of the two, and indicates that, in creating images, the wish to make something that may stand for something else comes before a refined search after visual equivalents. Likeness does not have to play an important role in representation, or any role at all. The child may take a stick to stand for a horse, the soldier may grab a box of matches to indicate the position of the enemy.[5]

A radical example, it seems to me, of how making comes before matching is provided by a sheet with drawings by a boy of three years and four months old, published in a book on children's drawings by Claire Golomb (fig. 1).[6] The scribbles were made in the company of a psychologist, while the child explained the drawings. The boy had acquired the motor skills to produce more or less oval shapes, and these stood for the following. The huge shape in the middle was 'baby', who perhaps had just arrived in the family, and demanded a lot of attention. We also see 'mother' and 'kitty', all conjured up (or should one say 'made') by the same shape, merely changing in size. But then we have 'giraffe' where a very tentative bulging of the shape may be detected, inspired by the animal's long neck; and wonderful too is the oval, unrolled as it were, to form a more or less horizontal line, which has the telling caption: 'snake'.

Apart from this snake example, there is clearly more 'making' than 'matching' in these drawings. The same goes for a drawing produced by a ten-year-old asked to draw 'mamma' (fig. 2). Although Mamma was present, the girl never looked at her. Then she was requested to draw mamma 'as she really looked', while observing the model, and this led to a different result (fig. 3) – a little less flattering for mamma perhaps.

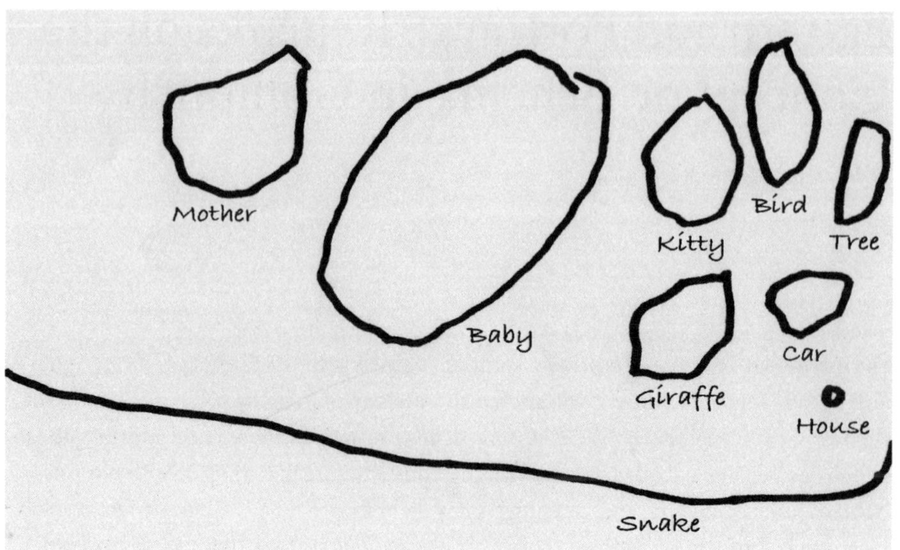

FIG.1 After drawings produced on request by a three-year-old boy, in Claire Golomb, *The Child's Creation of a Pictorial World*, 2nd edn, Mahwah (NJ), 2004, p. 23

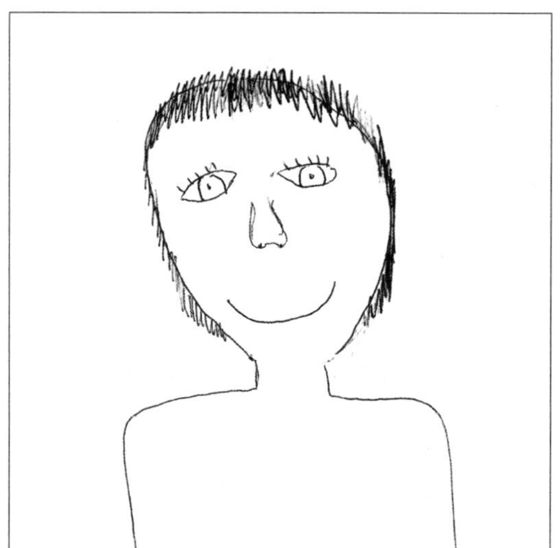

FIG.2 Ten-year-old girl, Portrait of her mother, private collection, The Netherlands

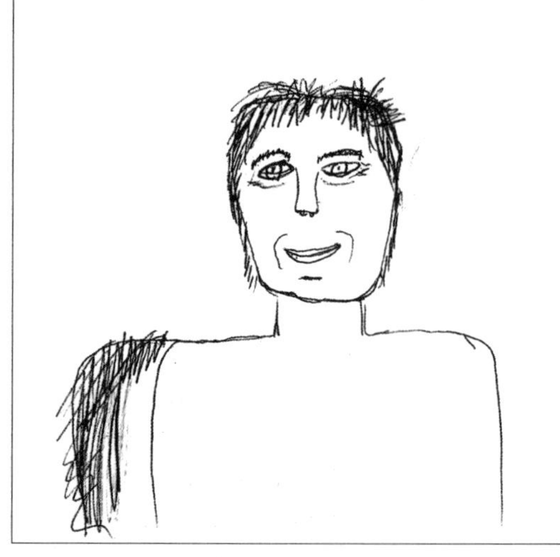

FIG.3 Ten-year old girl, Portrait of her mother, private collection, The Netherlands

　　Jeroen Stumpel

It was perhaps for this latter type of situation, actual portrayal, or working 'after life', that Gombrich intended to use the concept of schema and correction. Here we not only have simplified shapes modelled more or less to become an acceptable figure – drawings, that is, largely of a diagrammatic nature – we also have the obvious intent to modify the diagram or schema to make it comply better with observed features. In Gombrich this process becomes paradigmatic for essential aspects of artistic creation, as well as for art historical developments over several generations.

The concept of 'schema' may be used by him for discussing the motor skills necessary for guiding and steering the pencil,[7] as well as for the structuring of the process of observation to facilitate and inform this process.[8] In Gombrich's text, the schema in principle allows for a connection between the features of an image, and features of visual perception.

Long before Gombrich turned to the word 'schema' (originally a Greek word meaning 'form') the concept existed both in the field of art and in the study of the psychology of perception. Ultimately, it was derived from Kant's philosophy, where something rather complex is meant with the term – in the case of visual perception not features of the image itself, but the representation of rules necessary to form an image at all.[9]

The notion that something prior to perception may be responsible for the formal aspects of an image was passed from philosophy to psychology through the work of the British psychologist Henry Head.[10] This meaning has entered the standard dictionaries: in the OED we find the following meaning for the neurological and psychological senses of 'schema':

> An automatic, unconscious coding or organization of incoming physiological or psychological stimuli, giving rise to a particular response or effect.

Gombrich refers in his writings to the term 'schema' in the work of various psychologists, such as Ayer[11] and Boring,[12] and to the work of Bartlett on memory.[13] But more importantly, as we have seen, he also used the term to refer to artistic phenomena. For art history this was no novelty, as art too had inherited the term for relatively simple or simplified representations, of a diagrammatic nature.[14] Such schemata also occur in books specifically meant for draughtsmen and the instruction of artists, and examples of these constructions starting from a diagram were reproduced in Gombrich.[15] But as a term of art history proper, we owe its acceptance, I believe, to Heinrich Wölfflin. In Wölfflin's *Grundbegriffe*, published in 1915, we find the word employed in a manner vaguely reminiscent of Kant's philosophy:

> The material and representational content may in itself be so diverse that it remains to be decided if, here and there, another 'optical' schema underlies the concept, a schema which is, however, much more deeply rooted than in the purely

        Pattern and Portrayal

imitative problem of evolution: it involves the appearance of architecture just as much as that of representational art, and a Roman Baroque façade has the same optical denominator as a landscape of Van Goyen.[16]

At the same time the schemata in Wölfflin are different, since they are not fixed, but changeable. In fact, it is precisely their change over time that in Wölfflin's view might explain the change of styles of paintings in time. As is well known, Wölfflin argued that the history of art (in the periods at least which he discussed, Renaissance, Baroque and the Golden Age) was somehow equivalent to a history of seeing; he even went so far as to state that art history *was*, ultimately and in principle, a history of seeing.[17] This was a very bold suggestion, which understandably became rather famous (in fairness, one has to say that Wölfflin wrote this only once).

In Gombrich, too, the term schema is related both to acts of vision and the analysis of style, but his views are in many ways opposed to those of Wölfflin. First of all there is Gombrich's well known distrust of explanations in terms of collectives and epoch mentalities, an attitude or position that distinguishes his work clearly from Wölffin's. But there is also his use of the term schema. Gombrich seems to use the term in a more humble, down-to-earth sense, and he did not restrict the notion of 'schemata of vision' to a particular class of lofty artistic modes of perception. And yet, at the same time, in Gombrich the schema concept had an even grander role to fulfil than in Wölfflin. In the latter, the actual change of the schema, the *reason* why the artistic perception of the world in the fifteenth century was structured differently from seventeenth-century vision, was ultimately left unexplained. Wölfflin's ambition was merely to indicate and describe these perceptual structures in basic terms (*Grundbegriffe*).

Gombrich stressed on numerous occasions that he intended to help answer the question 'why there was a history of representation at all'.[18] In other words, his use of the psychology of the schema was directed at answering a historical question – not the psychology of the individual acquiring a certain set of skills, but changes over generations; not so much personal development as historical evolution. The impressionistic mode of representing is according to Gombrich the result of a long history, and one of the things he set out to do in *Art and Illusion* was to explain the mechanisms behind this gradual conquest of reality.

That the history of art could be seen 'as the history of the gradual discovery of appearances' was not a new thought. In fact, the phrase just quoted is derived from a text written by Roger Fry in 1934. According to Fry, '… the conceptual habits, necessary to life, make it very difficult, even for artists, to discover what things really look like to an unbiassed eye. Indeed, it has taken from Neolithic times to the nineteenth century to perfect this discovery.' And, still according to Fry, with clear overtones of Vasari, 'European art from the time of Giotto progressed more or less

    Jeroen Stumpel

continuously in this direction, in which the discovery of linear perspective marks
an important stage, whilst the full exploration of atmospheric colour and colour
perspective had to await the work of the French impressionists'.[19]

Gombrich could have subscribed to much of this, as for him, too, the history of
art presented a history of visual discoveries, and in Gombrich the gradualness and
the stumbling pace of this history was related to the nature of the grave difficulties
which had to be overcome. But Gombrich certainly did not agree with the idea that
the overcoming of such difficulties, the actual process of conquering appearances, was
equivalent to a discarding of biases. If rendering the world of appearances could be
achieved with an unconditional surrender to sense impressions, Gombrich argued, it
would be hard to explain why the making of more or less naturalistic representations
had such a long and gradual history in the first place. The real purpose of his book,
he repeated in his preface for a second edition, was '… to explain the reasons for the
unexpected difficulty which artists encountered who clearly wanted to make their
images look like nature'.[20]

There are psychological and epistemological reasons why a mere removal of bias
or prejudice will never suffice, Gombrich contended, and time and again we read
that it was precisely the biases that allowed for progress at all. The artist cannot start
from scratch, and of necessity he will start with schemata – which may or may not be
corrected and improved later on in the process. 'Every artist', Gombrich declared, 'has
to know and construct a schema before he can adjust it to the needs of portrayal'.[21] In
such statements the use of 'schema' was inspired not by lofty Kantian notions, nor
Wölfflinian crystallizations of artistic vision, but by something much more basic: the
use of simplified shapes and diagrams by artists in training and practice.

In 1916, one year after Wölfflin published his *Grundbegriffe*, an American
psychologist, F.C. Ayer, published a thesis on the psychology of drawing – a
fascinating subject, on which surprisingly little work has been done. On the basis of
his research, Ayer argued that amongst other things 'The trained drawer acquires a
mass of schemata by which he can produce a schema of an animal, a flower or a house
quickly on paper. This serves as a support for the representation of his memory
images and he gradually modifies the schema until it corresponds with that which
he would express.'[22] In this description, which is about the process of drawing after
the model, the term 'schema' again seems to hover somewhere between the mental
representation of motor patterns, memory images, processes of perception, and the
material process of drawing.

In any case, Gombrich wholly accepted this psychological description, and it
became the basis, so it seems, of his ideas not only about the mystery of portrayal by
the individual, but also of the gradual mastery of representation as a continual process
throughout history, over different generations. On the basis of this idea, Gombrich
made pioneering remarks on Renaissance art education, a subject hardly studied

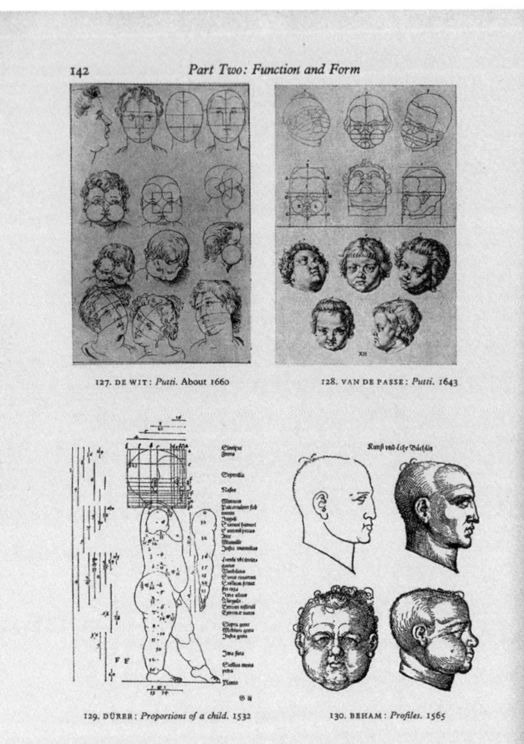

FIG.4 After E.H. Gombrich, *Art and Illusion*, London, 1960, pp. 142–43

until then. By turning to such older 'how to draw' texts, he could describe the work of Rubens as if it fitted precisely within the observational and experimental framework of Ayer's 'psychology of drawing'. He drew attention to sections in drawings books that had appeared in the sixteenth and seventeenth centuries, where in particular constructions for the chubby cheeks of children were schematically indicated;[23] he traced these patterns to instructive drawings by Dürer and Beham in the sixteenth century,[24] and argued that such articulate schemata could be detected in Rubens' portrayal of his own son (fig. 4).[25]

Here 'schema and correction' are entirely plausible tools of analysis: it seems likely that Rubens knew of such patterns, and indeed, may have trained himself in these when young; and it seems also convincing that the somewhat exaggerated, or in any case emphatic curvature of the child's cheeks is related to it. The case neatly illustrates Ayers description (here slightly modified for the occasion): 'The trained Rubens had acquired a mass of schemata by which he could produce a schema of a child quickly on paper. The schema served as a support for the representation of his memory images

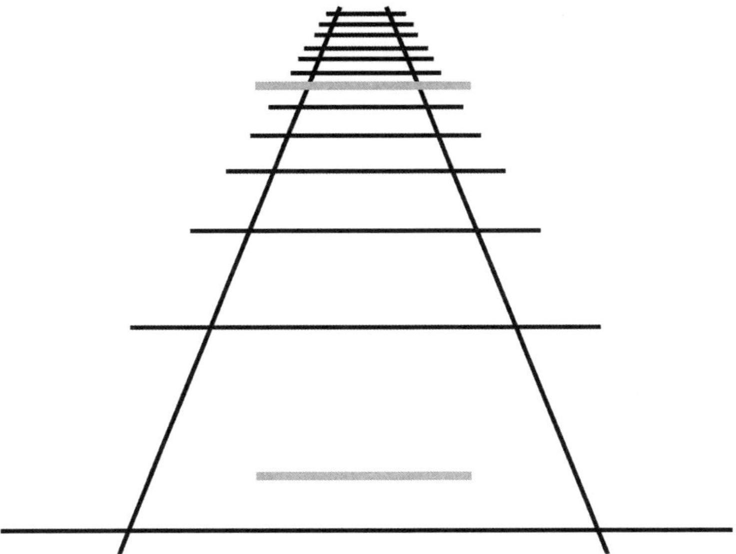

and he gradually modified the schema until it corresponded with that which he would express.'

But perhaps Gombrich's success in applying a psychology of drawing to elucidate stylistic features of a master like Rubens also presents a problem. If Rubens's act of portraying is so much like the way accomplished draughtsmen acted under Ayer's close observation in the beginning of the twentieth century, this type of schema and correction seems not qualified perhaps to explain the history of representation as a gradual discovery. This is a problem to which I shall return.

We have seen that the word 'schema' may have different meanings or overtones, one of which is related to the general psychology of perception, where it refers to a faculty for 'structuring vision'. Gombrich took this epistemological and psychological meaning and applied it to the question of the history of style as well.

Perhaps we should look more closely at the application of the term in different contexts, to see how and where it connects fruitfully to the idea that veristic representation must have a history because there are particular obstacles and problems to overcome related to the psychology of visual perception. In chapter IX of *Art and Illusion*, entitled 'The Analysis of Vision in Art', Gombrich argues that a psychological or cognitive mechanism which helps to keep our visual world stable is precisely a hindrance in producing correct or proper renderings of a three-dimensional spatial world on the flat plane. He is referring to the constancy phenomenon, which is also active in colour perception or perception of temperature; but in *Art and Illusion* it

    Pattern and Portrayal

is discussed in particular with regard to size constancy.[26] We all know the Ponzo
illusion, where, at least on a picture plane, objects supposedly further removed in the
pictorial world, appear larger (fig. 5).[27] Larger than what? Well, larger than they ought
to look, spoken unphilosophically. In the real world too, it seems that, for example,
sheep further away are seen as larger than a projection theory would predict.

According to Gombrich, this would hinder the draughtsman in creating
corresponding size relations when depicting a three-dimensional world. So
these ingrained constancies have to be broken down, as it were, in order for the
draughtsman to create a consistent world of comparative sizes; the eye has to try to
see the world as a camera does. The more depth cues there are, the stronger the size
compensation will be – the draughtsman therefore has to reduce depth cues, and
try to see the world as flat as possible, by closing one eye for instance (thus reducing
stereoscopic information about depth) or employing a ruler or even a transparent
screen to objectify the comparison of apparent sizes.

This can be achieved mechanically, as in the famous squared window depicted by
Dürer (fig. 6); but also the artist trained in this way will most likely develop the skills
to counteract his or her constancy impulses more easily – even without the help of a
measuring contraption. Certainly Impressionists like Pissarro will have practised such
tricks when they made their sketches or paintings after life.[28]

By referring to the constancy phenomenon Gombrich did give an explanation[29]
for an inherent difficulty of drawing the third dimension and objects in distances,
and it seems that he also gave an explanation as to why many pictures contain figures
the sizes of which are incongruously large with respect to their environment or to
each other (incongruously when judged by photographic criteria). This is, I believe, a
genuine and important contribution to the study of pictures by means of perceptual

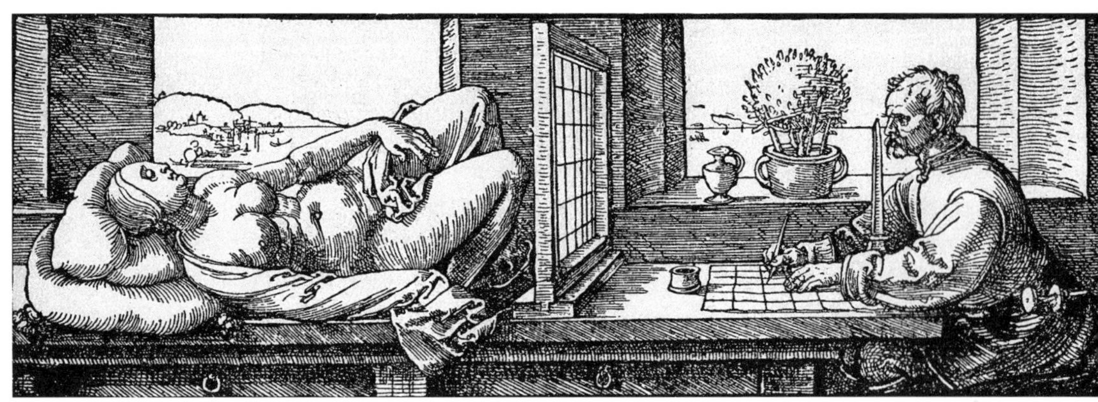

FIG.6 Albrecht Dürer, Drawing apparatus, 1525, Bartsch VII.160.149, British Museum, London.
Warburg Institute, Photographic Collection

     Jeroen Stumpel

psychology. But still one might wonder to what extent it is related to the schema, or perhaps even to the grand question of why image-making has a history at all. The need to overcome the constancies, after all, has only happened in a limited set of stylistic cultures in world history, and it is rather a matter of on and off: there seems to be no gradual development discernible as a result of a gradual conquest of constancies (or if there is, this history has not been written).

Also, the problem is not concerned with the drawing of objects in themselves, but of the proper coordination of object size with regard to a painted or drawn texture gradient surrounding it, on the basis of actual observation of real scenery. To produce such an image is a quite particular case of picture making. In *Art and Illusion*, however, this impressionistic, before-the-motif practice is made more paradigmatic than is warranted.[30] But for the moment I would like to return to question the concept of the schema in the portrayal of single objects, e.g. faces. We left this topic at the point where portrayal supposedly implied the easy mastering of a schema, which the good draughtsman was capable of modifying into a true and marvellous likeness. Such a likeness would suggest the full presence of an individual and yet not reveal the scaffolding of previous patterns.

It seems we encounter a problem here of an essential, perhaps even logical, nature, comparable to the infamous problem concerning Panofsky's concept of disguised symbolism, which denotes the disguise or adaption of symbols to make them make fit more easily into a naturalistic painting.[31] In this latter case, the better such disguises and adaptations succeed, the more difficult it is to discern, let alone prove their very presence. If we have, say, a Mary in a pleasurable garden which quite unobtrusively and naturally includes an apple tree, how can one say that this tree is an intentional allusion to the tree in paradise?

A parallel problem seems to hold for the use of schemata in portrayal that is truly successful. In the case of, say Van Eyck or Holbein, it is hard to perceive the schemata. Is this because they were not there in the first place, or because they have been modified in such a masterly way as to have become untraceable? To assume the latter, one would have to rely on the general validity of psychological propositions such as those made by Ayer, that each and every competent draughtsman operates with refined schemata – so also Holbein and Van Eyck. This may well be the case, but in neither master do we have the smallest hint of the nature or outlines of these schemata.

Another problem here concerns the transmission of the schemata; whether they can travel as it were from one mind to another. Even if it may well be true that Holbein operated by means of formulae and a set of refined schemata, these would be as hard to transmit as are the virtuoso motor skills of a trained pianist. Such skills have to be acquired by each individual again and again; and although the trainings methods may be transmissible, the individual results are not; so it is hard to see how this model could account for a gradual and cumulative process.

    Pattern and Portrayal

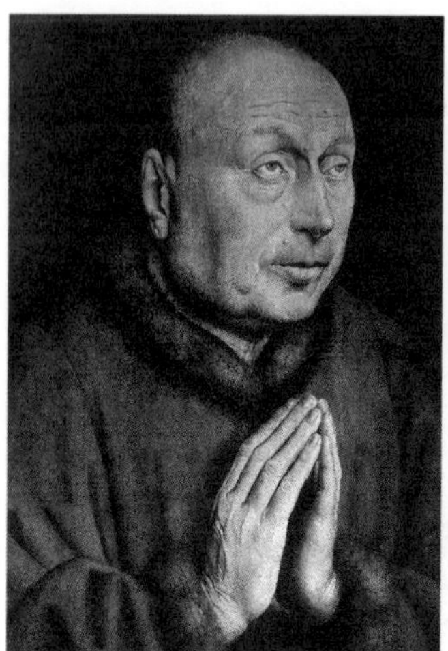 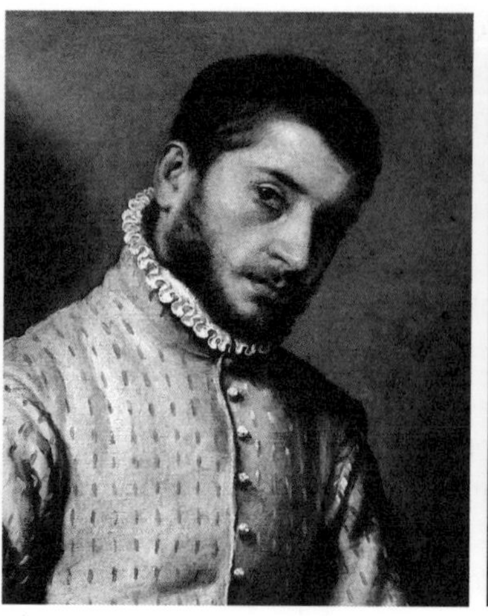 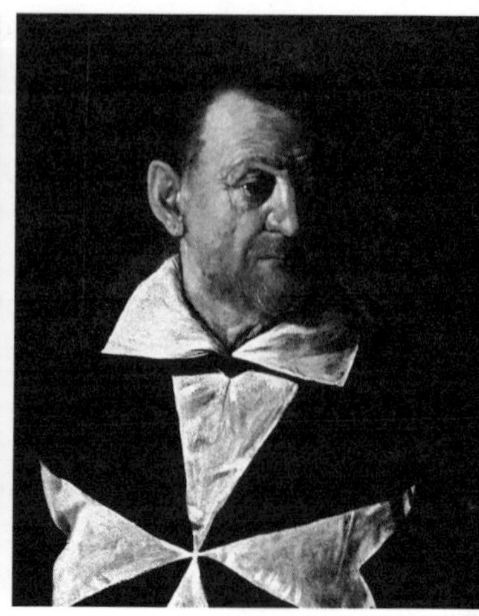

FIG.7 Jan van Eyck, Portrait of Jodoc Vyt, from the *Adoration of the Lamb* altarpiece, *c.* 1432, St Bavo's cathedral, Ghent

FIG.8 Giovanni Battista Moroni, Portrait of a tailor (detail), *c.* 1565-70, National Gallery, London

FIG.9 Michelangelo Merisi da Caravaggio, Portrait of a knight of Malta (Antonio Martelli?), (detail), 1607–08, Palazzo Pitti, Florence

This surely creates a problem for a history of gradual change in this type of internalized schemata; if these remarks are valid then schema and correction would not contribute to the question of why representation has a history at all, or how this history could be a cumulative one. Indeed, one could well argue that, as far as portrayal goes, there is no such history from, say, Van Eyck onward. Although for example Moroni in the sixteenth century used tricks (such as darker or lighter backgrounds) which differ from those used by either Caravaggio in the seventeenth or Van Eyck in the fifteenth, there is no way in which these achievements can be arranged in a line of gradual discovery over the course of three or four centuries. If these portraits were excavated, without label or date, how could an archeologist order them in chronological sequence (figs. 7, 8 and 9)?

The power of the case of Rubens in *Art and Illusion* is precisely that Gombrich could point to and trace fragments of a history of transmission; and that the Rubens portrait of his son (fig. 4) hovered perhaps on a borderline of schema and portrayal more than some of the portraits he made for adult patrons, where again the presence of schema eludes us – precisely as Rubens wished of course (fig. 10). Perhaps he cared a little less for adapting his formula in an informal painting of a child, particularly as he was to use the study – as one among more, presumably – to supply his Madonna in Munich with an appealing array of chubby putti, and may have been aiming for a type rather than a portrait from the start.

     Jeroen Stumpel

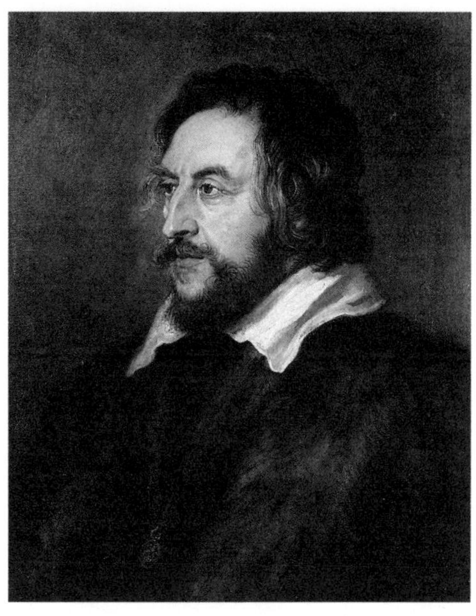

FIG.10 Peter Paul Rubens, Portrait of
Thomas Howard, Earl of Arundel, 1629-30,
National Gallery, London

The difficulty of discerning schemata precisely where, according to the theory, they
must be most successful is apparent not only when considering the portraits of Van
Eyck, but in many aspects of his oeuvre as we know it. Indeed, given the importance
for Gombrich of Popperian epistemology, he would certainly acknowledge the
importance of falsification – of finding, in the case of a general statement, the counter-
example, the proverbial black swan.[32] In my view Van Eyck is such a black swan with
regard to the interweaving of the schema and correction formula with explanations of
a gradual history of visual discovery in art.

Gombrich of course wrote about Van Eyck on several occasions, for instance in
one of his most important articles, 'Light, Form and Texture in Fifteenth-Century
Painting', first given as a lecture in 1962, and later reprinted in an expanded version
in his book *The Heritage of Apelles*.[33] Here he wrote about the difference between lustre
and shading; and how, as we can learn from written sources and from actual paintings
and mosaics preserved in Pompeii, this distinction had become known to classical
artists. The legendary Apelles may in fact have been a pioneer in producing effects of
lustre in his paintings, as Gombrich cogently argued.

In medieval times this 'heritage of Apelles' was lost, or frozen into formulas that
were a mere crude echo of classical finesse in this respect. Gombrich contended in
his article that, while the Italians rediscovered the subtlety of shading, in the North
the particular rediscoveries were lustre and shine. In this context he made his famous
comparison between Domenico Veneziano and Van Eyck (figs. 11 and 12). As for
Veneziano, one can well believe that his way of rendering drapery is a result of a more

     Pattern and Portrayal

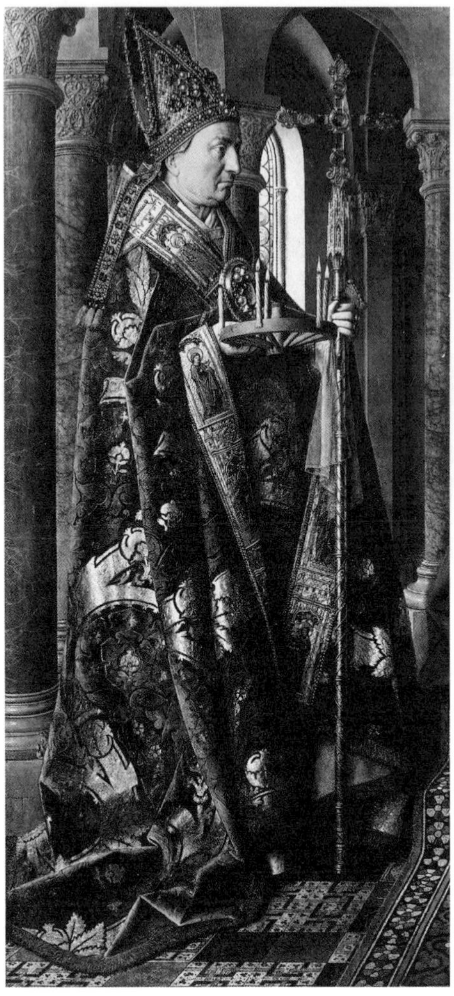

FIG.11 Jan van Eyck, *Van der Paele altarpiece* (detail of St Donatian), 1436, Groeningemuseum, Bruges

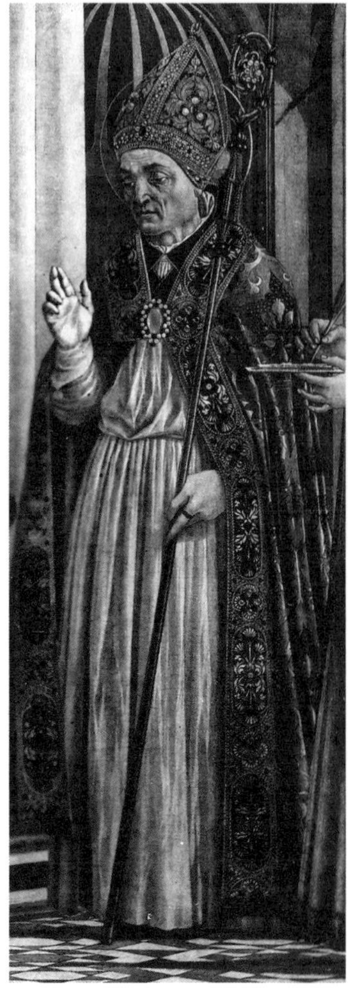

FIG.12 Domenico Veneziano, *St Lucy altarpiece* (detail of St Zenobius), c 1445-7, Galleria degli Uffizi, Florence

or less gradual increase in, let us say, visual competence since the so-called Greek manner of the thirteenth century – a stage in a discernible, Vasarian development, through Cimabue, Giotto and Masaccio; and we remember that Vasari was to write that the next generation (Raphael, Michelangelo) were to become even more proficient in the depiction of drapery than the generation of Veneziano had been. But a parallel statement of discovery over time cannot be made, surely, about Van Eyck's mastery. If we look at a detail of Van Eyck's painting (fig. 13), it is astounding to see the incredible richness of observation and suggestion, and the unbelievable completeness of the

     Jeroen Stumpel

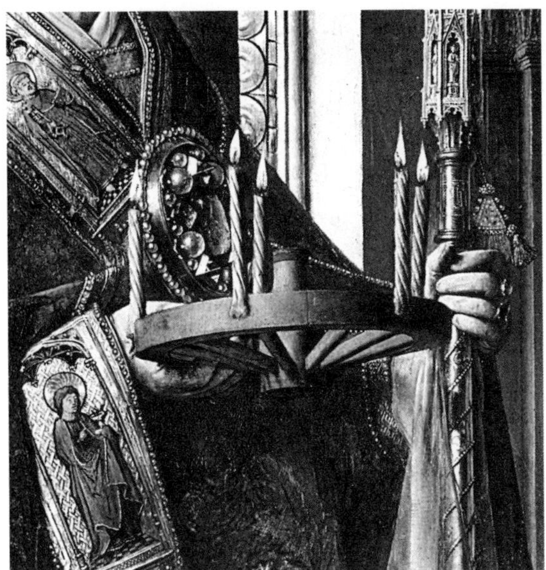

technique. Neither in the Limbourg brothers, nor in the paintings of Broederlam, do we find anything comparable to it.

The grand theme of *Art and Illusion* would demand that a predecessor must have been there; but, if we cannot trace such pathfinders and precursors, we may be forced to conclude that they never existed. After well over a century of research into early Netherlandish painting, it is less and less likely that it is due to a loss of information that we no longer have access to a prehistory of Van Eyck's manner. At this late date we probably have to abandon the thought that a missing link may be identified.

I hope the reader will not mind considering some other details of Van Eyck, to marvel with me. We have the famous, perhaps over-famous Arnolfini panel in London (fig. 14), where we may observe the way a chandelier is rendered in full competent and correct foreshortening (fig. 15), with the rich and suggestive play of shadows in different tones in each arm of the lamp, with the expressions of highlight in the proper and effective places: notice for instance how the larger reflections have been shaped in a form of hatching that very neatly corresponds with the surface quality of polished brass. Behind it we notice a string of beads hanging against the back wall. Thanks to published macro-photographs of the National Gallery, we may study the technique in which this detail was realised (fig. 16).[34] Each bead is shaped differently, but the behaviour of the light corresponds to the optical behaviour of light in such translucent globes: we have the incoming light, marked with a reflection near the light source; then we have light entering the crystal droplet, and exiting with a stronger light on the side opposite; furthermore we may see how this light interrupts the soft contoured,

     Pattern and Portrayal

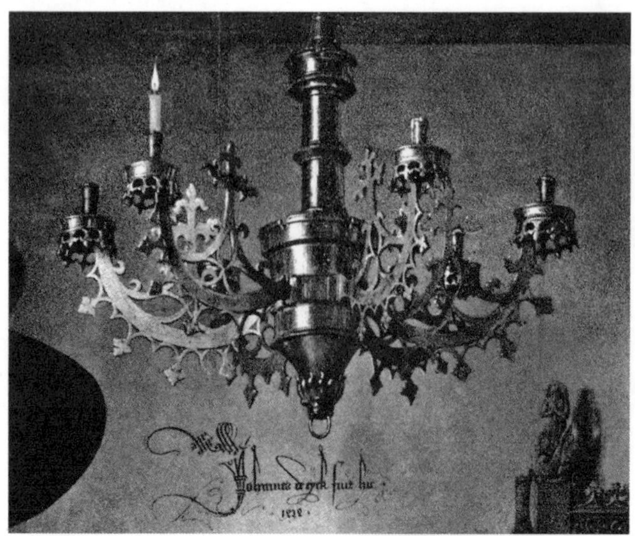

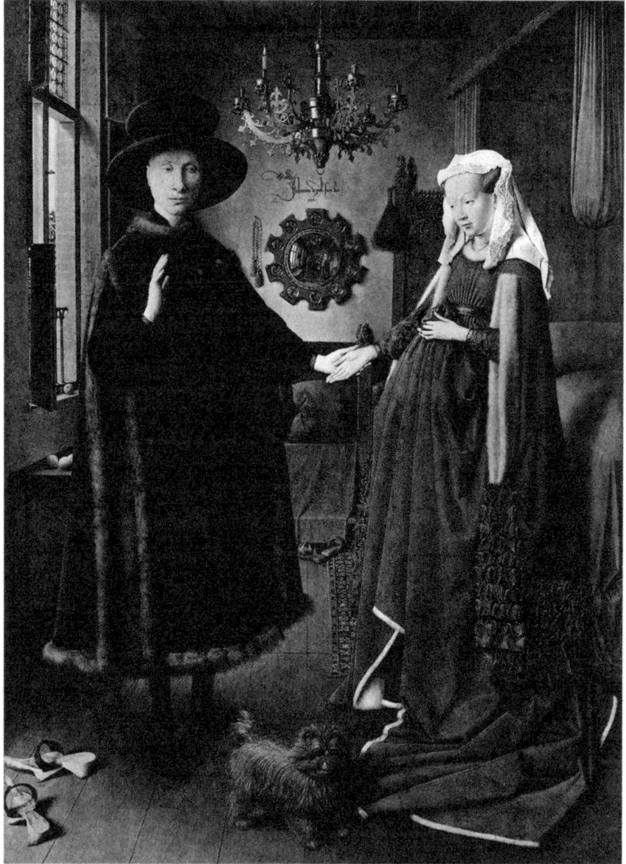

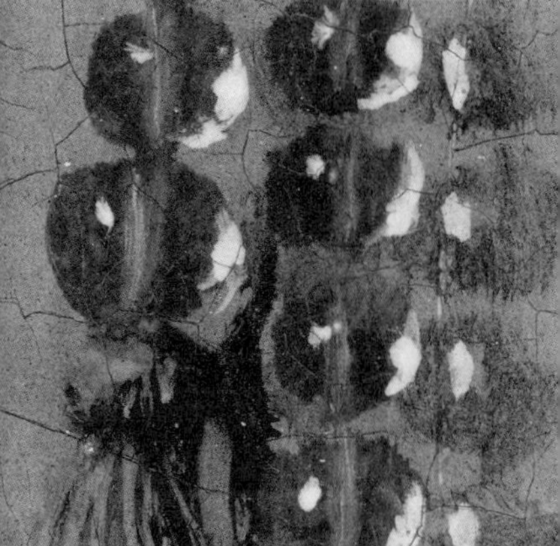

FIGS. 13–15 Jan van Eyck, The Arnolfini
portrait, 1434, National Gallery, London,
and details of chandelier and rosary

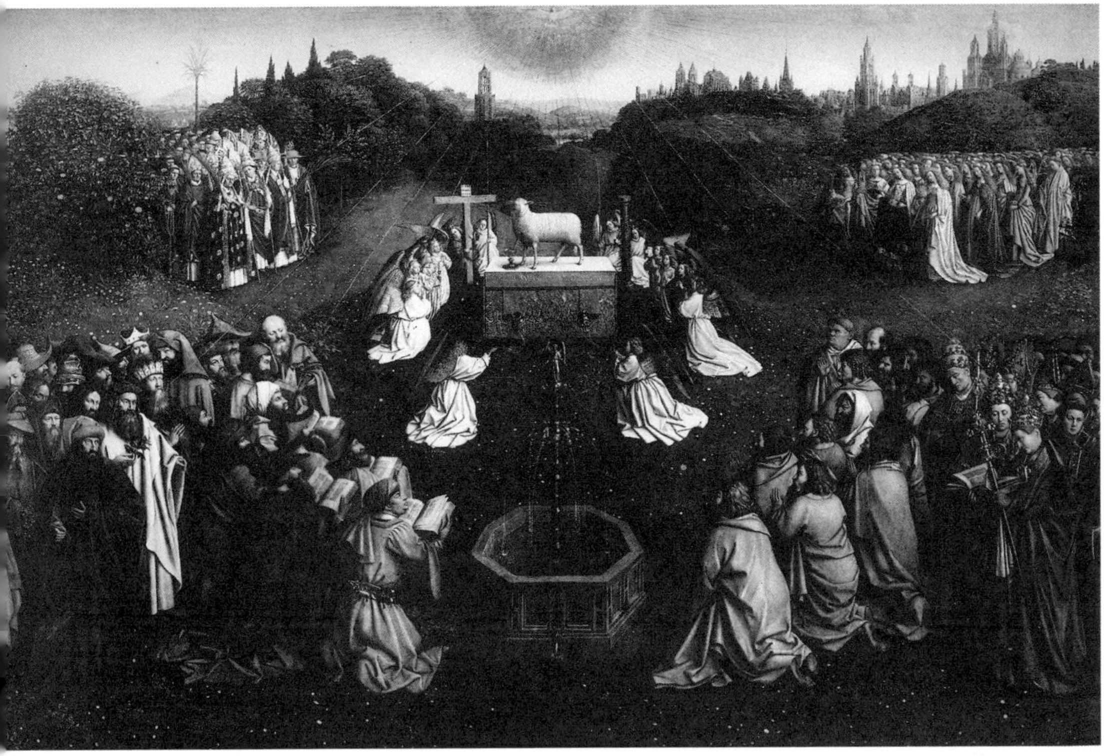

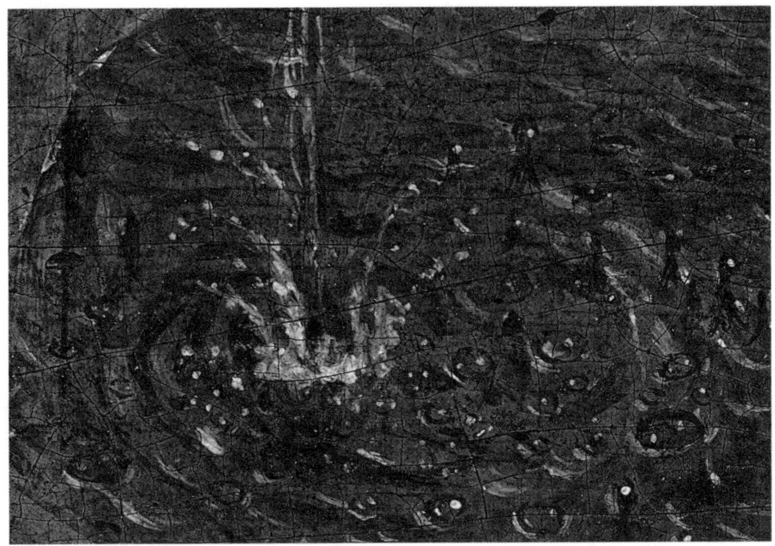

FIGS. 17–18 Hubrecht and Jan van Eyck, *The Adoration of the Lamb*, c. 1420-26, St Bavo's Cathedral, Ghent, and detail of fountain

     Pattern and Portrayal

half opaque shadow in the wall. All this not only demands an intense scrutiny of optical phenomena, but also a sophisticated, virtuoso brushwork on the tiniest surface imaginable – a mere handful of square millimetres.

In Van Eyck's oeuvre one may discover many such treasures. Here I show a lesser known case, which astounds me perhaps even more than the examples already mentioned. In the Ghent altarpiece, on the *Adoration of the Lamb* panel (fig. 17), we encounter a fountain. Droplets fall from high into a basin (fig. 18). The water has been rendered very well, and one may surmise how Van Eyck made clever use of the potential of oil painting to realise semi-transparency and glazing. But there is also his observation of the behaviour of water in motion, and the play of light on such a complex and reflective surface.

Most amazing however is the fact that the painter, having observed drops in detail, gives them the typical knob-shaped protrusion at the top of the local wave caused by a falling droplet. To us such shapes are familiar, indeed have become a cliché, through a plethora of slow motion movies and stroboscopic photographs. How different this must have been in the fifteenth century! And yet the phenomenon is rendered with great assurance by Van Eyck. Here again we have as I far as know no preceding formula. And in the case of these droplets it did not develop into a formula; on the panel in Madrid clearly derived from Van Eyck's famous example, the fountain does not contain this refined detail.

Certainly, Van Eyck became a painter of great prestige, whose work was followed by many painters. But unlike the Vasarian, general development in Italy, in the case of the Van Eycks it seems that they founded a school of portrayal, indeed hyper-portrayal, in one go. Jan van Eyck was not much improved upon, and it would seem rather as if parts of his works – his landscapes, his portraits, his reflections, his still lifes – were each formative for different branches of Netherlandish painting.

One could argue that, in Gombrich's *Art and Illusion*, not enough is made of the distinction between actual portrayal, working after life, and working from the head (and working from the head, incidentally, is what came to be praised particularly in the Tuscan-Italian tradition). Gombrich's study can be extremely helpful and suggestive when the correction seems *less* important than the schema, when formula presides over portrayal. In such cases, we can sometimes see very precisely how formulae acquire a life of their own.[35]

The love of impressionistic painting, the quasi-photographic rendering of reality, seems to have a too dominant position in *Art and Illusion*; Gombrich was perhaps too much concerned with the psychological wonders of adapting one's vision and knowledge to the task of working after life. On the one hand, I have argued, he overestimated the relevance of the perceptual constancies for the problems of portrayal, and also overestimated the scale of the difficulties of painting accurately from nature. As Jan van Eyck showed, this does not necessarily need centuries of preparation. What is more, the correction of the pre-existent schema is a special case of the modification of formulae, and there are many other kinds with which the art historian may legitimately be interested. Gombrich would not, of course, have denied this; on the contrary his works teach us to take interest in the life of formulae in general, in how they can be inherited from one master by another and change from one generation to another or from one culture to another. Such studies of cultural inheritance bring us back to what I believe to be the core business of art history: understanding the birth, the development, the modification and the discarding of visual traditions.

1   E.H. Gombrich, *Art and Illusion: A Study in the Psychology of Pictorial Representation*, London, 1960, pp. 58-67.

2   E.H. Gombrich, *The Sense of Order: A Study in the Psychology of Decorative Art*, 2nd edn, London, 1984 (1st edn Oxford, 1979), pp. 1, 87.

3   Gombrich, *Art and Illusion* (n. 1 above), esp. pp. 24, 121, 303.

4   Ibid., p. 99.

5   E.H. Gombrich, 'Meditations on a Hobby Horse or the Roots of Artistic Form', in *Aspects of Form, a Symposium on Form in Nature and Art*, ed. L. L. Whyte, London, 1951, pp. 209-24, reprinted in Gombrich, *Meditations on a Hobby Horse and Other Essays on the Theory of Art*, London, 1963, pp. 1-11.

6   C. Golomb, *The Child's Creation of a Pictorial World*, 2nd edn, Mahwah (NJ), 2004, p. 23. For other revealing examples of these phenomena, see J. Goodnow, *Children's Drawing*, London, 1977.

7   Gombrich, *Art and Illusion* (n. 1 above), pp. 63-64, 126-27, 144-45, 155, 298-300, 302.

8   Ibid., pp. 63-64, 76, 99.

9   I. Kant, *Kritik der reinen Vernunft*, Riga, 1781, I, 1. Theil, 1. Abteilung, 2. Buch, 1. Hauptstück, 'Von dem Schematismus des reinen Verstandes'.

10 H. Head and W.H.R. Rivers, *Studies in Neurology*, Oxford, 1920, II, p. 605.

11 Gombrich, *Art and Illusion* (n. 1 above), pp. 126-27.

12 Ibid., p. 260.

13 Ibid., p. 64.

14 E.g. G. Kerschensteiner, *Die Entwicklung der zeichnerischen Begabung*, Munich, 1905, p. 16; H. Read, *Education through Art*, London, 1943, p. 121.

15 Gombrich, *Art and Illusion* (n. 1 above), pp. 134-48.

16 H. Wölfflin, *Kunstgeschichtliche Grundbegriffe. Das Problem der Stilentwicklung in der neueren Kunst*, Munich, 1915, p. 14: '*Der stofflich-imitative Gehalt mag an sich noch so verschieden sein, das Entscheidende bleibt, daß der Auffassung da und dort ein anderes „optisches" Schema zugrunde liegt, ein Schema, das aber viel tiefer verankert ist als in den bloß imitativen Entwicklungsproblemen: es bedingt die Erscheinung der Architektur ebensogut wie die der darstellenden Kunst und eine römische Barockfassade hat denselben optischen Nenner wie eine Landschaft des van Goyen.*'

17 Ibid., pp. 11-12: '*Jeder Künstler findet bestimmte „optische" Möglichkeiten vor, an die er gebunden ist. Nicht alles ist zu allen Zeiten möglich. Das Sehen an sich hat seine Geschichte und die Aufdeckung dieser „optischen Schichten" muß als die elementarste Aufgabe der Kunstgeschichte betrachtet werden.*'

18 Gombrich, *Art and Illusion* (n. 1 above), pp. 3-4, 7-8, 24-25, 73, 304.

19 Roger Fry, *Reflections on British Painting*, London, 1934, pp. 134-35, quoted in Gombrich, *Art and Illusion* (n. 1 above), pp. 246-47.

20 Gombrich, *Art and Illusion: A Study in the Psychology of Pictorial Representation*, 2nd edn, London, 1961, p. XI.

21 Gombrich, *Art and Illusion* (n. 1 above), p. 99.

22 F.C. Ayer, *The Psychology of Drawing, with Special Reference to Laboratory Teaching*, Baltimore, 1916, quoted in Gombrich, *Art and Illusion* (n. 1 above), pp. 146-47.

23 Gombrich, *Art and Illusion* (n. 1 above), pp. 134-35.

24 Ibid., p. 143.

25 Ibid., pp. 143-44.

26 Ibid., pp. 253-54.

27 Ibid., pp. 237-38.

28 Gombrich told Didier Eribon, 'I am particularly fond of Pissarro. If you ask me what the world looks like to me, it looks like a painting by Pissarro': E.H. Gombrich and D. Eribon, *A Lifelong Interest: Conversations on Art and Science with Didier Eribon*, London, 1993, pp. 109-10.

29 He was I think the first to do so.

30 This paradigm of the Impressionist in Gombrich's oeuvre is worth further investigation.

31 E. Panofsky, *Early Netherlandish Painting*, Cambridge MA, 1953, ch. V, 'Reality and Symbol in Early Flemish Painting: "*Spiritualia sub metaphoris corporalium*"', pp. 131-48.

32 Gombrich, *Art and Illusion* (n. 1 above), pp. 23-24.

33 E.H. Gombrich, 'Light, Form and Texture in Fifteenth-Century Painting North and South of the Alps', in Gombrich, *The Heritage of Apelles: Studies in the Art of the Renaissance III*, London, 1976, pp. 19-35.

34 J. Dunkerton and R. Billinge, *Beyond the Naked Eye. Details from the National Gallery*, London, 2005.

35 One might give as an example the hook-like cast shadows of late antique mosaics.

Beholders' Shares and the Language of Art*

JOHN KULVICKI

GOMBRICH'S WORK WAS THE STARTING POINT for all philosophical theories of depiction that followed it. Richard Wollheim identifies Gombrich as one 'to whose thinking on these subjects I am so deeply, so transparently indebted'.[1] Kendall Walton claims that his account of depiction[2] is a direct descendant of Gombrich's paper 'Meditations on a Hobby Horse',[3] which itself was a precursor to *Art and Illusion*.[4] Nelson Goodman followed Gombrich's work closely, and initiated a correspondence with him in response to the 'Hobby Horse' essay in 1952, a full sixteen years before *Languages of Art* would see the light of day[5] and at least eight years before Goodman's first published essay on philosophy of art,[6] which was a review of *Art and Illusion*.[7]

This essay traces the theme of language in relation to art from Gombrich's work through some of its philosophical descendants, focusing on how Gombrich and Goodman disagreed about the issue. The famous point of contention between them concerned linear perspective. Gombrich insisted that linear perspective is *not* merely a convention for depicting space, and thus we cannot attribute its appeal merely to 'the beholder's share'. Goodman disagreed. This disagreement brings out very important issues in the study of images and representations of other kinds. The upshot of this paper is that there are at least three senses in which beholders have a share in representation and there are at least two important respects in which images can be like languages. Once we realize this we will be in a position to see that Gombrich and Goodman were quite a bit closer than one might imagine and that each of these thinkers had a much more subtle view than recent caricatures of them might suggest.

Section I sketches the debate between Goodman and Gombrich over the conventionality of linear perspective and the way in which that debate has been received by philosophers. Section II unpacks two senses in which Gombrich understood the beholder's share in understanding images. One of them concerns recognitional responses to images, and section III shows how this helps explain Goodman's puzzlement over Gombrich's treatment of perspective. Another beholder's share regards expectations concerning symbols. Section IV explains how Goodman developed this idea in a way quite different from Gombrich. It is here that a third kind of beholder's share becomes important, and two ways in which images can be like languages become apparent.

I. The Gombrich-Goodman controversy

Art and Illusion dedicates itself to unpacking the methods artists have devised for representing the world with images. This is a complicated affair. The challenge is not just rendering a three-dimensional world in two dimensions, but also rendering a world of light and shadow on a uniformly illuminated surface. Just as flat patterns must give the impression of depth, aspects of hue, saturation and brightness must be recruited in the service of rendering shadows, highlights and luminance. Gombrich suggests there are many ways of accomplishing these ends, and whether one way or another is convincing depends in large part on the habits of the day. Famously, Gombrich draws the line between what is conventional and what is not with linear perspective. While techniques for rendering light and shadow are highly conventionalized, certain ways of rendering space, of which linear perspective is the clearest example, are not: 'Now perspective may be a difficult skill, but its basis, as has been said, rests on a simple and incontrovertible fact of experience, the fact that we cannot look round a corner'.[8] Habits do not determine whether we can see around a corner. Linear perspective demands a certain spatial relationship between the picture surface and what it depicts. Though the appeal of linear perspective might be merely a matter of habits, its effectiveness is rooted more in biology than it is in culture.

Goodman wrote that Gombrich's 'treatment of this subject is often puzzling.'[9] He went on to argue that perspective is just as conventional as anything else in pictorial representation.[10] Claims of this sort are taken to ground Goodman's view that depiction and other kinds of representation are like languages. Goodman is a radical conventionalist in that he thinks linear perspective is no more privileged a way to represent space than 'dog' is a privileged way of representing canines. Here are a few passages that help to make this point about Goodman's view and how it has been received over the years:

> Almost any picture may represent almost anything; that is, given a picture and object there is usually a system of representation, a plan of correlation, under which the picture represents the object.[11]

> For [Goodman], any set of markings on the canvas can, given the appropriate conventions, represent anything. In this sense, painting is like a language.[12]

> According to conventionalism, the only representationally relevant relations between pictures and their objects are conventional. In this respect, they are like words. Nelson Goodman, the most influential proponent of conventionalism, is explicit about the similarity between language and depiction.[13]

The same gloss of Goodman is provided by almost every philosophical theorist of depiction since, including Flint Schier,[14] Karen Neander,[15] Dominic Lopes,[16] and John Hyman.[17] While not inaccurate, these summaries are at best partial truths because they leave out a key sense in which Goodman thought pictures were like languages. Since it is terribly implausible that linear perspective's significance is rooted merely in convention, it seems as though Gombrich has the upper hand. But Gombrich's view is also more subtle than his denial of the conventionality of perspective suggests. The next section aims to explain Goodman's puzzlement over Gombrich's treatment of perspective by emphasizing a line of thought in Gombrich that the philosophical community has neglected. This will clear the way for explaining the other sense in which Goodman thought that pictures are like languages and for appreciating its importance.

II. Recognition and Goodman's puzzlement

Michael Podro points out that 'for Gombrich, to understand how depiction works we must examine how the painter mobilizes the mechanisms of recognition'.[18] We are visually aware of a landscape when looking at an Impressionist painting, but we are also aware of an Impressionist painting. 'When we say that the blots and brushstrokes of the impressionist landscapes "suddenly come to life", we mean we have been led to project a landscape into these dabs of pigment.'[19] Projection suggests that we put something out there, so what is out there is not wholly independent of its observers. Projection is rooted in the deployment of capacities for recognition, which are quite important for how we see the world generally. Look, and you see the trees, as such, and the mountains, the house on the hill and so on.

Recognition is a perceptual ability that is subject to training and depends in no small measure on the context in which one finds oneself and on the interests that such contexts make salient. 'Whenever we receive a visual impression, we respond by docketing it, filing it, grouping it in one way or another, even if the impression is only that of an inkblot or a fingerprint.'[20] The specific character of one's response depends on what one has the ability to see, what one can recognize, so an important part of the beholder's share is just the set of those recognitional capacities. These are a result of both our natural endowment and the specific cultural context in which we find ourselves.

These thoughts form the core of what would later be called the 'recognition theory of depiction': *P depicts O only if P elicits appropriate observers' capacities visually to recognize O.*[21]

What makes something a picture of an apple is in part the fact that looking at it leads to a recognitional response for apples. The claim is not that pictures are recognitionally identical to apples – they don't fool us into thinking we are viewing apples – but that there is overlap between recognitional responses to apples and pictures thereof. When looking at the picture surface, one recognizes apples, a flat surface, patches of colour, and so on. Pictorial content is determined by some subset of the recognitional capacities the picture excites. Texts, like 'apple', are recognizable as such, and they can prompt imaginings of apples, but such texts do not secure visual recognition of apples.[22]

Gombrich's essays 'Meditations on a Hobby Horse'[23] and 'Image and Code'[24] are forerunners to the recognition theory of depiction and they anticipate a point about resemblance in pictures made by recognition theorists. Taking Konrad Lorenz's studies as his guide, Gombrich claims in the former essay that:

> The ball has nothing in common with the mouse except that it is chasable .… As 'substitutes' they fulfill certain demands of the organism. They are keys which happen to fit into biological or psychological locks, or counterfeit coins which make the machine work when dropped into the slot.[25]

In 'Image and Code', published thirty years later, he is still focused on the same point: 'the greater the biological relevance of a feature, the greater is also the ease of recognition, however remote the objective resemblance may be'.[26] Objective resemblance does little work as long as one has a suitably tuned recognitional capacity. He continues: 'The main point I wish to make here is that the fish which snaps at the artificial fly does not ask the logician in what respect it is like a fly and in what unlike'.[27] And from the earlier essay: 'An "image" in this biological sense, then, is not an imitation of an object's external form but an imitation of certain privileged or relevant aspects'.[28]

Schier, and then Lopes, would go on to unpack this point in some detail. 'The respect in which S resembles its depictum O is this: there is an overlap between the recognitional abilities triggered by S and O.'[29] Recognitional overlap accounts for the intuition that pictures resemble what they depict. Notice that this view places few, if any, concrete constraints on surface configuration. That is, it does not insist that pictures of red things must be red, or pictures of quadrilateral things be quadrilateral. Schier continues: 'I doubt that it will prove possible to give a simple, general account of the similarity between picture and depictum that does not essentially invoke the fact that S and O trigger some of the same recognitional abilities.'[30] Given suitable recognitional capacities, any configuration of colour on a canvas could depict anything else. 'Any design can depict any object provided it is recognizable as of that object.'[31] For example, a simple smiley face secures recognition of a face, but of no face in particular. It depicts a face, but not a bearded man's face, and certainly not Ernest Hemingway's face. Other, more detailed, images can secure recognition of a face, but also of facial features at a high level of detail. We say of the latter that they 'really look like' faces while the smiley face merely suggests a face. For the recognition theorist,

     John Kulvicki

this merely picks up on the fact that the detailed images secure recognition for more facial detail than the cartoonish ones do.

Once this aspect of Gombrich's work is made clear, it becomes easier to see why Goodman was puzzled by Gombrich's treatment of perspective. Recognition need not be *explained* by easily articulated, observer-independent similarities between the picture plane and what it depicts. As mentioned earlier, Goodman was first impressed by Gombrich's hobby horse essay, which clearly states that '"representation" does not depend on formal, that is, geometrical, qualities beyond the minimum requirements of function'.[32] That is to say, the most perspicuous specification of the relevant similarities might just be that they provoke similar responses in appropriate observers. Why insist, then, on a special *spatial* relation between the canvas and the scene it depicts? Linear perspective might be special because one can easily learn to interpret pictures made according to its rules, but that is not central to what makes linear perspective a way of making pictures. It is a pictorial technique only insofar as it secures the appropriate recognition responses from appropriate viewers.

While recognition is very important to Gombrich's view of depiction, it cannot do its work alone. Deployment of recognitional skills depends in no small part on what one is looking for, what one expects the world to deliver. We have developed a practice of using images and along with it we have trained ourselves to expect certain things from them. These expectations concerning representations are the core motivation for Goodman's discussion of symbol systems.

III. Symbol systems

It is standard to think of Goodman as the one who stresses the importance of symbol systems in his work, but the roots of this view can be found in Gombrich:

> There is a limit to the information language can convey without introducing such devices as quotation marks that differentiate between what logicians call 'language' and 'metalanguage'. There is a limit to what pictures can represent without differentiating between what belongs to the picture and what belongs to the intended reality.[33]

Viewers must differentiate between features of the picture surface and features of the 'intended reality'. This is no simple perceptual task, akin to ascertaining the colour of a patch of paint. This task involves one's sense of what makes a painting, drawing or print the picture that it happens to be.

> In visual representation, signs stand for objects of the visible world, and these can never be 'given' as such. Any picture, by its very nature, remains an appeal to the visual imagination .... Unless we know the conventions, we have no means of guessing which aspect is presented to us.[34]

   Beholders' Shares and the Language of Art

Pictures burden beholders with the task of knowing the conventions: sorting out what belongs to them as pieces of canvas and what belongs to the contents they present to us. One could imagine that Jenefer Robinson is talking of Gombrich when she says 'Understanding what a picture refers to is always a function of the system of symbolizing within which it functions'.[35] Her target is, of course, Goodman: 'Nothing is intrinsically a representation; status as representation is relative to symbol system'.[36]

But what is it we commit ourselves to when we insist that we must distinguish 'what belongs to the picture and what belongs to the intended reality'? There are at least two dimensions that matter here. First, one could be interested in piecemeal image-world correspondences. Given that we have such and such a picture what is the scene that it represents? Can we make rules for such correspondences across a range of pictures? The other dimension is the one that Goodman emphasized. To identify some object as a member of a symbol system is to make a (perhaps tacit) judgement about how it relates, semantically and syntactically, to other representations within such a system. To see the distinction between focusing on correlations between images and contents, on the one hand, and general semantic and syntactic constraints on the other, it helps to consider an ancient example of the conventionality debates: Plato's *Cratylus*.

Recently, Lynne Nygaard, Allison Cook and Laura Namy published a study that claimed to undermine 'a fundamental assumption regarding spoken language … [namely] that the sound structure of words bears an essentially arbitrary relationship to meaning.'[37] Hermogenes supports this fundamental assumption in the *Cratylus* but, unluckily for him, at the time it was neither an assumption nor fundamental. The Nygaard study suggests that Hermogenes' luck hasn't changed. Though many might assume Hermogenes was correct, he was wrong. Not only are there 'cross-linguistic sound-to-meaning correspondences to which listeners from unrelated language backgrounds are sensitive' but also these correspondences 'aid learning relative to entirely arbitrary sound-to-meaning pairings'.[38] In the *Cratylus*, Socrates comes closest to the view supported by this study, while Cratylus himself occupies a fairly radical position to the effect that a name cannot correspond to something unless it resembles that thing in rather significant respects.

What matters most for present purposes is the way in which Socrates tries to find a middle ground between Cratylus and Hermogenes:[39]

> … the signification of words is given by custom and not by likeness, for custom
> may indicate by the unlike as well as by the like … custom and convention must
> be supposed to contribute to the indication of our thoughts; for suppose we take
> the instance of number, how can you ever imagine, my good friend, that you will
> find names resembling every individual number, unless you allow that which you
> term convention and agreement to have authority in determining the correctness
> of names? I quite agree with you [Cratylus] that words should as far as possible

    John Kulvicki

resemble things; but I fear that this dragging in of resemblance, as Hermogenes says, is a shabby thing, which has to be supplemented by the mechanical aid of convention with a view to correctness.[40]

Convention is relevant, somehow, as a supplement to resemblance. Moreover, resemblance is a somewhat blunt instrument. It is far from obvious to Socrates that it can be used to pair all words with their meanings. This kind of middle ground is evident in the Nygaard study mentioned above. They do not claim that it is impossible for a word to refer to something in the absence of some significant relationship between word and object. They suggest that:

> Although arbitrariness certainly remains a central design characteristic of linguistic structure, these results indicate that language users also can and do exploit non-arbitrary relationships in the service of word learning and retrieval.[41]

Here they make use of a notion not available to Plato, and thus not something he could have given to Socrates in the dialogue. These scientists do not think it is essential to the structure of a language that the words in it resemble what they are about. In fact, the words can function syntactically and/or grammatically within the language irrespective of whether they bear non-arbitrary relationships to what they are about. They would not suggest that it is essential to being a *language* that elements within it resemble, or that they have any other kind of non-arbitrary relationship to, their referents. The languages we can learn well typically make use of non-arbitrary connections between words and what they are about,[42] even though that is not essential to being a language. One can, and should, I think, read Goodman as making a similar suggestion.

Gombrich focused on whether the picture/object connection is arbitrary, or conventional, and in this most philosophers have followed him. If this is the ground for debate, Goodman comes out as a clear loser, because it certainly seems as though there are non-arbitrary connections between pictures and their contents. In an essay responding to Goodman, Gombrich claims, 'At any rate it appears that learning to read an ordinary photograph is very unlike learning to master an arbitrary code. A better comparison would be with learning the use of an instrument'. In a Socratically concessive gesture, Gombrich continues:

> As soon as we approach our problem from this angle, the angle of the ease of acquisition, the traditional opposition between 'nature' and 'convention' turns out to be misleading. What we observe is rather a continuum between skills which come naturally to us and skills which may seem next to impossible for anyone to acquire.[43]

The point is that certain picture/object correspondences are impressively easy to learn while others are doubtless 'impossible for anyone to acquire'. In fact, it is difficult to deny this claim, even as it applies to language. With our limited phonetic

     Beholders' Shares and the Language of Art

and phonological potential one can imagine languages we simply could not learn, names we could never master. Or think about trying to name the integers in a non-compositional fashion: Ernst, Nelson, Gertrude, Frances, etc. That is not to say there is anything of the essence of spoken or written language that requires it to be easily learnable. As a matter of fact, the languages we use are reasonably learnable, but that is far from surprising. Similarly, we might be able to characterize what it is to be pictorial in a way that concerns itself with the structure of such a representational system, without an eye to whether any instance of such a system would be useful to or easily learned by creatures like us.

In response to the first published version of Gombrich's 'Image and Code' paper Goodman said:

> But I think as you do that it is 'not very helpful to divide meanings into those which exist "by nature" and others which are learned'. This seems to diminish the importance of the residual disagreement: I cannot believe that the standard rules of perspective embody the one native and easiest way of achieving and reading a realistic representation. But does innateness really matter much?[44]

Are there 'plans of correlation' between pictures and the world that are easier to learn than others? Probably. Perspective might be among them, but Goodman couldn't bring himself to believe this because, as he endeavoured to show in *Languages of Art*, perspective can seem quite artificial.[45] Regardless of whether he ultimately wins the day concerning perspective, the important point is that Goodman wants to move the focus in discussing representation away from specific symbol-meaning correspondences and on to the syntactic and semantic structure of representational systems.

For Goodman, pictorial systems of representation are semantically dense, syntactically dense and relatively replete. Linguistic systems of representation are syntactically finitely differentiated, not very replete, and they fail to be semantically finitely differentiated. Diagrammatic systems are often semantically and syntactically dense, but not very replete, and so on. It is beyond the scope of this paper to explicate these conditions. The point is that for Goodman the distinctive marks of representational kinds were not to be found at the level of individual representation-meaning correspondences, but rather in the syntactic and semantic relations that representations bear to one another. He thought that there was a structure to our representational practices, but he understood this structure in a fairly abstract way. It is possible that certain representation-meaning correspondences are easier to learn than others, but that fact will not help to distinguish depiction from language, since certain word-meaning correspondences are easier to learn than others too.[46] The point is not so much that, like languages, there is an arbitrary pairing of representation and content as that, like languages, there are syntactic and semantic constraints on how pictorial systems are structured.

     John Kulvicki

Our representational practices have developed this structure without the
benefit of our assistance. We never decided, in any interesting sense of the term,
that English should have a subject-verb-object word-order and we never decided to
make use of semantically and syntactically dense representations that are relatively
replete, like pictures. Things just happened that way. Our representational practices
are beholden to us, the creatures that do the representing, but the nature of this
dependence does not entail we could make pictures be anything we want them to be.
It might in some sense of the word be arbitrary that representational systems have
the structure Goodman finds them to have – God did not decree that pictures must
be this way – but they are not arbitrary in the sense that we could just decide to do
things differently. Goodman thinks he has found the joints at which practice with
representations is articulated. Rarely quoted,[47] even though it sits right in the middle
of Goodman's most radically conventionalist claims, he says:

> Among representational systems, 'naturalism' is a matter of habit but habituation
> does not carry us across the boundary between description and representation [i.e.
> depiction]. *No amount of familiarity turns a paragraph into a picture; and no degree of
> novelty makes a picture a paragraph.*[48]

There is a 'boundary between description and representation [depiction]' that
is not breached by familiarity with the system being employed. The boundary
is structural. Any individual object can be treated as a picture or as a letter in an
alphabet, or a word in some language, but only at the cost of accepting constraints
on what makes it similar to other possible representations within some system. One
cannot satisfy the pictorial and the linguistic constraints at once. Goodman is trying
to find the aspects of representations that are characteristic of pictures in a different
place than they are typically sought. He in this way responds to the challenge put by
Gombrich, who was keenly aware that we had to 'know the conventions' and have
a way of sorting out 'what belongs to the picture and what belongs to the intended
reality'. Goodman makes room for vast conventional variation within constraints that
nevertheless distinguish depiction from description. These constraints on syntactic
and semantic structure constitute a third beholder's share, and a rather important
one at that, because these constraints are those within which convention flourishes.
It does not seem as though Gombrich ever grasped this point, even though such a
theory of of symbolic structure complements Gombrich's discussion of recognition so
well. It fills out the notion of expectation, without which recognition could not do the
job required of it.

     Beholders' Shares and the Language of Art

Summary

One of Gombrich's well-known discussions of caricature also serves as a worthwhile warning.

> If these examples have suggested anything, it is that we generally do take in the mask before we notice the face. The mask here stands for the crude distinctions, the deviations from the norm which mark a person off from others. Any such deviation which attracts our attention may serve us as a tab of recognition and promises to save us the effort of further scrutiny.[49]

Gombrich and Goodman played a large role in shaping contemporary Anglophone aesthetics and philosophy of art, but with around half a century between us and their most important work, the danger is that masks replace faces. If the goal is to distinguish thinkers from one another, to have convenient places to put them, then the masks suffice. But if the goal is allowing their work to inform what has become a rather complex contemporary philosophical scene, then we need to remove the masks.

Gombrich thought that illusion was important for understanding the history of art and the nature of depiction, but exactly what he meant by illusion is a subtle affair,[50] and his work is more directly related to the recognition view of depiction than has been acknowledged. Indeed, recognitional capacities are a key beholder's share, though not the only one. The other beholder's share involves expectations concerning symbols. Which features of the object one encounters matter for it being the representation that it happens to be? As suggested above, this is where Gombrich makes room for the study of symbols as Goodman would come to understand it.

We cannot understand our expectations regarding representations without understanding what we encounter *as representations*. Goodman accepts this and tries to deepen our sense of what treating something as a representation involves. Yes, it involves knowing conventions concerning meaning-representation correspondences, just as Gombrich suggested. But our practice is a bit more complicated than that. Representational kinds are distinguished from one another syntactically and semantically. This impressive regularity in our practice reflects a third beholder's share. Something about us, as consumers of representations, makes certain kinds of syntactic and semantic structures salient for different purposes. This suggests avenues for investigation that have not been explored fully and thus merit further attention.

Gombrich and Goodman disagreed about linear perspective and related techniques, but this disagreement is an unfortunate foundation upon which to build an understanding of their respective views. Gombrich denied that perspective is conventional in the way that word/meaning correspondences are, but there are also excellent reasons for thinking that this is beside the point when Gombrich's understanding of depiction is at issue. Gombrich is in many respects the father of

    John Kulvicki

recognition views of depiction, after all, and these views need not privilege perspective constructions, even if they can agree that for reasons external to the theory such constructions are not merely conventional. Similarly, Goodman implausibly insists that linear perspective is merely a convention, not unlike the conventions governing word/meaning correspondences. But this fact obscures the positive account he offers of what pictures are, and the avenues of research such an account reveals. Goodman's beholder's share is distinct from the two articulated by Gombrich, not least insofar as it seems to set constraints within which conventions flourish, more than it reveals another set of conventions. All three are worth keeping in sight.

* Versions of this paper were read at conferences hosted by the National University of Singapore and the New School for Social Research. I thank the organizers – Ben Blumson in Singapore and Zed Adams in New York – and the participants for their helpful feedback.

1 R. Wollheim, 'On Drawing an Object', London, 1965; reprinted in Wollheim, *On Art and the Mind*, Cambridge, MA, 1974, pp. 3-30 (p. 24).

2 K. Walton, 'Pictures and Make-Believe', *Philosophical Review*, 82, no. 3, 1973, pp. 283-319 (p. 283, n. 1).

3 E.H. Gombrich, 'Meditations on a Hobby Horse or the Roots of Artistic Form', in *Aspects of Form, a Symposium on Form in Nature and Art*, ed. L.L. Whyte, London, 1951, pp. 209-24, reprinted in Gombrich, *Meditations on a Hobby Horse and Other Essays on the Theory of Art*, London, 1963, pp. 1-11.

4 E.H. Gombrich, *Art and Illusion: a Study in the Psychology of Pictorial Representation*, London, 1960.

5 N. Goodman, *Languages of Art*, Indianapolis, 1968.

6 N. Goodman, 'Review of Gombrich's *Art and Illusion*', *Journal of Philosophy*, 57, 1960, pp. 595-99, reprinted in Goodman, *Problems and Projects*, Indianapolis, 1972, pp. 141-46.

7 Gombrich's papers are being organized by Veronika Kopecky of the Warburg Institute,

and I thank her for showing me some of the Gombrich-Goodman correspondence.

8 *Art and Illusion* (n. 4 above), p. 211.

9 Goodman, 'Review' (n. 6 above), p. 145.

10 N. Goodman, *Languages of Art*, 2nd edn, Indianapolis, 1976, pp. 10-19.

11 Ibid., p. 38.

12 D. Carrier, 'A Reading of Goodman on Representation', *The Monist*, 58, no. 2, 1974, pp. 269-84 (p. 277), and cf. Carrier, 'Perspective as a Convention: on the Views of Nelson Goodman and Ernst Gombrich', *Leonardo*, 13, 1980, pp. 283-87 (p. 284).

13 C. Abell, 'Against Depictive Conventionalism', *American Philosophical Quarterly*, 42, no. 3), 2005, pp. 185-97 (p. 186).

14 F. Schier, *Deeper into Pictures*, Cambridge, 1986, p. 141.

15 K. Neander, 'Pictorial Representation: a Matter of Resemblance', *British Journal of Aesthetics*, 27, no. 3, 1987, pp. 213-26 (p. 221).

16 D. Lopes, *Understanding Pictures*, Oxford, 1996, p. 65.

17 J. Hyman, *The Objective Eye: Colour, Form and Reality in the Theory of Art*, Chicago 2006, p. 167.

18 M. Podro, *Depiction*, New Haven and London, 1998, p. 6.

19 *Art and Illusion* (n. 4 above), p. 170.

20 Ibid., p. 251.

21 See, e.g., Lopes, *Understanding* (n. 16 above), pp. 136-56; Lopes, *Sight and Sensibility*,

Oxford, 2005, p. 641, and Schier, *Deeper* (n. 14 above), pp. 50-51.

22 There is more to the recognition view than is discussed here. What makes an observer appropriate? What are sufficient (as opposed to mere necessary) conditions on something being a picture? For now, these issues can be left to one side since this core claim of the recognition theorists suffices to illustrate the point about resemblance below.

23 Gombrich, 'Hobby Horse' (n. 3 above).

24 E.H. Gombrich, 'Image and Code: Scope and Limits of Conventionalism in Pictorial Representation', lecture given at the International Conference on the Semiotics of Art, Ann Arbor, Michigan, 1978, published in Gombrich, *The Image and the Eye. Further Studies in the Psychology of Pictorial Representation*, Oxford 1982, pp. 278-97.

25 'Hobby Horse' (n. 3 above), p. 4.

26 'Image and Code' (n. 23 above), p. 285.

27 Ibid., p. 286.

28 'Hobby Horse' (n. 3 above), p. 6. Gombrich is not completely consistent on this point. He claims, 'Image and Code', p. 297, that 'Western art would not have developed the special tricks of naturalism if it had not been found that the incorporation *in the image* of all of the features which serve us in real life for the discovery and testing of meaning enabled the artist to do with fewer and fewer conventions' [italics added]. Incorporating features of the world in the image suggests pictures resemble their objects in a more profound way than envisaged by the recognition theorists. Lopes, *Understanding* (n. 16 above), §4.1, stresses a discontinuity between the hobby horse essay and *Art and Illusion* (he never mentions 'Image and Code'), and thus he sees Gombrich as a more distant forerunner of the recognition view than the present discussion suggests. Lopes, *Sensibility* (n. 21 above), ch. 1, seems more amenable to the present view of Gombrich, as is Patrick Maynard, *Drawing Distinctions*, Ithaca, 2005, p. 97.

29 Schier, *Deeper* (n. 14 above), pp. 186-87.

30 Ibid., p. 188.

31 Lopes, *Understanding* (n. 16 above), p. 151.

32 'Hobby Horse' (n. 3 above), p. 4.

33 *Art and Illusion* (n. 4 above), p. 201. Maynard (*Drawing Distinctions*, n. 28 above, p. 112) suggests that Gombrich misses this point. It is true that in this remark Gombrich has a specific set of examples in mind, but it seems a stretch to insist that he is unaware of how generally this point applies.

34 Ibid., p. 204.

35 J. Robinson, 'Languages of Art at the Turn of the Century', *Journal of Aesthetics and Art Criticism*, 58, no. 3, 2000, pp. 213-18 (p. 214).

36 Goodman, *Languages* (n. 10 above), p. 226.

37 L.C. Nygaard, A.E. Cook and L.L. Namy, 'Sound to meaning correspondences facilitate word learning', *Cognition*, 112, no. 1, 2009, pp. 181–86 (p. 181).

38 Ibid., p. 181.

39 It is controversial whether this is the right way to interpret the dialogue. See, e.g., the discussion by C.D.C. Reeve in Plato, *Cratylus*, tr. Reeve, Indianapolis, 1998, XXXIV, XL-XLII.

40 Plato, *Cratylus*, 435a-c, tr. Jowett (accessed at the Internet Classics Archive, http://classics.mit.edu/Plato/cratylus.html, 8/9/10).

41 Nygaard et al., 'Correspondences' (n. 37 above), p. 185.

42 See also R. Schwartz, 'Representation and Resemblance', *Philosophical Forum*, 4, 1974, pp. 499-512.

43 'Image and Code' (n. 23 above), p. 283.

44 Goodman quoted ibid., p. 284n.

45 Goodman, *Languages* (n. 10 above), pp. 10-19.

46 Cf. Lopes, *Understanding* (n. 16 above), pp. 66-68 and Robert Schwartz, 'Vision and cognition in picture perception', *Philosophy and Phenomenological Research*, LXII, no. 3, 2001, pp. 707-19 (p. 708).

47 However, see Lopes, *Understanding* (n. 16 above), p. 69.

48 Goodman, *Languages* (n. 10 above), p. 231. Italics added. And see Schwartz, 'Representation' (n.42 above).

49 E.H. Gombrich, 'The Mask and the Face', in *Art, Perception, and Reality*, ed. M. Mandelbaum, Baltimore, 1972, pp. 1-45 (p. 13).

50 K. Bantinaki, 'Pictorial Perception as Illusion', *British Journal of Aesthetics*, 47, no. 3, 2007, pp. 268-79.

Looking at Images and Reasoning about their Content

ROBERTO CASATI

THE COMPLEX AND MULTI-FACETED CONTRIBUTION of Gombrich to our understanding of pictures – in particular those pictures that count as works of art (with a sympathetic eye for the psychological side of the issue) – can hardly be summarized in a thesis or in a set of theses. This in itself will be no excuse for my own cherry-picking attitude towards the corpus of Gombrich's ideas. I have, however, a sufficiently circumscribed target here – shadow depiction and the inferential landscape that depicted shadows make possible – and I would like to pursue it in some detail. My hope is that by analysing some subtleties of the depiction of shadows in art, light will be cast on the viability of the larger Gombrichian programme of accounting for depiction and of our complex relationships to representational images.

Gombrich's programme: artists' toolboxes

In systematizing part of Gombrich's ideas, Patrick Maynard wrote: '... convincing depiction is largely a matter of building a toolbox of effective devices – dodges – passed on, studied, borrowed, stolen, or invented, though occasionally systematized'.[1] Gombrich himself eloquently wrote that:

> The history of art ... may be described as the forging of master keys for opening the mysterious locks of our sense to which only nature herself originally held the key .... Like the burglar who tries to break a safe, the artist has no direct access to the inner mechanisms.[2]

> The question is not whether nature 'really looks' like these pictorial devices but whether pictures with such features suggest a reading in terms of natural objects.[3]

A toolbox account of depiction is thus the thesis that artists have arranged certain physical properties of their productions so as to compel the viewer of those productions to imagine *visually* a certain situation and to *imagine that she is seeing* that situation. Triggering of recognitional abilities is certainly a useful ingredient of this imaginative relationship with pictures. But it is not enough – for instance, if we exclude triggering of motor responses we block the possibility of explaining the perspectivality of pictures. So let us be inclusive and accept that any tool that enables visual imagination and imagination of seeing is to be found in the toolbox.

It is no minor feat of Gombrich's project that at the same time it assumed and showed the impressive continuity between fine art and demotic art at all levels, from the productions of children to that of visual designers and cartoonists, to banausic endeavours by practitioners and amateurs. Nothing in the image production activity is alien to the scholar of art.[4] Thus opening the field to the investigation of all sorts of contributions unravels a vast body of knowledge that artists could choose to deploy at their will. But what is the point of the deployment? What are those tools good for?

There are three points worth emphasizing. First, 'convincing depiction' is a metacognitive, pragmatic term. It is a quality of the representational vehicle that is borrowed from a quality of the experience of the viewer. We have been sufficiently guarded against the risks of collapsing convincing depiction on to illusion. But we need some substantive account of convincing depiction – and one that preserves the idea that *depiction* is at stake. Second, the toolbox account predicts that some depictions will be convincing but not correct, if compared to some geometric or physical standards. Third, it also makes the dual prediction that some depictions are correct according to some standards, but still remain unconvincing. (Never mind, of course, the many correct and convincing depictions, and the even more numerous wrong and unconvincing depictions.)[5]

These predictions call for the study of some particular tools in the box. The representation of shadows appears to be an interesting candidate because shadows have a rich informational structure, a relatively straightforward geometry, and are very salient in terms of their luminance properties. At the same time the logic of mental shadow computations is quite idiosyncratic and deflects from the norms of geometry and physics. Let us introduce some pictorial representations of shadows. In *Shadows* Gombrich lists some *functions* of shadows by investigating paintings mostly in the collection of the National Gallery.[6] I have tried to enrich the classification by providing a more comprehensive list of functions of depicted shadows,[7] and there is still quite a lot of work ahead. But already at this point, out of the large number of examples of depicted shadows, some regularity emerges. At times shadows have been depicted almost for their own sake, for the pleasure of documenting an interesting visual phenomenon. One beautiful example is the shadow of the suspended candle in Crivelli's *Madonna della Candeletta* (fig. 1). Photographic art has pursued this approach – many beautiful aspects of the visual world have been registered accordingly.

In the spirit of the 'toolbox account', shadows have been mostly used to add vividness to pictures; their images have helped the viewer to represent a scene visually in such a way that she can imagine herself to be representing it visually; they have helped bestow on a depiction the character of convincing depiction. Most interesting of all for our purposes are those depictions that are not unconvincing in spite of the fact that

     Roberto Casati

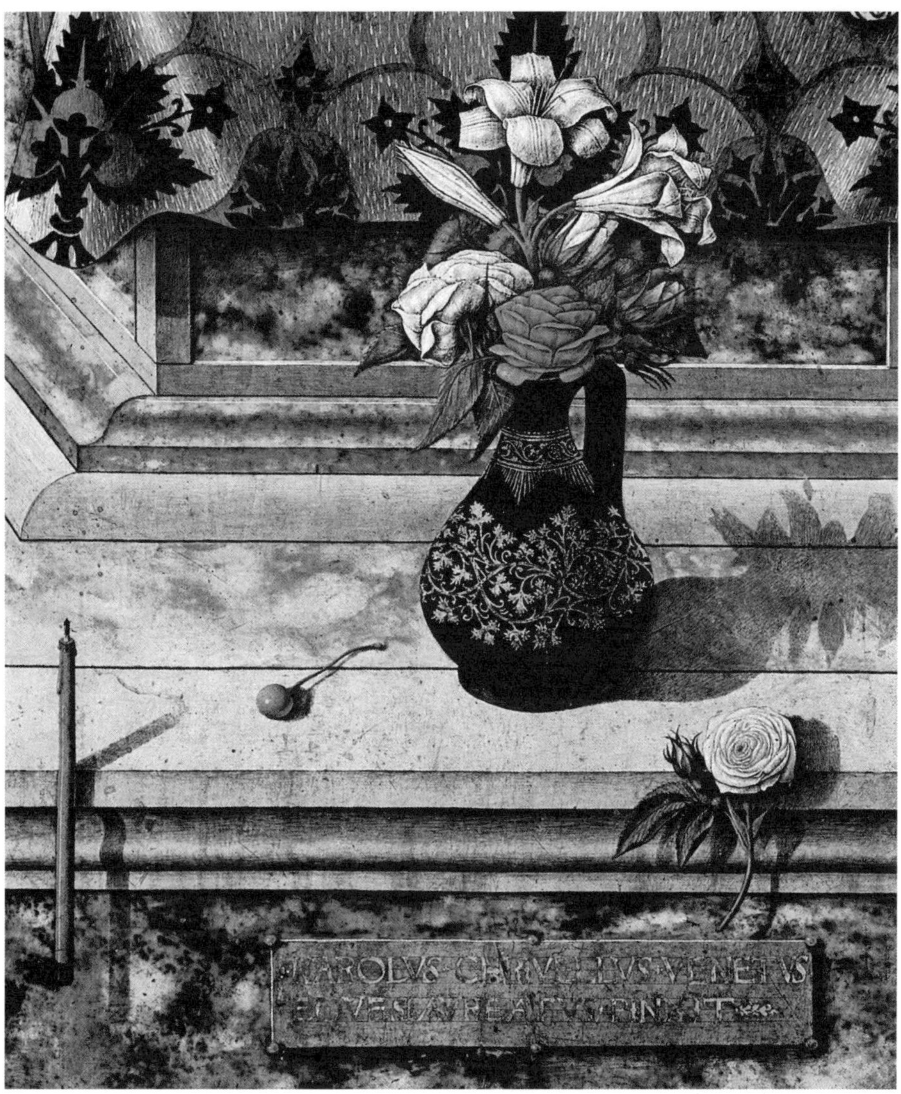

FIG. 1 Carlo Crivelli, *Madonna della Candeletta*, Milan, Pinacoteca di Brera

they are not of photorealistic quality and not even geometrically accurate.

I start from a comparison the interest of which lies in the fact that it provides a striking example of an actual double dissociation between convincing power and correctness. The two pictures in question are the *Nativity* of Filippo Lippi in Spoleto (1466-69; fig. 2) and the *Nativity* of his collaborator at Prato, Fra Diamante (*c.* 1465-70; fig. 3). Lippi presents us with very convincing shadows of poles protruding from the ruins of a building. The shadows are shown as parallel, indicating a source of light

     Looking at Images and Reasoning about their Content

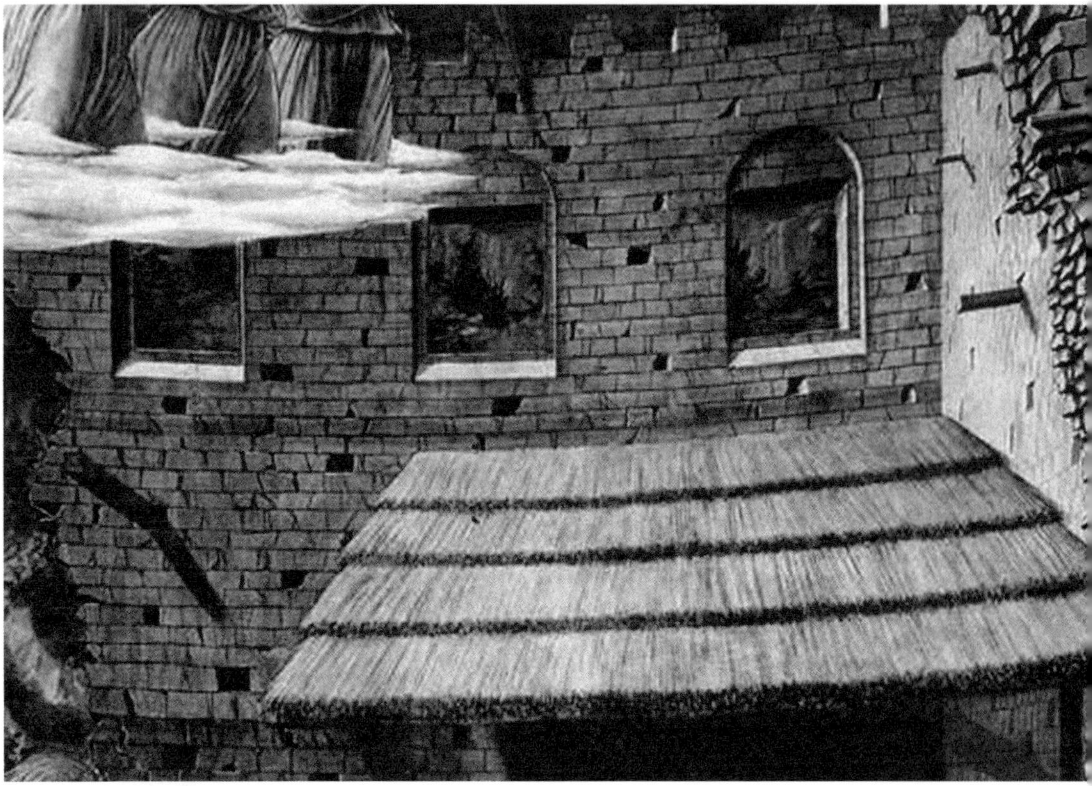

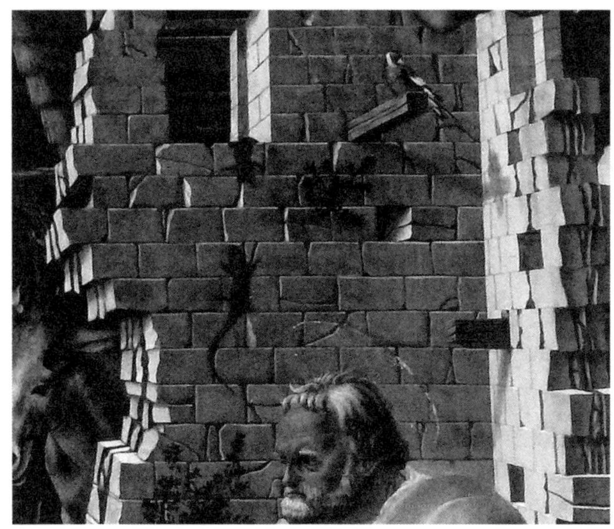

     Roberto Casati

(the sun) that is placed somewhere beyond the top left area of the represented space. However, these shadows are impossible, as they are projected on surfaces at right angles to one another, and hence are incompatible with the uniqueness of the light source. The fresco is convincing but incorrect. Fra Diamante's work, on the other hand, is correct but unconvincing. He represents a very similar situation, in which shadows are cast from poles protruding from two surfaces that form a right angle. The shadows appear to *converge*. Much as this may disturb the viewer, the convergence is consistent with the presence of a single light source and the relative positions of beams and walls.[8]

It is important to notice that much as the metacognitive predicates 'convincing' and 'unconvincing' are the result of some automatic processing of the visual scene, the normative predicates 'correct' and 'incorrect' require some reasoning. One has to spend time observing the painting, paying attention to details, and reasoning about the geometry, in order to find out that the shadows in the Lippi fresco are not normatively correct, whereas the shadows in the Fra Diamante painting are correct.

We can enlarge the picture a bit. If we look into general informational properties of shadows, we can see that many of those properties are not exploited by the visual system, which is blind to potentially useful information.[9] Call this the 'cherry-picking principle'. The fact that information is cherry-picked depends on many causes; we can only blame the random paths of selection that made us cherish some types of information when other, ideally more useful types were neglected. As an example, the size of the sun's images projected to the ground through foliage can tell you about the distance of leaves and branches from the ground. The beauty of this mathematical property of foliage in the sun apparently was shunned by evolution. Nobody seems to be able immediately to perceive the height of a tree upon inspection of the shadows of foliage on the ground.

Conversely, if we look into what the visual system considers as useful informational means, we discover that it is not only blind to many physical and other constraints, but that it positively speaks in favour of violations of these constraints. Call this the 'good enough principle'. In a picture, patches of colour that appear to be uniformly darker than their surroundings and are somewhat made to correspond to objects in the scene count as shadows even though they may be fantastically inaccurate from the physico-geometrical side.

Cherry-picking and good enough show that there are interesting idiosyncrasies of the visual system; it does not behave in an ideal way, but according to some internal logic. Patrick Cavanagh has written of the pictorial logic of images as 'simplified physics',[10] but in some cases the putative laws that are followed by the represented shadows are more complex than the actual laws of physics.[11] For a shadow to bend around a corner in the way that it does in Konrad Witz's *Adoration of the Magi* (fig. 4),

    Looking at Images and Reasoning about their Content

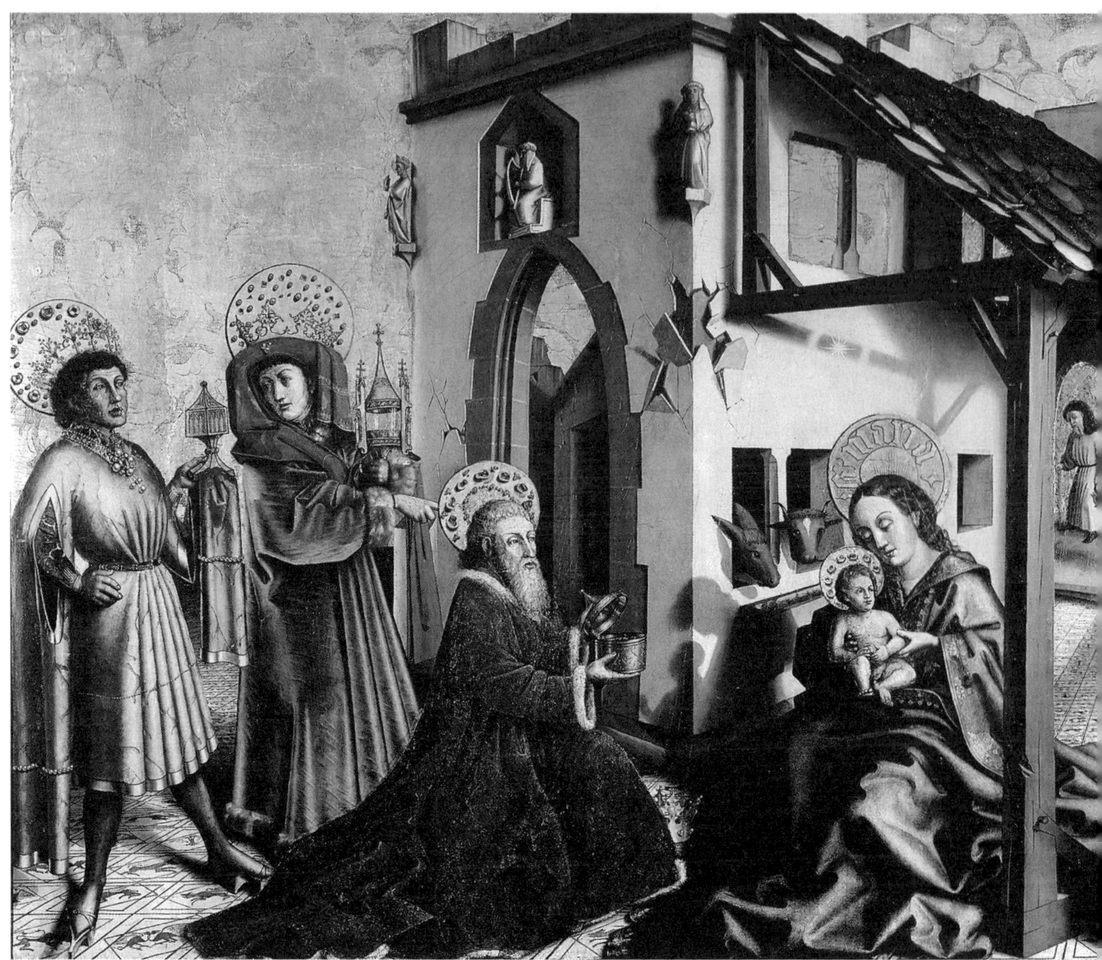

FIG. 4 Konrad Witz, *The Adoration of the Magi*, Geneva, Musée d'art et d'histoire

light rays must deviate in physically impossible ways. Witz's example is
particularly telling because of his association with naturalism. The *Adoration* is
depicted on the interior panel of a triptych one of whose exterior wings, representing
The Miraculous Draught of Fishes, is alleged to be one of the first European
representations of a real landscape – Lake Geneva, with its mountain Le Môle
in the background.[12]

Once we have set aside more anecdotal cases, we can see the liberating force of the
good enough principle. The visually possible does not coincide with the physically
possible. Painters have taken advantage of this fact in order to depict characters –
historical or fictional – whose behaviour defies the laws of physics. Panofsky famously

     Roberto Casati

used the example of Rogier van der Weyden's *Vision of the Magi* to make the point that we can draw inferences about the subject matter of a painting based on our knowledge of the laws of physics.[13] We would rule out the literal interpretation of a baby falling from the sky or projected into the air and settle for some supernatural event – a flying baby, or a flying divinity, or yet another, more complex fact.

The *visually* possible is certainly more heavily constrained by (some) physics than are other types of non-perceptual possibility. I can tell a tale about the jealousy number three feels for his fellow number four, but I cannot depict this tale (I may depict numerals, not numbers, but this would be another tale yet). But to what extent does visual possibility require physical possibility? Numbers cannot be depicted because they do not have a visual appearance. (Is this because they do not interact with light? Can there be visual appearances that do not depend somehow on interaction with light and on light transmission? These are further questions.)

Possible worlds exist in which colours as they appear to viewers are instantiated by different types of physical properties than the ones we find in our environment (say, pressure waves instead of surface reflectances). These worlds would be perceptually close to ours but physically remote. They could still be depictable. Indeed, many pictures show how a visual world could be made that defied the lights of physics yet was still conceptually acceptable. Of course, much has to be said about the sense of 'conceptually acceptable'. In a weak sense we may want to operationalize conceptual acceptability based on the triggering of sufficiently rich recognitional and interpretive abilities. No visual stimulus is probably such as to elicit no recognition at all: colour concepts will be always activated when looking at a visual display. But richer, more structured concepts may not be activated.

Shadows in paintings are in many cases instances of this discrepancy between the conceptually acceptable and the physically acceptable. However, it is not only recognitional factors that play a hand in the game; so too do inferential factors in general. The following sections thus deal with inferences concerning the spatial and material layout of represented space. There are more complex inferences one may want to study, related for instance to recognition of characters. In what follows I offer a fragment of a taxonomy.

Shadows of allegedly invisible or diaphanous objects

We start from shadows of figures that ought not to cast a shadow. Indeed, there is a conceptual problem here. Some paintings represent souls or angels which, being diaphanous or immaterial, ought not to cast shadows. However, if light is not blocked by those figures, they ought to be completely transparent, hence (virtually) invisible. If the characters were not totally but only somewhat transparent, they ought to cast weaker but in any event non-full shadows. A classic example is the Signorelli

     Looking at Images and Reasoning about their Content

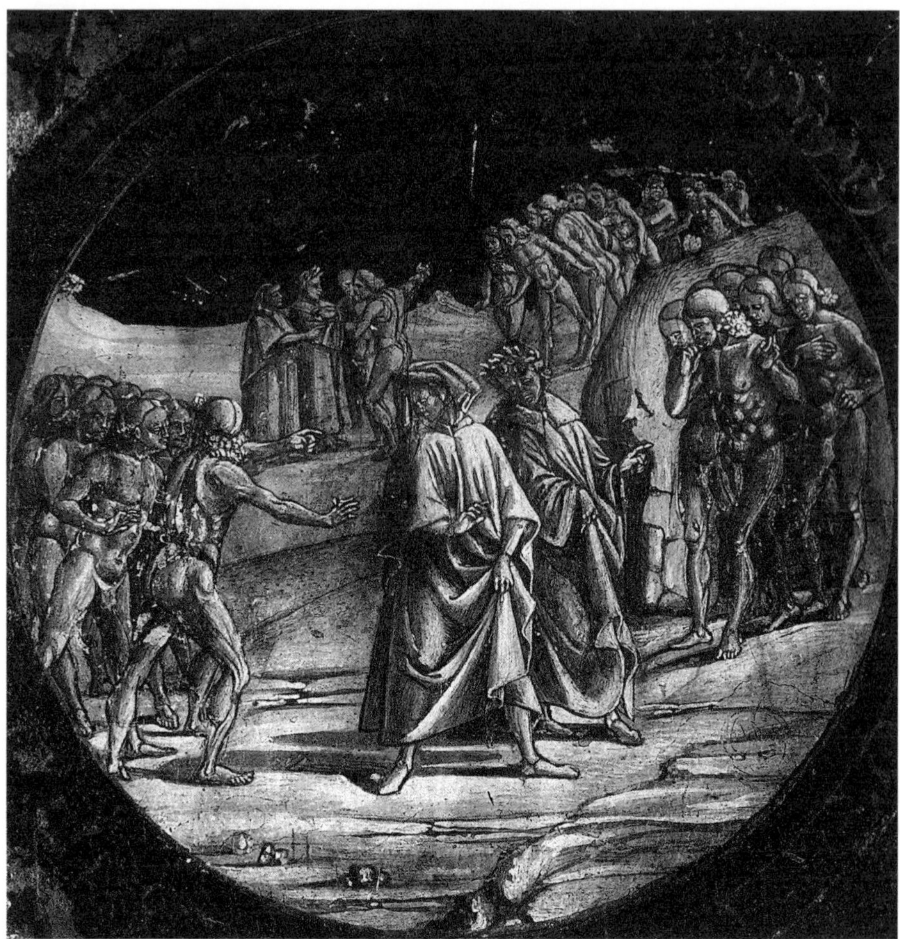

FIG. 5 Luca Signorelli, *Purgatory*, Orvieto Cathedral

representation of Canto V of Dante's *Purgatory* (fig. 5).[14] According to the verses of the poem, Dante casts a shadow and this betrays him; the souls of Purgatory discover his corporeal nature.[15] However, Signorelli has given the soul of Virgil as full a shadow as that of his living companion, as well as painting (admittedly shorter) shadows at the feet of all the other souls. Another paradigmatic example is the *Annunciation*, in which the angel generally casts a shadow, and is always defined by means of attached shadow. But aren't angels incorporeal entities?[16]

We find here an instance of the depiction of worlds that are physically different from ours but still conceptually accessible. Not only are they inhabited by immaterial characters, but these can cast shadows, although, as they are 'immaterial', they should let light pass through.

     Roberto Casati

This suggests in turn an intriguing cognitive hypothesis: that shadows are conceptually close to objects in the sense that they do not appear to be the result of a process (as opposed to, say, scratches on a surface, which wear on their face their processual origin). No matter how they are produced, we can recognize them as shadows. Even if we know and accept that immaterial objects ought not to produce them, we still accept them as shadows.

Shadows that indicate the presence of objects that are not visible in the painting

There are some masterly examples of this category. One, described in Gombrich's *Shadows,* is *Golgotha. Consummatum est* painted by Jean-Léon Gérôme (fig. 6), in which the three crosses are visible only via the shadows they cast. We know everything of the story, nothing is left to say, and the depiction of the material, wooden crosses would distract from the contemplation of an empty landscape. Another, earlier example (a precursor?) is the *View of Marseilles* of Emile Loubon (fig. 7). Barely readable, the shadows of two shepherds riding their horses are visible on the right in the foreground. This is a tale of power. The masters, unseen by us but whose presence is made

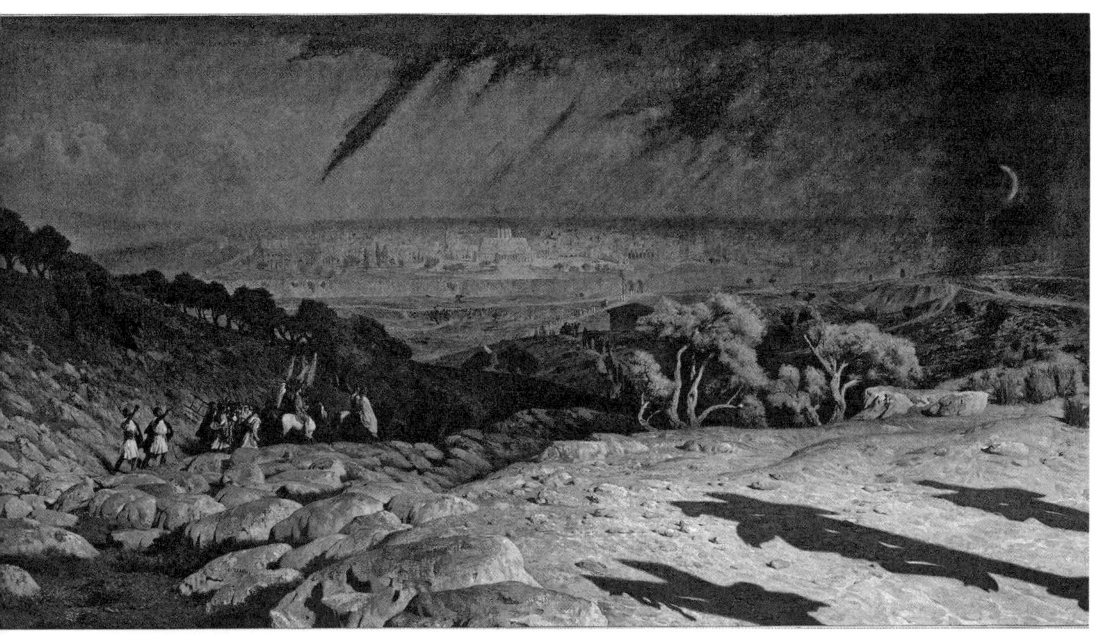

FIG. 6 Jean-Léon Gérôme, *Golgotha. Consummatum est (Jérusalem; La Crucifixion)*, Paris, Musée d'Orsay © RMN (Musée d'Orsay) / Hervé Lewandowski

     Looking at Images and Reasoning about their Content

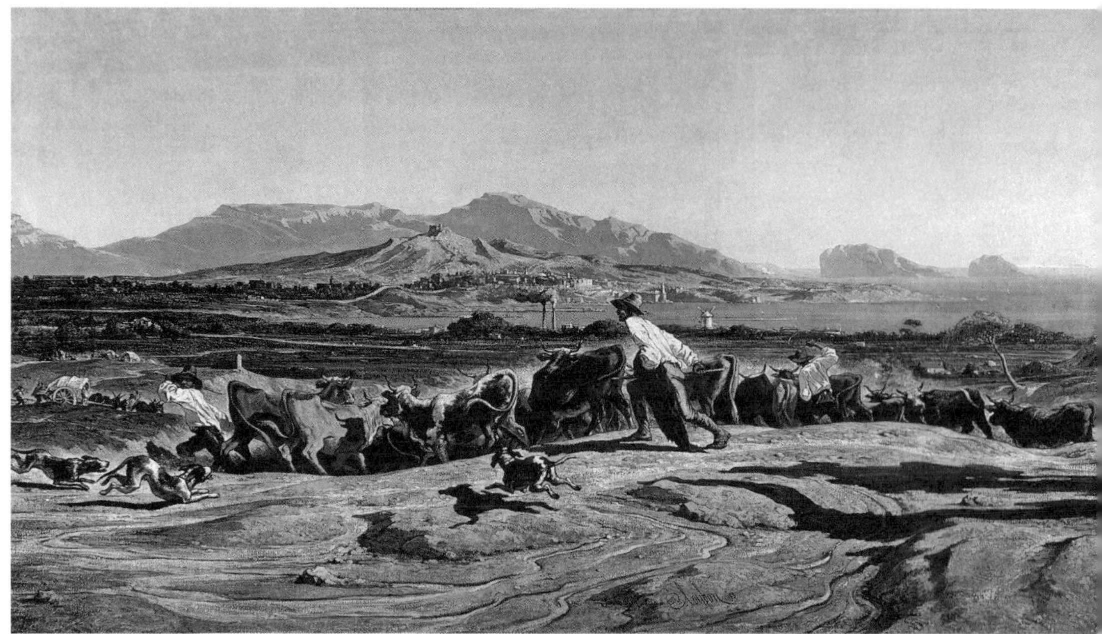

FIG. 7 Emile Loubon, *A view of Marseilles from the Aygalaldes, market day*, Marseilles, Musée des Beaux-Arts © Musée des Beaux-Arts / Jean Bernard

manifest by their shadows, control the activities of the servants. *Even if you cannot see us, we keep an eye on you.* The masters are all the more present as they are mysterious. In both examples, shadows that are so introduced are by default intended as key elements of the composition.

The 'small crowd' hypothesis

An interesting conceptual problem arises here as well. Consider what happens when one takes a casual picture of a crowd on a sunny day. One part of the crowd is framed in the picture. Some characters are inevitably outside the 'core' part, and in appropriate lighting conditions they would cast a shadow which is visible in the photograph.
If you are a painter who depicts a crowd you may not be willing to incorporate those shadows of unframed characters. The depicted crowd will be thus a small one. The 'small crowd' hypothesis is indeed a simple prediction we can make about crowded paintings. Building from this we can reason that the 'small crowd' effect of ancient paintings is just an inferential artefact. We are entitled to conclude that a crowd it is: that there are many more people around beyond those that are actually depicted, people who somehow need not cast a shadow.

     Roberto Casati

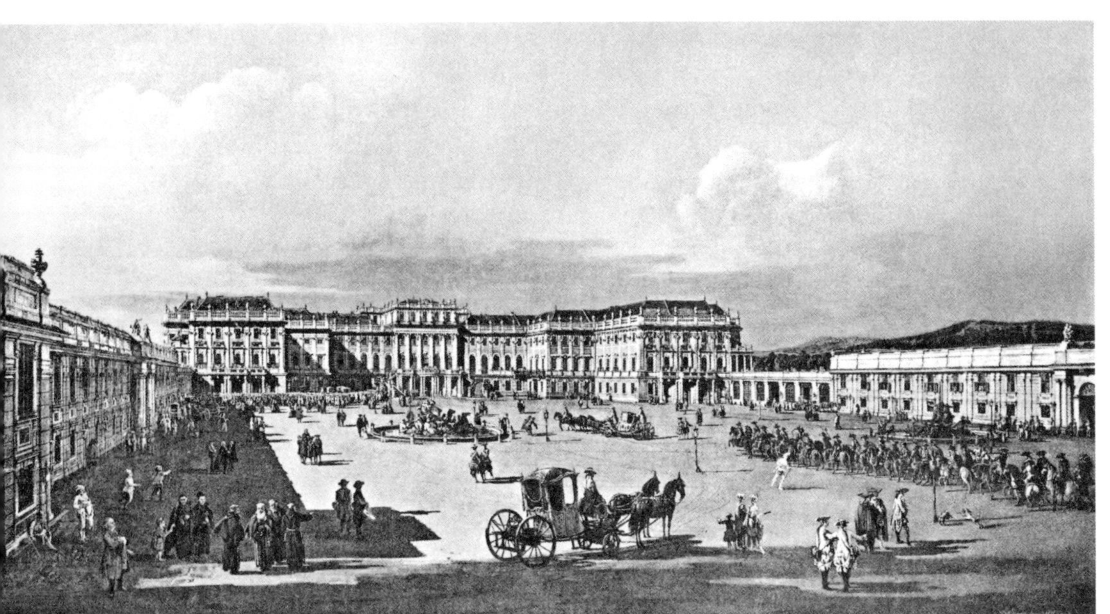

FIG. 8 Bernardo Bellotto, *Schönbrunn*, Vienna, Kunsthistorisches Museum

Because of the 'small crowd' assumption, shadows from unseen figures that are not provided with narrative justification will be interestingly informative. We will now see a couple of reasoning threads that build upon shadows (or their absence).

Shadows that may induce wrong inferences about unseen objects

The Bellotto 1758-61 painting *Kaiserliches Lustschloss Schönbrunn* (fig. 8) represents the shadow of an architectural detail, a portion of the wing of Schönbrunn castle. The shadow of an urn is visible, and we would expect by symmetry to find also the shadow of a sister urn. The second urn is indeed present on the building itself. However, it is not visible in the painting. Its shadow is not visible either. It looks as if shadows have been added later, only looking at what is visible in the painting and not checking the real scene. We are reminded of the fact that painted shadows are not photographed shadows.[17]

Shadows that can be used to infer the original properties of a painting

In Masaccio's Pisa polyptych shadows of non-displayed figures have been used by art historians to infer the shape of the original, now incomplete panel. Their reasoning can only work under the assumption that no shadow can be cast from a figure which

    Looking at Images and Reasoning about their Content

is not represented in the painting. In an article in the *Burlington Magazine* in 1966, John Shearman argued that the Madonna in the National Gallery was probably the central part of a single painting that had been broken into three pieces. Central to his argument were two faint shadows falling from the left on two levels – cast originally, he surmised, by figures standing on the steps which continued outside the confines of the present painting.[18]

Shadow-based inferential procedures are used in restoration techniques. Postulating consistent shadows helped the reconstitution of the frescoes in the Casa di Augusto in Rome – the pieces of which were found scattered on the floor.[19]

Shadow of the painter himself: 'forcing' pictorial content

In his *Shadows* Gombrich published a *Self-Portrait of the Author in the Setting Sun*, a photograph he took around 1990. It depicts a shadow of Gombrich himself taking a picture. He calls it a 'self-portrait', innocently, as if it were perfectly normal, first, to consider a photograph of a shadow of a person to be a portrait of that person, and second, to dub 'self-portrait' an image in which it is impossible to recognize the sitter. In the case in question, any person carrying a cane would have projected a similar shadow.

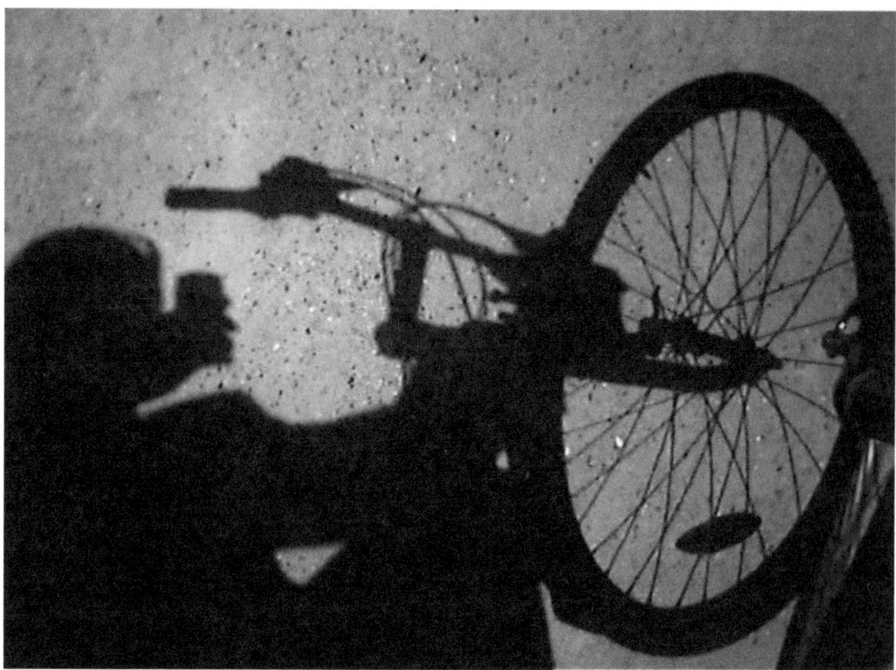

FIG. 9 Roberto Casati, 2004, *Self-portrait + bicycle*

     Roberto Casati

Indeed, the difficulty or near-impossibility of recognizing the sitter draws our attention to the importance of *labelling* pictures as portraits of a given person in order for us to take them as portraits of that person;[20] and in particular of stating that a certain portrait is a self-portrait in order for the viewer to take it as a self-portrait (fig. 9). It is an interesting fact about self-portraits that their content alone cannot in general be used to tell them from portraits that are not self-portraits. In general we need supplementary, non-pictorial information to ascertain whether the painter and the sitter are the same person. There are, though, cases in which a *prima facie* classification of the portrait as a self-portrait is made possible by visual inspection of the content. M.C. Escher's *Hand with Reflecting Sphere* (1935) belongs in this category. In it, a hand holds a sphere which reflects the hand itself and the person to whom the hand is attached. We are *prima facie* entitled to infer that this is a self-portrait.[21]

Of course, pictures are always underdetermined, whence the *prima facie* proviso. The lithograph could have been created by someone who pretended to be Escher. It could represent a hand carrying not a mirror, but a painted sphere representing someone who is very similar to Escher. Or it could represent a reflecting sphere which reflects a mannequin in whose eye is placed a periscope allowing the artist to take this very picture. But *prima facie* we are entitled to infer that this is a self-portrait.

Analogously, Gombrich's photo can *prima facie* be taken as a self portrait. It is of some importance that the sitter himself not be visible, as this fact forces the inference that the photo can only be taken from the viewpoint of the sitter. That very shadow is *prima facie* the shadow of the person who took the photograph, hence it is *prima facie* a self-portrait. There are countless alternative interpretations of the picture: the shadow could be that of a mannequin hiding a remotely operated camera, etc. But the *prima facie* interpretation stands.

Other shadow-based inferences

Some paintings represent shadows from sources of light that ought to be visible but are not. In Piero della Francesca's *Flagellation* (*c*. 1455-60, Urbino, Galleria Nazionale delle Marche) the beams cast shadows in the ceiling from a source (possibly two) situated somewhere to the right of the face of the Christ. But no such source is visible. We are entitled to infer the presence of an unseen lamp, or a possibly supernatural source of light.[22]

Conclusions

The augmentation of the Gombrichian toolbox took us on a path that moved away from purely perceptual and imaginative effects or uses of images, without requesting us to access the vast empires of semantic and episodic memory that are the preserves

    Looking at Images and Reasoning about their Content

of the art historian and of the connoisseur in general. The precise limits of background knowledge are of course hard to trace. For instance, a whole set of inferences would require technical knowledge of astronomy. A number of impossible moons and eclipses are suspended in the skies of many a painting. But many intriguing inferences can be triggered by simple careful observation. One need not be an iconographer in order to be able to appreciate that Dante's shadow is inconsistent with that of most other characters in Signorelli's depiction.

I would like to conclude with two programmatic points. The first is a plea for this strange, humble activity, that is, simple, untutored but patient and good-willed observation of a painting, or of an image more generally. A large panoply of interesting phenomena await description, located as they are between automatic recognition and the subtleties of erudite contemplation. No longer the immediate power of pictures; not yet the use of pictures for intellectual activities that do not engage predominantly their pictorial aspect. The second is a request to study the mechanisms that underpin patient observation that require the exercise of attention. We have little yet in terms of an account of how working memory is used in the act of looking at images; and even less of an account of how plans for managing the viewer's memory are represented in the intentions of she who produces an image. Saying that the toolbox is likely to be larger than was thought is not yet saying which tools belong in it.

1   P. Maynard, *Drawing Distinctions: The Varieties of Graphic Expression*, Ithaca, 2005, p. 98.

2   E.H. Gombrich, *Art and Illusion: a Study in the Psychology of Pictorial Representation*, London, 1960, p. 359.

3   Ibid., p. 360.

4   A point forcefully made about reception by David Freedberg in *The Power of Images*, Chicago, 1989.

5   As an example, line drawings provide one key to the dual set of predictions. Convincing line drawings in the norm do not correspond to all luminance discontinuities in the environment. Line drawings that respect all the discontinuities are in general hard to decipher.

6   E.H. Gombrich, *Shadows. The Depiction of Cast Shadows in Western Art*, London 1995.

7   R. Casati, poster for the conference 'Shadows – From Art to Neuroscience', Museo di arte moderna e contemporanea di Trento e Rovereto, 2003; R. Casati, 'Methodological Issues in the Study of the Depiction of Cast Shadows', *Journal of Aesthetics and Art Criticism*, 62, no. 2, 2004, pp. 163-74.

8   The fact that the wall behind Joseph's head is in shadow is of course inconsistent with the fall of light, especially since the post on which the goldcrest stands is casting a shadow within the shadow, which is impossible. A similar effect, though not quite as striking, can be found in the Lippi. I confine my attention here

to the projective geometry of the shadows of the posts.

9 R. Casati, 'The shadow knows: a primer on the informational structure of cast shadows', *Perception*, 33, no. 11, 2004, pp. 1385-96; M. Baxandall, *Shadows and Enlightenment*, New Haven, 1995, pp. 32-75.

10 P. Cavanagh, 'The artist as neuroscientist', *Nature*, 434, 2005, pp. 301-07.

11 The copycat effect provides another example. A copycat shadow can be inaccurate and convincing, where the correct shadows can be unconvincing. No simplified physics could account for the impossible position of the shadows in the convincing but inaccurate picture. See R. Casati, 'The *copycat* solution to the shadow correspondence problem', *Perception*, 37, no. 4, 2007, pp. 495-503.

12 K. Clark, *Landscape into Art*, London, 1949, p. 19. I am grateful to Pascal Mamassian for having drawn my attention to Witz's impossible shadows.

13 E. Panofsky, *Studies in Iconology*, New York, 1939, p. 10.

14 Discussed in R. Casati, *The Shadow Club*, New York, 2002.

15 Dante Alighieri, *La divina commedia*, Canto v: '*Io era già da quell'ombre partito, | e seguitava l'orme del mio duca, | quando di retro a me, drizzando 'l dito, | una gridò: "Ve' che non par che luca |lo raggio da sinistra a quel di sotto, |e come vivo par che si conduca!" | Li occhi rivolsi al suon di questo motto, | e vidile guardar per maraviglia |pur me, pur me, e 'l lume ch'era rotto*' (1-9) .... '*Quando s'accorser ch'i' non dava loco| per lo mio corpo al trapassar d'i raggi, | mutar lor canto in un "oh!" lungo e roco*' (25-27); Dante, *The Divine Comedy*, tr. R. Kirkpatrick, London, 2006: 'Now had I left those spirits, and pursued/ The steps of my Conductor, when behold/ Pointing the finger at me one exclaim'd:/ "See how it seems as if the light not shine/ From the left hand of him beneath, and he,/ As living, seems to be led on." Mine eyes/ I at that sound reverting, saw them gaze/ Through wonder first at me, and then at me/ And the light broken underneath, by turns .... When they perceiv'd that through my body I/ Gave way not for the rays to pass, their song/ Straight to a long and hoarse exclaim they chang'd.'

16 I leave theological niceties to one side. According to Thomas Aquinas, although angels are incorporeal, they can 'assume bodies of air, condensing it by the Divine power in so far as is needful for forming the assumed body', in order to be seen by humans. Although the saint does not mention the subject, it presumably follows that, like clouds, they can cast shadows. See *Summa Theologica*, I, 51, 2.

17 Casati, *Shadow Club* (n. 14 above).

18 J. Shearman, 'Masaccio's Pisa Altar-piece: an Alternative Reconstruction', *The Burlington Magazine*, cviii, 1966, pp. 446-57. For refinements and developments since Shearman's article, see D. Gordon, *The Fifteenth-Century Italian Paintings, Volume One*, National Gallery Catalogues, London, 2003, pp. 201-23.

19 Gianna Musatti, personal communication.

20 Certain conventional features of the sitter's pose can be used to infer that the portrait is indeed a self-portrait.

21 R. Casati, *L'immagine*, Florence, 1990. Pictures in which the sitter is painting at an easel with his left hand are of course also likely candidates.

22 For further discussion see Marilyn Aronberg Lavin, *Piero della Francesca: The Flagellation*, Chicago, 1990, pp. 46-48.

Gombrich and Leonardo:
A Natural Affinity

MARTIN KEMP

LEONARDO occupied a special and perhaps unique position in Ernst Gombrich's thought. Indeed, if we look at his citing of Leonardo over the full span of his writings we are presented with something like a *speculum Gombrichianum* or *microcosmus Gombrichianus*. Not only was Gombrich endlessly fascinated by Leonardo's paintings, drawings and writings, but he had recurrent recourse to the great Tuscan as a historical exemplar who consciously and unconsciously demonstrated the truth of concepts that were central to his own beliefs. We gain the impression that when the going became tough, the Leonardo light cavalry, armed with an unparalleled array of ingenious weapons, galloped across the plain to rout Gombrich's ideological enemies, who were only equipped with ponderous metaphysical artillery. The cavalry go into battle under two proudly fluttering banners; the first is "the greatest of all visual explorers"; the second is "the greatest wizard of them all". These designations occur nine pages apart in *Art and Illusion*.[1]

Under the "explorer" banner, Leonardo exemplifies the value of visual knowledge, acting as:

> the supreme maker and matcher;
> the perfect exemplar of Karl Popper's scientific method of hypothesis and testing;
> a persistent searcher for universal laws in nature;
> a systematic classifier of variations of natural forms and processes;
> a dogmatic advocate of experience and practice;
> a salutary exemplar of the recurrent recourse to nature;
> an unswerving advocate of rationalism;
> a committed exponent of natural magic as opposed to metaphysical magic;
> a dedicated pricker of metaphysical balloons.

Under the "wizard" banner, Leonardo exemplifies the power of imagination, acting as:

> a notably potent re-former of schemata;
> a supremely imaginative inventor of form;
> a pioneering exploiter of serendipity in graphic invention;

the first to separate graphic motif from predetermined meaning in formal
invention;
a great explorer of imaginative projection;
the first consciously to exploit visual indeterminacy;
the first to use art as a fully self-conscious *dimostrazione* of visual knowledge;
the supreme reformer of the power of art to communicate actors' feelings;
the earliest writer to probe the untrammelled nature of the creative imagination
in the visual arts.

It would require more space than is available here to explore all eighteen of these
roles. Instead, I will cluster them under four headings: 1) schemata and universals;
2) making and matching; 3) the power of art; 4) for better or for worse.

Schemata and universals

It is not hard to demonstrate that Leonardo used a series of recurrent schemata.
Aligning heads of women from his drawings and paintings, as Gombrich did, suffices
to show the kind of formulas that he used. Yet Gombrich emphasized that Leonardo
sought for universals in a way that led him to reform inherited schemata. Let us take
the example of trees as adduced in *Art and Illusion* (fig.1):

> The most illustrious instance of …[the] natural union between knowledge and art
> is of course Leonardo da Vinci… [He] was obviously dissatisfied with the current
> method of drawing trees. He knew a better way. 'Remember,' he taught, 'that
> wherever a branch divides, the stem grows correspondingly thinner, so that if you
> draw a circle round the crown of a tree, the sections of every twig must add up to
> the thickness of the trunk'. I do not know if this law holds. I do not think it quite
> does. But as a hint on 'how to draw trees', Leonardo's observation is invaluable.
> By teaching the assumed laws of growth he has given the artist a formula for
> constructing a tree – and so he can still feel like the creator, 'the Lord and Master
> of all things', who knows the secrets of nature and can 'make trees' as he hoped
> to 'make' a bird that would fly.
>
> I believe what we call the Renaissance artists' preoccupation with structure has
> a very practical basis in their needs to know the schema of things.[2]

At this stage Gombrich was not acknowledging the extent to which Leonardo was
searching for universals on the basis of general dynamic laws, but this was something
he was to accomplish in his 1969 paper on Leonardo's water drawings. In this classic
study, Leonardo serves Gombrich's enduring concern with seeing and knowing:

> What prompted me to take up the study of these astonishing drawings was the
> relation between seeing and knowing or more accurately between thought and
> perception, to which I have devoted my book, *Art and Illusion*. There can be no

107. UCCELLO: *The Hunt*. Detail. About 1460

classes of living things could not rely on such roundabout methods. He had to strive for a greater knowledge of universals and master the structure of things so thoroughly that he could visualize them in any spatial context.

The most illustrious instance of this natural union between knowledge and art is of course Leonardo da Vinci. It seems a far cry from Villard's geometric tricks and his heraldic lion to Leonardo's incessant search for the secret of organic form, and yet they belong together, for both are directed towards the 'universal'. One example must suffice. Leonardo was obviously dissatisfied with the current method of drawing trees. He knew a better way. 'Remember,' he taught, 'that wherever a branch divides, the stem grows correspondingly thinner, so that, if you draw a circle round the crown of the tree, the sections of every twig must add up to the thickness of the trunk' [108]. I do not know if this law holds. I do not think it quite does. But as a hint on 'how to draw trees', Leonardo's observation is invaluable. By teaching the assumed laws of growth he has given the artist a formula for constructing a tree—and so he can still feel like the creator, 'Lord and Master of all things', who knows the secrets of nature and can 'make' trees as he hoped to 'make' a bird that would fly.

I believe what we call the Renaissance artists' preoccupation with structure has a very practical basis in their needs to know the schema of things. For in a way our very concept of 'structure', the idea of some basic scaffolding or armature that

determines the 'essence' of things, reflects our need for a scheme with which to grasp the infinite variety of this world of change. No wonder these issues have become somewhat clouded by a metaphysical fog which settled over the discussions of art in the sixteenth and seventeenth centuries.

IV

THE MEDIEVAL DISTINCTION between universals and particulars was mainly a matter of logic. In these terms, Leonardo had discovered a law about the biological class called 'trees' to which every individual tree belonged. Those who wanted to portray a tree in their garden had first to know about the structure and proportion of trees. But thanks in part to the influence of Platonism, the whole distinction could be given a different twist. For Plato, the universal is the idea, the perfect pattern of the tree exists somewhere in a place beyond the heavens, or, to use the technical term, in the intelligible world. Individual trees or horses or men, such as the painter may encounter in real life, are only imperfect copies of these eternal patterns, imperfect because base matter will always resist the flawless seal and prevent the idea from realizing itself. It was on these grounds that Plato himself denied art its validity, for what value can there be in copying an imperfect copy of the idea? But on the same grounds, Neoplatonism tried to assign to art a new place that was eagerly seized upon by the emerging academies. It is just the point, they argued, that the painter, unlike ordinary mortals, is a person endowed with the divine gift of perceiving, not the imperfect and shifting world of individuals, but the eternal patterns themselves. He must purify the world of matter, erase its flaws, and approximate it to the idea. He is aided in this by the knowledge of the laws of beauty, which are those of harmonious, simple geometrical relationships, and by the study of those antiques that already represent reality 'idealized', i.e., approximated to the Platonic idea.

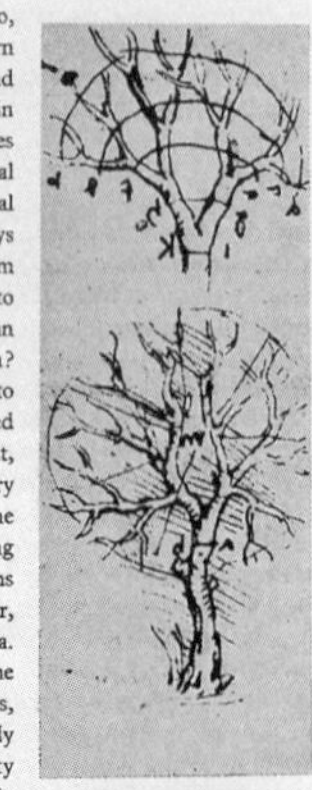

108. LEONARDO DA VINCI: *Diagram of the growth of trees*

FIG. 1 Gombrich, *Art and Illusion*, pp. 132–33, showing a detail of Paolo Uccello's *Hunt in the Forest* and Leonardo's theory of the branching of trees

more important witness for the student of this problem than Leonardo. He represents a test case for those of us who are interested in the interaction of theory and observation and are convinced that the correct representation of nature rests on intellectual understanding as much as on good eyesight.[3]

Gombrich is also looking in this paper at the universality and 'unity' of Leonardo's thought. This unity centres on a set of fundamentally Aristotelian principles of the forms and forces in nature. He quotes what he calls a 'tortuous passage' from Leonardo's notebooks to show how an Aristotelian theory of motion found direct expression in his drawings of turbulent water. Leonardo himself makes a conveniently Gombrichian point about knowing and representing:

At this point [we read in the *Trattato*] the opponent says he does not want so much *scienza*, that practice is enough for him in order to draw the things in nature. The answer to this is that there is nothing that deceives us more easily than our confidence in our own judgement, divorced from reasoning, as experience shows, which is the enemy of the alchemists, the necromancer, and other simple minds.[4]

A few lines later, accompanied by a footnote reference to Karl Popper, Gombrich tells us that 'it is increasingly recognized that science does not progress by looking, but by taking thought, by the testing of theories and not by the collection of random observations'. One of these testable theories is a law that was not to be formulated in print (albeit in a rather different way) until over a century later. He quotes Leonardo to the effect that 'a river of uniform depth will have a more rapid flow at the narrower section than at the wider, to the extent that the greater width surpasses the latter'.[5] It is a little surprising that Gombrich does not refer back to the rule of branching trees, which would have served splendidly to illustrate the unity of Leonardo's thought.

The main problem with the 1969 paper is that Gombrich juxtaposes Leonardo's statements directly with Aristotle's ideas, in particular the Greek philosopher's theory of antiperistasis, rather than with the impetus dynamics of medieval natural philosophers, most notably Buridan. However imperfect was Leonardo's knowledge of the medieval texts, his framework of explanation for how bodies and fluids moved according to proportional laws was founded on impetus dynamics rather than the theories of Aristotle himself. This recourse to classical antiquity rather than the Middle Ages is broadly characteristic of how Gombrich generally articulates the Renaissance in relation to the classical tradition rather than looking in addition at innovations in medieval thought.

Regardless of such quibbles, the essay on the water drawings remains compelling in method. It was his loan to me of his then unpublished paper on the water drawings that drew me into Leonardo studies and essentially pointed me in the direction of asking what still seem to me to be the right questions. He sees clearly how he can exploit his close focus on the water drawings as a base from which to reach out into questions of the dynamics of the elements in nature as whole and even more widely into philosophical topics of the kind that Leonardo rarely embraced. The key motif was provided by the micro- and macrocosms. In looking at 'Leonardo da Vinci's Method of Analysis and Permutation', he noted how Leonardo equated the 'desire' of the elements to return to their original position with the desires of the soul. He quotes what he calls 'one of his [Leonardo's] most poetic notes':

> Now look at the hope and the desire to seek the home and to return to the primal chaos, which acts like the moth to the light, and man, who with constant longing always joyfully waits for the new spring, the new summer, always the next months and the next years … does not see that he desires his own undoing. But this inheres in that quintessence, the spirit of the elements, which finding itself shut up as the soul of the human body desires always to return to him who sent it there; and I want you to know that this same desire is that quintessence, companion of nature, and man is a model of the world.[6]

   Gombrich and Leonardo: a Natural Affinity

Gombrich is served reasonably well by J.P. Richter's translation in this instance, but two pages later the translation leads him to miss the sense of what he calls 'one of the more mysterious of Leonardo's notes', which he does 'not pretend quite to understand':

> On the Soul: The movement of earth against earth in collision results in little movement on impact. Water hit by water circles around the point of impact. The voice in the air creates the same along a greater distance; even larger ones in fire, and longer still the mind in the universe, but since the universe is finite the impulse does not extend to the infinite.[7]

The last section should read, 'but since the mind is finite, it does not extend to the infinite'. This aligns Leonardo with aspects of the philosophy of Albertus Magnus and Thomas Aquinas in the way that they separate the reach of the human mind from God's infinity. Although Gombrich recognises Leonardo's description of the circularity of the ripples of water in Dante's *Paradiso*, he is again prone to miss the centrality of the medieval legacy in Leonardo's thought.

However, such detailed problems do nothing to diminish Gombrich's deep insight into the relationships between *scienza*, seeing and representation in Leonardo's drawings, and the support that these relationships lent to his theories of schemata and making and matching.

Making and matching

Gombrich demonstrated Leonardo's resort to schemata in places where it is least obvious, most notably in the famous early drawing of the 'Val d'Arno', made as Leonardo himself testified on the 'day of Saint Mary of the Snows / day of 5 August 1473'. The inscription has led almost all commentators to think that the drawing was made on the spot and is therefore a record of what the draughtsman could see. Gombrich begged to differ:

> It seems to me impossible to reconstruct from the drawing even the roughest sketchmap of the landscape in which he is supposed to have sat. Judging by the height of the tress in the foreground and on the ledge, the bank of rocks must be very close to the viewer and cannot be much higher than three to four times the height of those trees. Yet the waterfall that descends from this rock out of an implausible river course into a deep pool suggests a very different scale. Trying to follow the water, which presumably descends down another ledge into the plane, presents new problems, and once we are thus alerted we shall also be at a loss to account for the foreground and its curving into depth on the left. That sizeable country seat with its walls and turrets must surely be more distant than the structure of this land suggests, and the relation of the promontory on which it stands to the lake or flooded fields below remains puzzling. I grant that even photographs of real views may sometimes present similar posers, but if we return from the drawing to the setting of Jan van Eyck's *St Francis*, the basic kinship of the lay-out offers the easiest explanation of these inconsistencies.[8]

The topography is thus based more on Netherlandish schemata than a real view. I had myself reached the conclusion that the Leonardo drawing does not show an actual place, but is rather a *fantasia* referring to the oratory of S. Maria della Neve in the vicinity of the destroyed Gherardini castle near Greve in Chianti.[9] But I had forgotten Gombrich's earlier demolition job, which would have helped my argument a good deal. The passage I have quoted also serves to remind us just how intensively Gombrich looked at both art and nature.

A similar conviction about the need for schemata lay behind what Gombrich called a 'rather cruel question' he asked of Ludwig Heydenreich. He told me how he was once discussing Leonardo's 'imitation of nature' with the great Leonardo scholar, who was extolling Leonardo's naturalism. Gombrich invited his companion to look out of the window. He asked him if anything out there looked like a Leonardo. I do not think that Heydenreich's response was part of the story.

Matching is the process through which old schemata are modified and new ones established. In a true process of matching, the schemata must be revised to some degree, which is a notably difficult thing to accomplish. Gombrich interpreted Leonardo's obsessive drawing of grotesque heads as (amongst other things) a way of violating the facial formulas that he adopted for his various stock types – the virginal woman, the pretty youth, the belligerent warrior and so on: 'far from being free observations, the grotesque heads look like frantic avoiding actions, almost desperate struggles to get away from the compulsion of once more repeating the features of the 'nutcracker' head'.[10] The extreme variations also help to negate what I have called 'automimesis', that is to say the reflex imitation of one's own 'look', which Leonardo regarded as a great fault of artists.

Leonardo is one of the great 'matchers'. When sketching Leonardo strives 'to learn, to make and match and remake till the portrayal ceases to be a second-hand formula and reflects the unique and unrepeatable experience that the artists wishes to seize and hold'.[11] When we can look over Leonardo's shoulder, as it were, as in the miraculous little drawings of the River Adda near the Villa Melzi, we can see the kind of rigorous matching that it is impossible to accomplish with the Val d'Arno drawing.[12] In this respect, Leonardo features as a kind of precocious Constable, able to overcome not only the schemata but also the inbuilt perceptual tendencies that lead to 'constancy scaling' and other gravitational pulls that make it so difficult to depict just "what we see". Essentially the same point about matching is made when Gombrich notes Leonardo's innovative observation that 'lustre' (*lustro* or *splendore*) moves on the surface of a shiny object in response to varied positions of the eye, compared to the conventional schema of illumination in which form is modelled in light and shade in such a way that it depends only on the direction of the light source.[13]

There is one other major Leonardesque dimension in making and matching that tends to be overlooked in the discussion of Gombrich's ideas. This concerns the

     Gombrich and Leonardo: a Natural Affinity

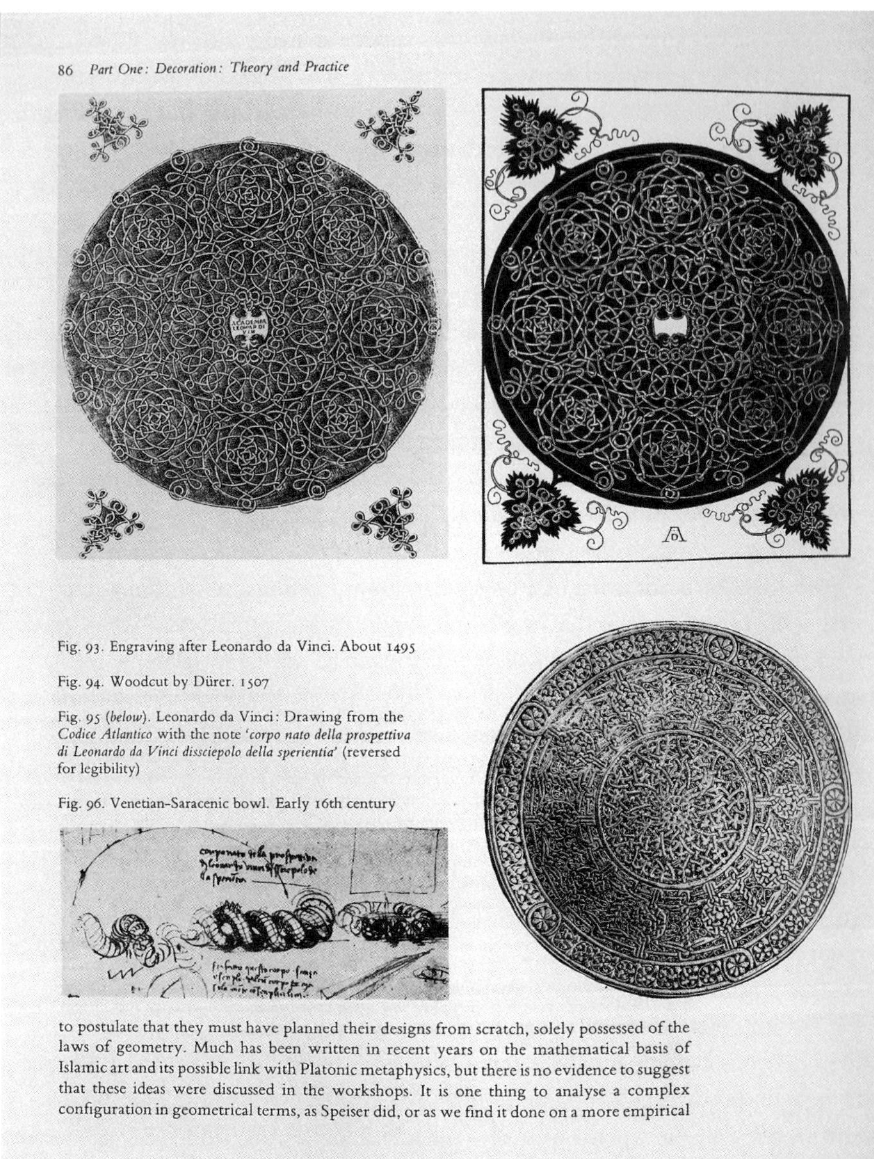

Fig. 93. Engraving after Leonardo da Vinci. About 1495

Fig. 94. Woodcut by Dürer. 1507

Fig. 95 (*below*). Leonardo da Vinci: Drawing from the *Codice Atlantico* with the note '*corpo nato della prospettiva di Leonardo da Vinci dissciepolo della sperientia*' (reversed for legibility)

Fig. 96. Venetian-Saracenic bowl. Early 16th century

to postulate that they must have planned their designs from scratch, solely possessed of the laws of geometry. Much has been written in recent years on the mathematical basis of Islamic art and its possible link with Platonic metaphysics, but there is no evidence to suggest that these ideas were discussed in the workshops. It is one thing to analyse a complex configuration in geometrical terms, as Speiser did, or as we find it done on a more empirical

Martin Kemp

FIG. 2 Gombrich, *The Sense of Order,* p. 86, illustrating Leonardo's knot designs, a Veneto-Saracenic bowl, and the '*corpo nato della prospettiva di Leonardo da Vinci discepolo della sperientia*'

physical acts of production – they way that line, surface, texture, solid and motion are rendered as marks on a surface. Gombrich is adducing a kind of physically integrated intelligence that operates in conjuction with the artist's trained and skilled hand. Examples are provided by Leonardo's knot designs, whose physical intertwinings are set by Gombrich beside a Veneto-Saracenic plate (fig. 2).

He is particularly delighted by Leonardo's 'body born of perspective by Leonardo da Vinci, the disciple of experience'. The extravagantly twisted *mazzocchio*, which knowingly out-Uccellos Uccello, is seen as a supreme example of a step-by-step skill that relies upon an incredible persistence in the application of practical *disegno*: 'it looks as if he wanted to counter the pride of the Platonic Academy in Florence by demonstrating his manual skill'.[14] Given that such geometrical exercises, as in the truncated and stellated solids that Leonardo illustrated in Luca Pacioli's *De divina proportione*, were thoroughly Platonic in tone (as Pacioli himself emphasized), this anti-Platonic interpretation is not one of Gombrich's most convincing.

Again, the problematic details in Gombrich's commentaries do nothing to lessen the fundamental efficacy with which he exploits Leonardo as a witness on his behalf. There is hardly any aspect of Leonardo's drawings, ranging from the exploratory questing of his 'brainstorm' drawing style – which Gombrich compares to Leonardo's account of a poet crossing out unsatisfactory lines – to his wonderfully sharp and super-real portraits of plants that does not serve Gombrich's conviction that Leonardo could make and match and make like no other.

The power of art (and of writing)

Leonardo also comes in handy when Gombrich wants to emphasize that there is actually more to art than the kind of making and matching that serves Popperian science so well. Looking at Leonardo's Louvre *Madonna of the Rocks*, he lays down an important principle:

> It is … important, in my view, to clarify in what respect it [art] differs from the principle of scientific experimentation. It differs, I would claim, because the goal which the artist seeks with such self-critical persistence is not a true proposition (as in science), but a psychological effect. Such effects can be discussed, but they cannot be demonstrated.

He goes on in the next paragraph to say that

> We need not stray further than the art of Leonardo to give substance to these general considerations. For however intent the master may have been in making his pictures conform to visual reality, there are limits to this aspiration.[15]

We are back with the 'cruel question' he put to Heydenreich. He is asking all of us if we really expect to see anything in nature that really looks like the *mise-en-scène* in

     Gombrich and Leonardo: a Natural Affinity

Leonardo's altarpiece. The use, reform and even the limits of schemata thus are linked in successive paragraphs to the psychological power of art. The schema is not just a visual convention but can act in the hands of an artist as a potent unit of psychological communication.

The psychological power of art brings us to Leonardo the 'wizard'. Gombrich was repeatedly drawn to those passages in Leonardo's notes on painting that conjure up the artist's magical powers:

> The divinity which belongs to the science of painting transmutes the painter's mind into a likeness of the divine mind. With untrammelled power he can reason about the generation of the various natures of the diverse animals, plants, fruits, landscapes, fields, landslides in the mountains, places fearful and frightful, which bring terror to those who view them; also pleasant places, soft and delightful with flowery meadows in various colours, swayed by the soft waves of breezes, looking beyond the wind that escapes from them, rivers that descend from high mountains with the impetus of great deluges, dragging along uprooted plants mixed with stones, roots, earth and foam, carrying away everything that opposes its own ruin. And also the sea with its storms, which battle and contend with the winds that fight with the sea; having reared itself up in proud waves, it falls, crushing the wind that beats against the base of the waves, enclosing and imprisoning it beneath itself it splits and tears it; mixing it with muddy foam.[16]

Gombrich quotes a further eleven lines, clearly delighting in Leonardo's propulsive lyricism. We sense that he is happy for Leonardo to operate with the kinds of hyperbole that he is himself reluctant to unleash in his own prose.

The long quotation supports Gombrich's contention that the conventional distinction between 'verbal types' and 'visual types' is inapplicable in Leonardo's case. To prove his point, when looking at 'Leonardo and the Magicians' in *New Light on Old Masters* he illustrates three pages of 'pure text' by Leonardo.[17] This verbal dimension is vital to Gombrich's argument that the water drawings are as much based on written theory as visual observation. And the theory was expressed with literary power.

He also stresses that the 'brainstorm' drawings are not only ways of seeking novel forms for the sake of matching but also provide a means to rival the poet in invention of content. They are exercises in *fantasia*, the high poetic faculty that Dante valued so highly – as Leonardo well knew. The drawings themselves, exploiting the kind of manual intelligence that we have already noted, serendipitously suggest new forms and compositions to the artist's imagination as a kind of feedback. It is inevitable that Gombrich was much drawn to Leonardo's famous accounts of imaginative projection when looking at stains in walls and clouds:

> I have seen shapes in clouds and on patchy walls which have roused me to beautiful inventions of various things, and even though such shapes totally lack finish

     Martin Kemp

in any single part they were not devoid of perfection in their gestures or other movements.[18]

The indeterminacy of such semi-choate images was something that Leonardo carried over into his painting in the form of veiled *sfumato*: 'his discovery of the "indeterminate" and its power over the mind ... made him the inventor of *sfumato* and the half-guessed form'.[19] This accords Leonardo a key place in the history of the invention of 'the beholder's share', the factor in viewing pictures that was absolutely central to the collaboration that transforms paint on a flat surface into Gombrich's beloved illusion. As so often, Leonardo provides vital testimony in support of one of the historian's key notions.

Indeterminacy does not stop with elusive form. It also embraces those gestures that Leonardo emphasized as necessary to convey *il concetto dell'anima* (the intention of the mind) of each of the actors in his painted dramas. In the *Last Supper* these gestures hover between the spontaneous expression of emotions as observed in nature and the conventions of art through which we recognise how the painted actors are behaving.[20] The disciples illustrate to perfection Gombrich's theory of the language of art and the way that great artists draw us into their manipulation of the language for meaning that is at once structured and open, conventional and experimental.

For better or for worse

These three categories – schemata and universals, making and matching, and the power of art – serve to illustrate the role that Leonardo played in Gombrich's theory of the way that images work. But they are not the end of the story, or even its most momentous part. Leonardo occupied a very special position in the moral and political foundations of Gombrich's theory of knowledge. Leonardo is repeatedly called on when Gombrich needs to berate one of those thinkers whom we might call 'totalizers', that is to say, those who advocate absolute theories of human nature and society in defiance of the humane and liberal values that allow us to operate with open minds. There is a recognisable stock of *bêtes noires* running through his writings. One of these is Sigmund Freud.

Freud, who held a special fascination for him, is neatly put in his place in *Tributes*, when Gombrich discusses the famous essay in which Freud attempts to psychoanalyse Leonardo. The put-down, to the Freudians as much as Freud himself, is all the more effective because of its ostensible tone of generosity:

> I wish to stress... that Freud's wide culture and his insights saved him here and
> elsewhere from the mistake of confusing the biography of an artist with the theory
> of the arts. What he says about this point could not possibly be more explicit. 'It
> must be confessed to the layman, who may possibly expect too much of analysis
> in this respect, that it does not throw any light on two problems which probably

interest him most. Analysis has nothing to contribute to the explanation of an
artist's gifts, not is it competent to lay bare his method, his artistic technique'.[21]
With these words Freud decisively indicated the frontiers between his insights and
the concerns of the art historian. For if he did not want to enter into a discussion of
artistic gift, he thereby eliminated the problems of value.[21]

In other words, Freudian analysis cannot aspire to reach to the heart of those things
that constitute the real power of art – those things, as Gombrich pointed out, that
differentiate a Leonardo from a Luini. This distinction was not merely one of style or
of market value but of the highest levels of human communication.

Freud, at the end of the day, proves not to be one of the most dangerous of the
bêtes noires in the world of art, but is something of a yappy dog, who is not biting into
the biggest issues. The real monsters are the proponents of the great metaphysical
theories of everything. Historically, high Platonism is in the vanguard of such theories.
Even the apparently blameless branching tree in Leonardo's drawing can potentially
lead us in the pernicious direction of false idealism. The idealist will maintain that

individual trees or horses or men, such the painter may encounter in real life, are
only imperfect copies of these eternal patterns, imperfect because base matter will
always resist the flawless seal and prevent the idea from realising itself. It was on
these grounds that Plato himself denied art its validity, for what value can there be
in copying an imperfect copy of the idea? But on the same grounds Neoplatonism
tries to assign art a new place that was eagerly seized upon by emerging academies.
It is just the point, they argued, that the painter, unlike ordinary mortals, is a
person endowed with the divine gift of perceiving, not the imperfect and shifting
world of individuals, but the eternal patterns themselves. He must *purify* the
world of matter, erase its flaws, and approximate it to the idea. He is aided in this
by the knowledge of the laws of beauty, which are those of harmonious, simple
geometrical relationships, and by the study of those antiques that already represent
reality 'idealised', i.e. approximated to the Platonic idea.[22]

I have emphasized 'purify' in this strongly angled passage because it helps us to
see where Gombrich is going, by implication at least. The 'pure' master-race of the
ideal society lurks not far below the surface. On the next page he says that 'if the tree
or the man in front of you does not conform to that geometrical scaffolding now
presented as the perfect canon, so much the worse for the tree or the man'. The danger
of Leonardo's law for tree branching is that in the wrong hands it can be used to try to
engineer the 'true' and 'beautiful' tree, just as the Nazis (and the Communists) aspired
through social and educational engineering to propagate a human race that conformed
to their rules of superiority. The tyranny of aesthetic absolutes propagated by Platonic
art theory in the academies resulted in a 'metaphysical fog which settled over the
discussions of art in the sixteenth and seventeenth centuries'. This fog has the

     Martin Kemp

same dense and threatening obscurity as clouded totalitarian thinking in Gombrich's own time.

The stakes are high and they do not only involve aesthetics. The sculptures of Arno Becker and the buildings of Albert Speer, respectively the favoured sculptor and architect of Hitler, were repulsive because of their meanings, and it was *style* that carried these meanings. The 'lessons' of ancient art and architecture had ossified into a tyrannical theory of absolute beauty that was inseparable from tyrannical rule.

Gombrich, like a number of his colleagues at the Warburg, and indeed Warburg himself, used their scholarship to probe into these 'metaphysical fogs'. Gombrich's distaste for later Platonic fogs is not brought specifically to bear on his famous study of Botticelli's limpid mythologies in *Symbolic Images*, in which Marsilio Ficino's rapturous letter to young Lorenzino de' Medici plays a key role. He praised Frances Yates and D.P. (Perkin) Walker for their objective analyses of Neoplatonic and Hermetic dimensions in 'the Renaissance imagination'.[23] At this historical distance we can perhaps be indulgent with spurious ideas. But there is a sense that the closer the fogs come to our time the more they are seen as obscuring the truth in a dangerous manner, becoming less a legitimate subject for disinterested history than an urgent concern for those who wished to protect humane values.

The praise for Yates and Walker comes in Gombrich's essay on 'Leonardo and the Magicians', in which he emphasizes that Leonardo, for all his visual 'wizardry', was an unforgiving critic of mystical systems like astrology, alchemy and necromancy. He quotes with relish Leonardo's satirical demolition of the necromancer's claims. His extended quotation ends resoundingly:

No lock or fortress, though impregnable, would be able to save anyone against the will of the necromancer. He would have himself carried through the air from east to west and through all the opposite sides of the universe. But why should I enlarge further on this? What is there that could not be accomplished by such artifice? Almost nothing, except to escape death.[24]

Gombrich then goes on to say that 'Neo-Platonism blurred the difference between magic and science by propagating faith in the philosopher whose superior insights have turned him to a miracle worker'. Historically it is less than simple to differentiate 'science' from 'magic' without imposing anachronistic definitions, but for Gombrich it was essential to be able to do so, since he had a keen sense where the superiority claimed by advocates of totalizing dogmas had led in his own century. He could, as he acknowledged in a conversation with me, metaphorically hear the sound of the jack-boots marching as the armies of the unjust loomed up through the oppressive metaphysical fogs.

Our defence against the legions of the totalizers is twofold, reason and nature. Reason is that which allows us to see clearly – however difficult this may be. It allows

   Gombrich and Leonardo: a Natural Affinity

science to be science, and in the realm of art it allows us to define the imaginative realms of art – its scope for extending rational thought into other communicative dimensions. It is this definition that allows Gombrich to delight in the 'splendid poetic description of Shakespeare's Prospero in *The Tempest*. Prospero too commands the winds and can cause shipwreck, and he too can cast spells and bind Ariel, the sprite to his service and purpose'.[25] Great art uses imagination in the service of the same great ideal as reason. Scientific reason allows us to know other things; the arts allows us to 'know ourselves', to paraphrase the famous Delphic tag, *nosce te ipsum*. Nature is where we can seek the complementary truths of science and of art.

We should remind ourselves that Gombrich and many leading intellectuals and artists of his generation in Europe had witnessed what happens when the imaginative freedoms of the arts and humanities are violated. For them, humanist studies were not simply engrossing pursuits that make each of us a whole person but rather bastions of humane values and guardians of very special kinds of truth. In their own way the heroic 'matchers' who question the received wisdom of the 'schemata' are part of the great quest to negate stereotypes. Unflinching mimesis implicitly carries a huge ethical charge in the context of the wider need to see honestly. The last paragraph of his essay 'Light, Form and Texture in Fifteenth-Century Painting' reminds us that he is unafraid to use the terms 'good or bad, true or false' when discussing the imitation of nature:

> We art historians might do worse than to follow Leonardo's advice and turn to nature in order to confirm for ourselves the reasons of what the artist had learned. We have concentrated so long on the morphology of different styles and visual idioms that we neglected to probe their descriptive potentialities for matching the visible world. It is true that the variety of styles which we encounter in the history of art confirms the idea that nature can be described in many different languages, but it happens to be wrong to infer from this premise that these descriptions cannot be either good or bad, true or false.[26]

1 E.H. Gombrich, *Art and Illusion: A Study in the Psychology of Pictorial Representation*, London, 1960, pp. 72 and 81.

2 Ibid., p. 132.

3 E.H. Gombrich, 'Leonardo's Method of Analysis and Permutation: The Form of Movement in Water and Air', in Gombrich, *The Heritage of Apelles: Studies in the Art of the Renaissance III*, London, 1976, pp. 39-56 (p. 40).

4 Ibid., p. 40.

5 Ibid., p. 41.

6 Ibid., p. 52.

7 Ibid., p. 54. It is worth noting that Gombrich was intimately acquainted with the two-volume edition of J.P. Richter's *The Literary Works of Leonardo da Vinci*, Oxford, 1939, since he had prepared its remarkable indices, which are themselves a research tool.

8 E.H. Gombrich, 'Light, Form and Texture in Fifteenth-Century Painting North and South of the Alps', in Gombrich, *Apelles* (n. 3 above), pp. 19-35 (p. 34).

9 M. Kemp, *Leonardo*, Oxford, 2005, pp. 218-19.

10 E.H. Gombrich, 'The Grotesque Heads', in Gombrich, *Apelles* (n. 3 above), pp. 57-75 (p. 68).

11 Gombrich, *Art and Illusion* (n. 1 above), p. 148.

12 A. Vezzozi, *Leonardo da Vinci: Renaissance Man*, London, 1997, p. 114.

13 Gombrich, 'Light, Form and Texture' (n. 8 above), p. 19.

14 E.H. Gombrich, *The Sense of Order: A Study in the Psychology of Decorative Art*, Oxford, 1979, p. 85.

15 E.H. Gombrich, 'Experiment and Experience in the Arts', in Gombrich, *The Image and the Eye. Further Studies in the Psychology of Pictorial Representation*, Oxford 1982, pp. 215-43 (p. 228).

16 E.H. Gombrich, 'Leonardo and the Magicians: Polemics and Rivalry', in Gombrich, *New Light on Old Masters: Studies in the Art of the Renaissance IV*, Oxford 1986, pp. 61-88 (p. 71).

17 Ibid., pp. 62-63.

18 E.H. Gombrich, 'Leonardo's Method for Working Out Compositions', in *Norm and Form: Studies in the Art of the Renaissance I*, London, 1966, pp. 58-63 (p. 60).

19 Ibid., p. 61.

20 E.H. Gombrich, 'Ritualized Gesture and Expression in Art', in Gombrich, *Image and Eye* (n. 15 above), pp. 63-77 (p. 69).

21 E.H. Gombrich, 'Verbal Wit as a Paradigm of Art: The Aesthetic Theories of Sigmund Freud', in Gombrich, *Tributes: Interpreters of our Cultural Tradition*, Oxford, 1984, pp. 93-105 (p. 96).

22 Gombrich, *Art and Illusion* (n. 1 above), p. 133.

23 Gombrich, 'Grotesque Heads' (n. 10 above), p. 69.

24 Gombrich, 'Leonardo and the Magicians' (n. 16 above), p. 69.

25 Ibid., p. 69.

26 Gombrich, 'Light, Form and Texture' (n. 8 above), p. 35.

Index